RED LIPS AND BOTTOMS UP

Mereo Books

2nd Floor, 6-8 Dyer Street, Cirencester, Gloucestershire, GL7 2PF
An imprint of Memoirs Books. www.mereobooks.com
and www.memoirsbooks.co.uk

RED LIPS AND BOTTOMS UP
ISBN: 978-1-86151-930-6

First published in Great Britain in 2025
by Mereo Books, an imprint of Memoirs Books.

Copyright ©2025

Bernard Barnes has asserted his right under the Copyright Designs
and Patents Act 1988 to be identified as the author of this work.

The names of some characters have been changed.

A CIP catalogue record for this book is available from the British Library.
This book is sold subject to the condition that it shall not by way of trade or
otherwise be lent, resold, hired out or otherwise circulated without the publisher's
prior consent in any form of binding or cover, other than that in which it is
published and without a similar condition, including this condition being imposed
on the subsequent purchaser.

The address for Memoirs Books can be
found at www.mereobooks.com

Mereo Books Ltd. Reg. No. 12157152

Typeset in 10/16pt Garamond
by Wiltshire Associates.
Printed and bound in Great Britain

Bernard Barnes
RED LIPS & BOTTOMS UP

Four years of adventure working in
the Far East in the mid-1980s

Contents

1. From the UK to Hong Kong 1
2. The Tokyo experience 12
3. Settling in 25
4. Life in the office 37
5. Oxelotel II 50
6. September 1983, Black Saturday and the fallout from 1997 62
7. Singapore and Manila 75
8. The Greasy Goose, hairy crabs, Round Table and a new car 86
9. Trials and tribulations - meeting Lita 97
10. 1984 - building the team 108
11. Paradise Beach 132
12. Mr Wong, new friends & a difficult colleague 144
13. The real Philippines 156
14. My new role, Australia and around the world in a month 167
15. 'Cousin Ken', dodgy PCs and visiting China 179
16. Business travel, and Lita requests a hangover 190
17. Winding down, a Mini Moke and a big decision 203
18. Fun & Games - Christmas and New Year in the Philippines 213
19. The final weeks 225

Introduction

It was September 1983, and I was 30 and single. I had been living in Hong Kong for a few months, my company having relocated me there that February. I was having a great time, although working very hard and travelling continuously.

Living in Hong Kong was obviously exotic, and there was so much variety in so many areas. Whether it was the sights of the city and the harbour, the tiny cottage industries operating out of shop fronts in the side streets, the markets, the food options, ranging from stalls in the street to world-class restaurants or the completely different experience of the outlying islands, every day was an experience.

For a single expatriate like myself bars were clearly a key part of one's social life, and while there were many I used, the three that stood out head and shoulders above the rest as being memorable were Bottoms Up, Red Lips and the Bull and Bear. Each delivered a uniquely different experience, especially the first two, with Bottoms Up being quite well known from 1974 due to its inclusion in a James Bond film, *The Man with the Golden Gun*.

Bottoms Up was located in Kowloon, across the harbour from the Central district, a short walk from where the ferry docked. At first sight you would think it was only for single men, given its four circular dimly lit rooms, with a topless girl sitting in a round bar in the centre of each one. But that was not the case. Yes, the majority of the customers were male, but there were usually couples as well. It was not at all sleazy, you would not be ripped off and it was an interesting place to pop into for a drink; there was usually a good mix of people and the round bar format encouraged you to talk to others.

I had been there quite soon after getting to Hong Kong, as it was somewhere new arrivals would be taken to. But some months after I arrived the situation arose for me to help out the manager, an English lady called Pat Sephton, which resulted in my standing being boosted whenever I took people there. Pat would not only always welcome me like a long-lost friend, but had given me a card giving me a very sizeable discount, so large in fact that the bar girls were always impressed when I handed it over when paying the bill.

The event that resulted in this was a Typhoon. After causing very substantial damage to the Philippines, it then headed in our direction. There was a clearly defined procedure when typhoons threatened Hong Kong, based on how far away they were and their strength. Three signals were given before a typhoon hit and then two to denote how bad it would be on arrival.

No. 1:   Typhoon within 400 nautical miles of Hong Kong
No. 3:   Strong wind signal, typhoon approaching
          Hong Kong and c. 250 nautical miles away
No. 8:   Typhoon will hit Hong Kong, 3-4 hours away

Then when it arrived:

No. 9:   Gale force winds
No. 10:   Hurricane force winds

I was at the office when the No. 8 signal was given. This was the trigger for people to go home, shelters to be opened, public transport and ferries to be stopped very soon and precautions being taken such as putting up typhoon shutters on windows and the like. I still had a lot to finish and, as I had a car, I decided to carry on working, keeping an eye on the weather in case I felt I should head home. I managed to finish what I had wanted to do so I packed up and left. By then Hong Kong had already 'shut down' in preparation.

It was eerie. There was no one to be seen in the building except a security guard and outside not a person in sight, with only the very occasional car going by and no taxis. All the shops were closed, as well as the Bull & Bear pub in the bottom of my office block, with wooden typhoon shutters in place to protect any glass. The rain was pouring down and the wind was strong, but not worryingly so.

As I drove out of the multi-storey car park I saw a lone woman standing by the corner of the office. I realised that unless someone was coming to get her she was stranded, so I pulled up and asked if she was all right. It was Pat Sephton, and she explained that she had taken the last ferry across the harbour, expecting to get a taxi, and hadn't realised that they had all stopped operating. She lived in the mid-levels, which was quite a long steep walk. I therefore offered to give her a lift home, which of course she jumped at. Once in the car she explained who she was, which was really interesting to me, as she was quite well known in Hong Kong, and when we arrived at her apartment block she asked if I wanted to come in to have a drink and meet her husband.

As the weather conditions were still reasonable, I did. Her husband, Vic, was apparently a musician in a local band and we had an interesting talk about her background as a Windmill girl at the famous theatre in London, and what life was like running Bottoms Up. As I was leaving she thanked me once again and gave me a discount card, saying that anytime I was in the bar I must be sure to ask for her.

Of all my visits to Bottoms Up the most memorable was just before the final race of the 1983 Americas Cup. This was a race for large, extremely expensive sailing boats and the 'Cup' (in reality a ewer) had the distinction of being the oldest international sporting trophy, first having been won in 1851 by the New York Yacht Club (NYYC). Up until 1983 the race was little known outside the yachting fraternity, but press and TV coverage had exploded that year. The reason was that the NYYC had achieved the longest winning streak in sporting history, never having been beaten in 132 years. However that year the Australians had fielded a challenger which, against all the odds, was even, at three wins each *with* the NYYC with the seventh race being the decider. This was the first time a sixth race had ever been needed, let alone a seventh.

I went into Bottoms Up with a couple of friends and we found that one of the bars was packed with two groups of businessmen, one US and the other Australian. Virtually all the talk was of the America's Cup, this topic being uppermost in both these groups' minds given the situation. This was all good natured and both groups had some excellent wits amongst them, so it was a very sociable environment. We of course joined them.

The girl on our bar that night was from Europe, quite well endowed, and she had a party trick which I had seen before that went down a treat with these guys and made her a decent amount of money in the process. One of the swizzle sticks that Bottoms Up used was in the shape of a girl's leg, very long and with a stiletto shoe on. It was made of bright pink plastic and if reversed so the foot was pointing upwards, the bend of the foot and shoe allowed it to hang on, for instance, a nail. She had found a much better use for this feature. She would start by demonstrating that if she rubbed her nipple (remember she was topless) so it firmed up, the swizzle stick could be hung on it. Then, when her nipple had softened, off it would drop! She then explained that she would be hanging one on each nipple, after taking bets from those in the bar as to how long it would be before each pink leg fell off. The money taken for each of these would be split in two, half to the winner closest to the correct time and half to her. To increase her income she also auctioned off to the highest bidders the right to do the rubbing of each nipple and the hanging of the swizzle stick. Brilliant!

When I'd seen it before it was a big draw and people would move from the other bars to hers. On this night, with the already lively atmosphere in the bar, the nipple hanging game was really well received and was done a number of times, with the procedure subject to much banter and laughter, and she made a lot of money.

Helping to fuel the party atmosphere were many orders for the house cocktail. Called a Typhoon it came in a very large tulip shaped glass with its name emblazoned in blue. Whatever went into this drink definitely included a goodly amount of alcohol, as previous evenings when I had been drinking them had demonstrated. The price included the glass and I still have a few of them, together with two examples of that famous pink swizzle stick to remind me of those evenings.

The second of these particularly memorable places was the Red Lips Bar which, like Bottoms Up, was also on Kowloon side, in a small alley. It was very different from the other two, being a former R&R (rest and recuperation) bar. Its heyday had been during the Vietnam War (mid 1960s to the mid 1970s) when Hong Kong was a popular location for US servicemen on leave.

American military personnel were eligible for an R&R break during a tour of duty and if they were in Vietnam and chose an Asian destination, which was the preference of most single GIs, it lasted five days. The Vietnam War resulted in a massive number of US servicemen coming to Hong Kong for their R&R; they had money in their pockets and wanted to party. Many other bars opened up specifically to cater to them, but by the time I was in Hong Kong Red Lips was the last of the originals.

The ladies in Red Lips were definitely not the reason you went there, the local saying being that not only was the bar the same as it had been in the 60s, but the 'girls' in it were the originals as well. I had been told that it was started by a US military man at the end of the Korean War in 1953 as a place for retired prostitutes to work, and if so perhaps the hostesses in it have always been aged.

Red Lips was however full of character, as were the ladies who worked there. It looked and felt sleazy and run down, but it was an honest bar and the beer was cold and cheap. You would not stay there too long, but you would definitely visit if you were giving someone a tour of the nightlife.

It was small, with dim red lighting, and the most rewarding trips there were when I took individuals who were 'sensitive' to getting up close to the fleshpots of Asia. The ambience was distinctly down market and the 'girls' treated you as if they were attractive young hostesses looking for a chance to be taken somewhere for the night, which made for some interesting discussions.

The best visit I had of this nature was with someone from my company who was in Hong Kong for the first time. John was known to be quite religious and very straight, and was in fact the treasurer of his church. I told him I would take him to a couple of interesting bars and then we would have dinner.

We started off at Bottoms Up, which he had no problem with, but, when we entered Red Lips, he was immediately on his guard. 'What sort of place is this, Bernard?' he said nervously. 'I don't like the look of it.'

'Don't worry John, you're absolutely safe ' I replied, 'this is a Hong Kong institution and you must have a drink here.'

Red Lips had banquette seating for four people against the walls with room for two people either side of the table. I guided John to one of these and we sat opposite each other. The waitress came up and I ordered two beers. Less than a minute later two hostesses came and sat down with us, pushing us towards the wall so they could sit, effectively blocking us in.

'We don't want any company, thank you' John said to them tensely, 'please leave us alone.'

I was very pleased that the two 'girls' were just about the oldest and most wizened who worked there, well wrinkled and plastered with make-up and far too much bright red lipstick.

'It's OK John, it will be interesting talking to them,' I said. 'They usually have some fascinating stories about life in Hong Kong when they were younger.'

'I bet they have,' he replied, 'but I'm not interested in them, can we please leave and go somewhere nicer?'

'Ok, but let's drink our beers first as we've ordered them,' I responded, and as if on cue they turned up.

While the waitress was there the hostess next to John piped up 'please buy us a drink if you will, velly cheap here for girlie drink.'

I knew that the tiny glasses of girlie drink, which were tea but purported to be whisky, were not 'velly cheap', being about twice the price of the beers. This was not particularly expensive and as I knew it meant the girls would show us more interest, I agreed.

'Tank you very much' they both said in unison, 'you velly nice gentlemen.'

'Bernard, I'm not enjoying this,' said John. 'Why can't we just leave our beers and go?'

'You not enjoying it here?' said his girl, putting her hand on his leg and stroking it. 'Why not, we are velly friendly girls, can make you so happy.'

John visibly cringed and took her hand off his thigh just as the girlie drinks arrived.

'You gentlemen here on business?' my hostess asked.

'I live here' I replied, 'but my friend is only visiting and is looking for a good time.'

John was by now looking at me with some annoyance.

"Ooh, I can show him a very good time,' his girl said. 'What hotel you staying at?' she asked John.

'He's at the Furama, room nine one seven' I responded before John could say anything.

'Bernard, this is ridiculous!' John said, now getting quite uptight with me. 'What are you doing giving them my hotel and room number? I've had enough, I'm leaving with or without you,' and he started to get up.

I decided it wasn't fair to carry on as he was getting so upset. I calmed him down, apologised for winding him up and explained that he had no need to worry; she would not be knocking on his door in the early hours of the morning. I gave the girls a tip and said they could go. We finished our drinks before we left, with John now much more relaxed.

The last of the three, the Bull & Bear, was an English bar on the ground floor of my office block in the central business district on Hong Kong Island. Located where it was, it would have seen a fair amount of my salary going into its tills whatever it was like, but it was also the best 'English Pub' style venue in Hong Kong. With everything around you so different from the UK, its Tudor decor was comforting, and it served English beer and food. While I really enjoyed foreign cooking of every style, it couldn't be denied that every now and then a plate of sausages and baked beans or a pie and mash was a very welcome change.

However the English beer tended to be something I passed up on. Back home I was mostly a bitter drinker, but I didn't feel tempted by it in Asia and stuck to the lager type beers. The Bull & Bear did however advertise that it served draught Guinness, and on my second or third visit there I decided to have one. Luckily I was seated facing the bar and therefore able to see how it was served.

The barmaid took our orders, went behind the bar and was putting our drinks on a tray when I happened to notice her opening a normal bottle of Guinness. This made me take more notice as I had definitely ordered draught, not bottled. I saw that, surprisingly, she was pouring the bottle into a square metal container on the bar. I then realised that the container had a Guinness advert and a handle similar to a beer pump. She placed a glass below the container, pulled the handle a few times and then put the now full glass on the tray with our other drinks, so it was clearly for me. Bottled Guinness is quite a different drink from its draught version, and I wondered what, if any, difference this procedure would make. Well, on trying it, there was no difference to pouring it direct from the bottle, apart perhaps from a frothier head, and draught Guinness did not have a frothy head but a dense, creamy one. It was not at all like the real thing - what a disappointment! I suppose it was good marketing to offer draught as well as bottled, and many of those who would try it in Hong Kong would never have had the real thing, and would be none the wiser.

The marketing of some of the beers in Hong Kong was actually quite dubious. I was in the Bull & Bear one evening having a drink with the local manager (a New Zealander) of my direct competitor. Despite this, we had become friends. The subject of beer came up.

'It must be due to getting older, John' I said to him. 'Nowadays I seem to get more headaches for the same quantity of beer than I used to.'

'It's not your age, Bernard' he replied, 'it's because you're drinking San Miguel. It may be the most popular brand here, but it's brewed locally and it's not the same beer as in Spain, where it originates.'

'Really? Perhaps I should switch to Löwenbrau then, which I see they sell here. Given the strict German beer laws that will have to be only hops, barley and water.'

'No good I'm afraid' he said, 'those laws only apply to beer brewed in Germany. What you get here is again locally brewed, and it's pretty much the same as the San Miguel. And next time you're shopping look at the Heineken cans, you'll see it says that it's imported.'

'There's obviously a catch there,' I said.

'Absolutely' he replied. 'It's true it is imported, but from Singapore, where again it's brewed under licence and not the same beer as in Europe. But that's not made clear on the can. But there is one excellent lager beer available, it's called Tsing Tao. It's brewed in China, but they follow the German brewing law so there are no additives and I'd recommend that. And sometimes you can find Philippines San Miguel,' he went on, 'it will be in squat bottles and although it's brewed there, they do it well and that's a good beer.'

I was interested therefore in the Tsing Tao and looked into it. Despite being brewed in China, which did raise some question marks on its quality in my mind, it transpired the brewery had been started in 1903 by German settlers, hence the quality as they did still brew it, as John had said, to the famous German purity law of 1516.

The Bull & Bear was not just a place for homesick British expats however; you could always find a range of nationalities there, including a lot of local Chinese, and most times we went out with the staff after work for a drink they would want to go there, attracted by the English pub experience.

While memorable, Bottoms Up and Red Lips were clearly not places I would use on a regular basis. With the exception of the Bull & Bear, where I did spend a fair bit of time, I didn't use any other normal bar much either, only going to them on an ad hoc basis, usually when picked as a meeting place for a night out. An alternative, as with expatriate life elsewhere in the world, was to join a club, which would give you somewhere to go to regularly.

The bigger, more prestigious clubs were the places long-term residents or senior expatriate businessman and their families belonged to. They had long waiting lists for normal membership unless you were able to take one of the routes that allowed payment of a very large amount of money to get in quickly (often given as part of a senior expatriate compensation package), or could show you had relevant background in their area of focus (for example sailing skills in the case of the Yacht Club). These however were not the places for me, being single, and with the amount of travel I did, I would not use them enough to justify the expensive entry option (even if I could afford it), and I was unlikely to be in Hong Kong long enough to get in via the long-term waiting list route.

The closest I came to joining one of these was when, in early May 1983, I had lunch at the Hong Kong Club with the owner of a flat I had rented, who was a member. This was the most prestigious club of all and, of course, not easy to get into. John suggested I put my name down. He was happy to propose me, and said that it would be quite a long wait for my name to come up and I could decide then if I still wanted to join. I didn't have to make that decision as when I left four years later I had still not been contacted.

Then there were a reasonable number of smaller clubs catering to specific groups, often without a full range of facilities, but always with a bar and dining options. These were easier to get into, but the better ones still required a sizeable joining payment, together with an annual or monthly fee. Some could be amazingly good value though; for example The China Fleet Club, which was established for UK navy personnel, and which I occasionally went to events at, charged the equivalent of ten pence for a pint of beer. This when the 1983 retail price index in the UK showed the average cost of a pint of lager to be seventy-two pence!

The month after I arrived I did join a club in the building next door to the office. The 'I Club' was very new and very modern, but in reality a city bar and dining venue rather than a real club. Its target market was affluent youngish Chinese, many looking for the additional status of belonging to a smart private club in Central. On its opening there was a joining fee of c. £4,000, a very large amount of money indeed, but this 'status setting' pricing had clearly not pulled in enough people and I heard that they were offering memberships for the equivalent of £35 per month, with no down payment and no minimum period, which for Hong Kong was a bargain.

While rather too modern for me the bar was comfortable and the food was good, and I felt that being next door to the office it would be a good place to pop into if I was working late. In addition they had a function room which was the perfect size for a staff get together and dinner. So I joined. I stayed a member for some months and did use it for one staff dinner, but then received a letter from the club with revised terms requiring, if I can remember, having to put a holding deposit with them and setting a minimum monthly spend. I was sure they were in financial difficulty in doing this, which meant I didn't want them to be holding any of my money, and I also doubted I could easily achieve the minimum spend, so I resigned. Sure enough, some time later it folded.

Almost a year after I arrived I did join a conventional club, but one of the smaller ones. The Foreign Correspondents Club (FCC) was formed in China in 1943 and moved to Hong Kong in 1949. As the name indicates it was established as a base for media people, but (as with many clubs) they had opened membership to others as more income was needed to pay for the facilities than the media membership would generate. The FCC was housed in an attractive old building which had been built in 1892 as a cold storage warehouse, and then expanded over time, ending up as the head office of local company Dairy Farm. They moved out in 1970 and the FCC moved there in 1982 from Sutherland House, which had been next door to my office building. The Sutherland House location was famed in some guide books of the time as having the best view in the world from a men's toilet - looking right across the harbour!

The FCC was primarily a drinking and dining venue and was in the Central district and therefore good for business socialising. In fact this was the reason I joined, as a number of people I saw regularly in a work capacity were members, and it was a good place for networking. Given this I put the £500 joining fee on my expenses without asking, reasoning that if it was queried I had a good justification.

The only other bar I would visit reasonably often was, surprisingly, in one of the Government housing blocks in Kennedy Road, which was in the mid-levels, halfway up the steep hill behind Central. This building, called The Hermitage, was used to house single expatriates who had Government jobs. A less fitting name could hardly have been chosen, given that the vast majority of the residents had social lives that were about as far from being a hermit as was possible. This was a Friday lunchtime venue for me, as a regular group would get together then. The bar was on the 11th floor and though nothing special the drinks were a sensible price and the food, while basic, was good. Given the venue it was no surprise that the majority of this group were employed by the Government. It was interesting to be with such a group rather than the normal set of people I mixed with, who were in the commercial sector.

Chapter 1

From the UK to Hong Kong

My move to Hong Kong had commenced at the end of 1982 when the company I was with asked if I would relocate there to run the branch office.

I had worked in computing since leaving school. No degree for me, to the disappointment of my parents, although going to university had been my plan until the opportunity to do IT arose. I had joined my present company as a programmer six years earlier. They were a computer software house who became specialists in writing IT systems for the overseas banks who had setup in London. After a time they realised they were doing the same thing over and over again and created a software package that sold like the proverbial hot cakes. It transpired that it was not just the overseas banks in London who wanted the product; it met the needs of the overseas banks in every financial centre around the world. The company had only thirty people when I joined, but their rapid success meant that in under ten years they would have 900+ staff and many overseas offices.

But that was the future. It was now the end of 1982, and despite my relatively young age and shortage of management experience I was asked to take over as the General Manager of the Hong Kong branch, which was also responsible for China, Japan, Korea, Thailand, Taiwan, The Philippines and Macau. Such are the opportunities available if you get into a fast-growing company early.

The financial year-end was February and they wanted me to be in place first week in March, so I had to make arrangements rapidly. I rented out my house fully furnished, sold my car (a bright red Triumph TR6 2 seater which I was very sorry to see go), packed up some boxes to go in my parents' attic and decided that apart from what I would take in my suitcase, everything else for Hong Kong would fill a tea chest. This I arranged to go sea freight, and I didn't see it again for almost a year, mostly due to the low priority the shipping company gave to a single tea chest.

I reported to the Regional Manager, who was based in Singapore. Charlie ended up being a good friend, but at that time I only knew him from the London office. He suggested I should come via Singapore so we could run through the role and we could then travel to Hong Kong together. At a 'bonding session' in Singapore the night before we flew we consumed a fair bit of alcohol, finishing off at his house with a bottle of brandy. It turned out that Charlie liked brandy but it did not like him. The next day saw him feeling wretched, not helped by my being 100%, which he was none too happy about, I diplomatically blamed my lack of a hangover on the jet lag.

Arriving at Hong Kong we came into land at the old Kai Tak airport at what turned out to be a magical time of day, just as the sun was setting. The plane descended on the relatively undeveloped south side of Hong Kong Island and was bathed in the deep yellow setting sun. It then made a turn to come round the island and back towards the harbour. Almost immediately the setting sun was lost behind the high island and dusk was upon us, with a fairy-tale view of thousands of twinkling lights now visible from the densely packed buildings and roads of Kowloon and the side of Hong Kong Island that faced the harbour.

Landing at Kai Tak airport was an experience in itself as the single runway was situated right on the harbour, with densely packed tower blocks of apartments on the approach. The final landing required a very tight 47 degree turn to the right with the plane banked over so steeply that staring down through the windows on the right hand side you looked straight onto the roofs of the tower blocks, with the wing tip seeming only yards away from touching them. The aircraft suddenly righted itself and a few seconds later we were on the runway. Having come to a stop the plane had to make its way all the way back by the side of the runway to the terminal. I recalled reading that Hong Kong was one of the most dangerous airports in the world not, strangely, because of the frightening turn over the tall buildings but because the taxiway was so close to the runway, with the risk of a landing plane colliding with one coming back along the taxiway. The same article had also stated that a number of the nearby tower blocks we had passed had been built to be able to act as emergency hospitals, in case a landing plane did ever crash in one of the most densely populated areas in the world.

We were staying at the Furama Intercontinental Hotel right in the central business district, by the water and next door to the building where the office was – Hutchison House. The terms of my relocation allowed me to stay there for up to a month while I sorted out somewhere to live. Interestingly, some years later (in 2001), the hotel suffered a fate that demonstrated the impact of changing property values in a place like Hong Kong. Although there were no financial issues with it as a hotel, it was demolished and replaced with an office block, commercial space having become so valuable due to a shortage that this was a financially more attractive option.

The next day we went into the office and I was introduced to the staff, numbering just over twenty locals plus a couple of expatriates. My predecessor, Clive, was still in Hong Kong. I knew him and his wife reasonably well, as we had in the past socialised together outside work and we were quite friendly. Charlie left that afternoon to go back to Singapore and I sat down with Clive to sort out various handover meetings that required the two of us, as he was leaving in a couple of weeks.

That first weekend I was invited by Joanna, one of the Chinese staff, and her husband (I had known them when they were in London) to come over to their house on Saturday afternoon and then for dinner.

They lived on Peng Chau, a smallish island 8 kilometres west of Hong Kong, and I had to take a ferry. Luckily Joanna had invited some other staff as well so I joined them on the trip there. They met us off the boat and the first thing we did was to go to the market by the ferry pier to buy seafood, as the way it worked was you took this to the restaurant and they cooked it. The seafood having been selected, to much lively discussion in Cantonese as to what we should eat, we trooped off to the chosen restaurant, where further discussions took place as to how to cook the seafood and the additional dishes we wanted, and a price was agreed to. Next stop was Joanna's apartment to play bridge and mah jong until it was time for dinner. No knife and fork options were available, but luckily I had learned how to use chopsticks a few years earlier in London so I was ok. The food was stunning: incredibly tasty, well cooked and a far cry from the Chinese food I was used to in London.

From the moment I went into work on that first Monday (7th March) I was completely swamped. Not having had a job at this level before I was quite unprepared for the number of activities I had to deal with simultaneously. I had to learn all the office/staff/customer administration, which once grasped was straightforward, but initially was mind boggling. I was being taken round to meet customers and prospects, including an evening cocktail party to introduce me to a range of people associated with the company. I had arranged to sit down with each of the staff for a one on one, and was also finalising a major launch event for the following Monday to kick off the start of the year. Senior people from London were flying out to attend this, so it was important it went well.

Therefore it wasn't until the end of my second week that I had time to breathe and start to think about where to live. I had planned to rent somewhere fully furnished but on getting in touch with a couple of agents it transpired such flats were few and far between and the best places would be unfurnished - more complexity, which I could well do without. They suggested I consider renting a 'leave flat' in the interim. I had not come across this term before, but it was explained that due to the very high cost of flat rentals and because most expatriates took long holidays, many of them rented out their flats while they were away as it was so lucrative.

One of the agents was aware of a fantastic place right on the Peak (the highest point of Hong Kong Island) which was available for five weeks from the 26th March. I went for a look and was completely bowled over. 2,500 square feet, four bedrooms, two bedroom maids' quarters and a massive balcony with views down the south side of the island to the sunset. It was incredibly well furnished with antiques, Persian rugs, solid silverware, crystal glasses, bone china, jade, ivory and every conceivable gadget in the kitchen. Apparently it was the norm to leave everything in the leave flat and trust the tenants. I would also have use of the owner's car, which was a Rover 3500 - very nice. As it was within my budget, it was a complete no brainer to go for this, although the agent said it would spoil me for anywhere else as it was so exceptional.

The owners, John and Mimi, in their late 50s I thought, had been based in Hong Kong for many years. We seemed to hit it off and they said they were happy for me to rent it. I left them feeling excited and relieved, not only that I had somewhere to live for April, but in such an incredible place.

The previous night I had experienced a very odd situation. Clive and his wife had a leaving party at a local restaurant and I was introduced to a friend of theirs, Frank, who worked at the British Council. Late in the evening I heard him say he needed to book into a hotel, as his last ferry home had left. It transpired he lived on an island near Hong Kong called Cheung Chau. I had two double beds in my hotel room so I said he was welcome to stay with me.

At around 4 am I woke up and realised he was not in his bed, and all the bedclothes were on the floor - strange. I turned the light on. His clothes were still there but he was nowhere to be seen and the bathroom was empty - stranger still. I checked all over the room, even under the beds – he had disappeared! I was completely flummoxed as to what could be going on.

I put on some clothes and went into the hallway, no sign of him, so I checked the emergency stairs and then took the lift down to the lobby. He was nowhere to be seen. I was now really concerned as to what was going on, as from what I could tell, all he had on was his underpants! Nothing else I could do but go back to the room and see what transpired.

As I left the lift on my floor I saw him ahead of me walking towards the room, and as I had thought, he was wearing just his Y fronts.

'Frank - what the hell is going on'? I called out, 'I've been tearing my hair out wondering what happened to you.'

'Sorry Bernard' he said, turning round, 'I should have warned you that I sleepwalk!' He was most apologetic about the matter and we went back to bed, but I couldn't get back to sleep.

Frank was a nice enough guy, but although I bumped into him a few times over the next couple of years I could never bring myself to become particularly friendly with him after this, as the memories of that night came back to me whenever I saw him.

The following week I broadened my experience of Hong Kong food by eating at a Dai Pai Dong. These are one man/woman restaurants set up in the street, with very basic tables and chairs and a small cart for cooking food. One of the girls at the office had introduced this cuisine to me. 'Bernard, I heard you saying you wanted to try real local food and I'm going for some on my way to my evening class tonight,' said Cynthia, one of the programmers. 'Do you want to join me?'

Of course I said yes. Off we went and were soon seated on tiny stools around a very small table set up in a side street.

'What do you want to eat?' said Cynthia.

'I don't know' I replied. 'You order me something really local that you doubt I would have had in London.'

She did, and after a short time two bowls of food appeared with a teapot and handle-less tea cups. Chopsticks and Chinese style ceramic spoons were in containers on the table. I helped myself.

'You must wash them with the tea before you use them,' said Cynthia, 'the tea has a disinfectant quality and these will not have been washed well.' I did so.

The bowl of food in front of me was congee (a very wet rice porridge) with pieces of something unidentifiable sitting on top of the rice.

'What are these, Cynthia?' I said, pointing to the strange grey lumps.

'I don't know the English name' she replied, 'but it's from a cow.' She thought for a bit. 'You know, the backbone is bone, something, bone, something - this is the something.'

So it was the cartilage, obviously cooked a long time to be tender and yes, having a faint beefy taste. It was edible, just, but not something I would order again.

'You don't like the texture, do you?' Cynthia said enquiringly.

'It's not my favourite,' I said.

'You see texture is as important as flavour to us Chinese, and sometimes more important, and a lot of textures we like you don't eat in the Western world.'

I discovered the truth of this as I broadened my sampling of Cantonese dishes. Foods such as sea slug, chicken's feet, jellyfish, sharks' fin and fish maw were commonplace items at restaurants and had textures I doubted 99 out of 100 westerners would like, even if they were willing to eat them. They varied from the consistency of almost-set jelly to rubber bands, and in general these texture-based foods had little or no flavour of their own, with taste coming from what was added, for instance chicken soup, soy sauce or sesame oil.

On Saturday 26th March I moved into Carolina Gardens. John & Mimi showed me where everything was and then left, leaving me basking in comfort. I explored the flat in more depth now they were gone. One interesting thing about living so high up was that they had a dry room - a very large storage room without windows that was constantly dehumidified. This was necessary because of the extremely high humidity, even greater than it was normally in Hong Kong in the summer, due to low cloud which could completely envelop the Peak. This made mildew a real problem in stored items and they had therefore suggested I use this room for most of my clothes.

One difference now was that I had to commute to work, rather than walk the twenty yards between the hotel and the office. When Clive had left I had taken over his car and driving this around I had realised that the tortuous and confusing road network in Hong Kong, often due to the steep slopes, made navigation very difficult. You could often see where you wanted to go to but getting there might mean driving past your destination and then doubling back via some obscure one-way street. In other cases there would be a relatively direct route there, but as this road was one way only with no corresponding road in the other direction you had to take a totally different route back again. I realised very quickly that the best way to address this was to take a taxi the first time you were going somewhere and make sure you remembered the route it took.

As I had a car, I drove to work. Not just to save waiting for taxis (buses were a problem up at the Peak), but there was a multi-storey car park next door to the office and the company were paying my petrol and parking costs, whereas they would not have stumped up the taxi fares. The drive to and from the office was interesting, with much of it being on steep 1 in 3 roads with switchbacks to handle the slopes. Even for the ordinary Mitsubishi car I had, the effect of these gradients and having the air-con on meant petrol consumption was terrible - c. twelve miles to the gallon. I mostly used my company car as I didn't want to risk any damage to the Rover, although John had asked me to drive it to keep it running well.

The humidity in Hong Kong and the problems it could cause became apparent one day when I decided I would take the Rover to work, as it had been about ten days since I had given it a run. On opening the door I saw that the seats had mildew all over them - being leather, even a short time such as this was enough for it to form in the moist warm air.

The mildew in the car was also a factor of the terribly wet weather Hong Kong had been experiencing since I arrived - and in fact the December to March period had been the worst weather on record. Many days you could not see across the harbour from the office and looking up at the Peak it was constantly shrouded in cloud. I had of course looked into what weather I could expect before arriving. It fell into four distinct seasons with the climate overall being classed as humid sub-tropical. Winter (November to February) was usually dry with average daily temperatures of just over 20°C, spring (March to April) slightly warmer with increasing humidity and rain. Summer (May to August) was very hot with over 30°C during the day and high humidity and autumn (September to October) was 25°C to 30°C during the day with lower humidity. For Europeans October to December were the best months, dry with blue skies, low humidity and good temperatures. Discussing the weather with people I was told that although winter temperatures were never that cold, with 10°C being the lowest usually experienced and averages of 15°C, as apartments had no proper heating you did feel these colder periods. I was told to wait for winter when, on what I would think of as a nice warm day, many of the locals would have very thick sweaters or jackets on.

Easter Day was the 3rd April and it was a five-day holiday in Hong Kong, from Good Friday to the Tuesday. The reason for the extended break was that the Chinese festival of Ching Ming was on the Tuesday. Most of the year the cemeteries are avoided, but on this festival families go to the ancestral graves to clean and tidy them - in fact Ching Ming translates as 'clean and bright'. They also light incense, make offerings of food and burn fake money for their ancestors to use in the afterlife. Bus companies have to put on extra services to the cemetery locations due to the volume of people going to them at this time.

I was on my own over the break as the people I knew had either gone on holiday or were taking part in a major yacht race to San Fernando in the Philippines. I had been invited to stay with an ex-colleague and his wife who now lived and worked in Macau, which took about an hour to get to by jetfoil. Unfortunately on trying to book seats I was told all ferries, jetfoils and hydrofoils had been booked weeks in advance.

I had another option though. Clive, the previous manager, had been in the local Round Table (a social/charity group for those up to forty years old) and had taken me to one of their meetings. They had asked if I wanted to help at a big Easter Fair they organised each year. The setup was on Good Friday and the fair the following day. Thankfully after the terrible weather so far, both days were gorgeous, and it was fun getting involved and meeting new people.

Easter Day itself I was totally on my own but I decided that was no reason not to have a nice lunch so, feeling a bit of a sad case, I made myself a three-course meal with a roast chicken as the centrepiece, a nice bottle of wine and an Easter egg my parents had given me before leaving as the pudding. Of course it was beautifully presented using all the upmarket crockery, crystal and solid silverware I had access to.

Over the holiday I sat down and properly thought about the options for where I should live. I had brought together a fair bit of material, with a good deal of input from others, and there were basically five locations to consider. The first and most expensive was the north side of the island facing the harbour and around the central business district, and of course the closer you were to the centre the higher the cost, with places on the Peak with some space around and views being particularly costly. The south side was less developed, took longer to get into work from and was generally favoured by families rather than single people like myself. The other side of the harbour on the mainland, Kowloon, was possible but not ideal. Living there I would either have to take the harbour ferry to get to Central, or use the very congested tunnel if I drove. Cheaper options were the two bigger islands Lantau and Cheung Chau – 'chau' means island. Lantau was very large but undeveloped historically as it had no fresh water, but developers had started building houses and apartments and there was a quality new option called Discovery Bay with a golf course and its own ferry. Cheung Chau was interesting and one of our expatriate staff lived there with his wife. It was a dumbbell-shaped island with most of the property built on the flat narrow middle between the two hills at either end. Its history was as a fishing village, given the two large bays either side of the narrow strip, and there were no cars as the village was made up of small lanes. In terms of 'going local' it would be fun, but realistically, being single and with a lengthy ferry ride to get to work, it was not practical for me. These two reasons and its quietness also excluded Lantau.

Looking at living on the harbour-facing side of the island the area I would be considering was called, accurately, the Mid-Levels. This was a wide band of apartment blocks built on the steep slopes between the business district and the peak area. Prices here were based as you would expect on size, view and quality of the building. Because of the stunning view down into the harbour there was a significant price difference for the same size apartment in the same block, dependant on if it had the view or not, although typically the maid's quarters, kitchen etc. would be the ones looking at the hillside. One thing you had to be careful of though was summed up by the saying 'you are never guaranteed a view'. There were no planning restrictions in Hong Kong that would stop a developer knocking down the building below and in front of you and putting in its place a much higher one that completely blocked your view. In such a case, not only would you lose your view but you would have to suffer all the noise of a building site while it was going up. Therefore, even if you were renting and not buying, you needed good local knowledge to minimise the risk of having a blighted apartment.

I then looked at dates and it was clear that there was little chance of me finding and moving into a permanent apartment before my last day here on the 30th April. Tomorrow when I was back at work was the 6th April, I was scheduled to be in Tokyo 21st to 27th April and I didn't have anything at all to furnish a place with - not even a bed! So in parallel with the main flat hunt I needed to find another temporary one.

Chapter 2

The Tokyo experience

My responsibilities included Japan and therefore liaising with our Japanese agents Toppan Moore Business Systems (TMBS). They were a subsidiary of a major Japanese printing company and had been formed to develop an IT business in addition to their printing activities. TMBS handled our sales and support in Japan (effectively Tokyo only) and had also transferred staff to London to assist in the projects that were under way with Japanese banks in Europe.

While we had a number of Japanese bank customers elsewhere, sales in Japan itself had not been forthcoming. Part of my brief therefore was to assist TMBS in their sales activity in Tokyo and provide training and assistance on the installation and support of our software.

There had been virtually no operational activity thus far to support them in Japan, so Charlie and I decided that the first requirement was to travel to Tokyo to meet the key people and get a feel for the situation and what was required. This was arranged over a weekend with us arriving late on a Thursday night and leaving the following Wednesday, as we also wanted to experience Tokyo as tourists while we were there.

After an uneventful flight we jumped into a taxi to take us to our hotel. We had been travelling about ten minutes and were on a motorway type road when we saw a large sign in English – 'Tokyo 66 kilometres'! Never having been before, neither of us had any idea that the new Narita airport was so far from the city. We realised that apart from the long journey we might also have a cash problem, as Japan was one of the most expensive places in the world and the taxi fare was clearly going to be a very large one.

The journey took about fifty minutes and we later found out that this was unusually quick, due both to the lateness of our arrival at 10 pm and that our driver had really put his foot down; with the terrible traffic possible in Tokyo the journey at a busy time could take three hours. By pooling our cash we had enough to pay him, and we checked in and had a quick drink before bed.

Hideaki Nishimura (Nishi) was the manager of the TMBS division we dealt with and he met us in the hotel reception the next morning. Charlie and I both knew him from London were he had been the senior TMBS person. I had worked with him quite closely there and we had a good relationship.

About nine months earlier in London he had come over to my desk. 'Barnes-san, I have something to tell you' he said, using the honorific title 'san' after my name, which implies respect and is typically used between equals of any age.

'Sit down Nishi - what is it?' I said, expecting something to do with work.

'I have to go back to Tokyo, Barnes-san, as I need to get married,' he answered, as if disappointed.

'Nishi, that's great news,' I said. 'Congratulations. Will you be coming back here with your wife or does this mean you will stay in Japan?'

'No Barnes-san, you do not understand' he replied. 'I am now senior enough that I need to have a wife but I do not know a suitable girl. So the company is going to find me a wife, and that is why I have to go back to Tokyo.'

'I'm surprised, Nishi,' I responded. 'You have a good job, I would have thought you would not have a problem finding a wife yourself.'

'It is difficult, Barnes-san,' he explained. 'In Japan IT is seen as new and therefore does not have credibility in the eyes of the parents of daughters who would make a suitable wife for me; they want them to marry someone from an honourable profession such as banking or the sogo shoshas, which are the large trading companies.'

So off he had gone, and some time later he contacted us to say he was now married and would be staying in Tokyo. TMBS had indeed found him a wife, not part of the benefits you get with a European company!

When we had been arranging the trip Nishi had proposed that on the Friday evening he and his wife would take us out to dinner so we could meet her, and that on the Saturday they would like to take us round Tokyo. This, we were told, showed how much Nishi liked us, as it was not usual to involve wives in this way at the weekend.

That first morning we were going to the TMBS offices. Nishi met us in reception to take us there as it was difficult to get to a specific building in Tokyo, due to the quirkiness of the address system and the lack of English of the taxi drivers.

On arriving at the offices he took us to a formal meeting room, laid out in the standard Japanese fashion. There was a three-seater sofa with a coffee table in front, facing the sofa were three armchairs, and at each end of the table was an armchair. The visitors would sit on the sofa with the most senior in the centre, the armchairs being used for the hosts. Before the main work of the day we were going to be introduced to the Chairman and the CEO, hence the meeting room. The first formality was to exchange business cards, and this was done standing, holding the card with both hands, with each person bowing and in a strict order: most senior visitor with most senior host, then second most senior visitor with most senior host and so on. How low you bowed depended on your seniority and although this was not particularly relevant with westerners we did bow our heads a bit as we exchanged cards.

Interestingly in respect of the bowing, on a future visit to Tokyo I was present at a meeting IBM had arranged with a very senior director of one of the major banks, and IBM had with them a young engineer.

When the time came for him to exchange business cards with the top man from the bank the director just moved his head downwards a tiny bit, while the young engineer bowed so low I wondered if his head would actually touch the floor!

After the exchange of cards we took our seats and green tea was served. We had been reminded by Nishi that when drinking the tea we needed to make a slurping noise to show we appreciated it – drinking it silently would have been seen as very poor manners. We exchanged pleasantries, with Nishi translating. Charlie and I knew from our previous dealings with the Japanese that there was a way to discuss matters and a way not to. Basically the Japanese would not give you an answer which they felt could cause offence. If for instance you said you wanted to do a certain activity but they disagreed with this, they would not say so outright but would come back with something along the lines of 'that's interesting'. You needed to ask them open questions to see if they were prepared to let you know their position but, again, if they felt you would not like the truth they could still be evasive. Stories were commonplace about inexperienced Western companies coming away from a meeting thinking that what they wanted done matched that of the Japanese company, and then finding out over the coming months that nothing they thought had been agreed was being actioned. So it could be a bit of an art form to handle tricky subjects successfully.

This meeting was straightforward however, as it was to introduce us to each other and talk high level about 'mutual benefits' and the like, not to discuss anything important. We would be working with Nishi and his team to determine what the opportunities and issues were and what we proposed, and it would be later in the process when any thorny negotiation meetings might be required with his superiors.

After this meeting Nishi took us on a tour of the offices. There wasn't much to see – everywhere he took us was basically the same, open plan with densely packed tiny grey desks, even managers sitting at the same desks amongst everyone else – I wondered how they handled confidential business or staff discussions. These conditions were standard across all Japanese companies, whatever business area they were in.

That evening Nishi and his wife met us at the hotel. She seemed rather nervous and Nishi, realising this, explained that she was from the country and not used to being with westerners. We went to a lovely restaurant, but it was very traditional and we had to sit cross-legged on tatami (reed) mats on the floor, not a position my legs were used to. The food was mostly excellent, with many small courses, some very palatable but some a bit odd for Western palates, such as savoury egg custard containing fish. There were a couple of interesting moments with Nishi's wife, who was sitting opposite me. The first was when we were drinking warm sake out of ceramic cups and I lifted my cup to take a drink, but found it was empty so put it down again. Nishi at once said a couple of words, quite harshly to his wife, who jumped and immediately picked up the sake carafe and filled my cup. I realised then that she had been topping me up all through the meal and I hadn't had to do it myself.

The second time was some way into the meal when I had almost finished a delicious plate of fried fish which she had not touched.

'Do you not like this fish?' I asked her, 'It's very tasty.'

'Oh I like it very much' she replied 'in fact it is my favourite dish.'

'You must have what's left then,' I said, and passed the plate to her.

'No' she answered putting the plate back near me, 'you are the guests and I will not eat any of the food until it is clear you do not want any more.'

At this point it struck me that much of what I had seen as nervousness was not that; she was being deferential. This was a business dinner for Nishi to introduce his wife to us, and certain rules of etiquette therefore applied. I then realised that she had hardly eaten anything, due to Charlie and I polishing off most of the food, and not appreciating that we were expected to stop eating each dish while there was still some left, so she would be able to partake.

At the end of the meal, after no little difficulty in getting up after so long sitting cross-legged on the floor, we confirmed arrangements to meet the next morning. We said our goodbyes and Nishi put us in a taxi and told the driver where to take us.

The next day, a Saturday, we met Nishi and his wife again at the hotel for them to take us round the City. As we were walking around the small side streets it became immediately apparent that Nishi's wife was behaving completely differently. She was relaxed and chatty, with none of the deference of the previous night. I asked Nishi about this and he confirmed that the previous night had been, effectively, an extension of the working day with him formally introducing his wife to us, and despite it only being the four of us, certain rules applied. Taking us out today though was seen as something between friends and the invitation had been given on this basis.

While on the surface Tokyo appeared rather grey and drab, as we had seen in the taxi rides we had taken so far, once you were on foot exploring it was completely different. Whether it was going into a temple, a shop, a tiny restaurant or a coffee house, everything was attractive, beautifully presented and spotlessly clean. Of course language was an issue and we were so lucky to have the two of them to explain everything to us. In terms of eating out, however, you could exist quite happily without any translation being required. All the restaurants had plastic reproductions of their dishes on display in their windows, so it was easy to go outside and point out what dish you wanted. These displays were clearly not done just for the benefit of tourists but were a standard feature of most of the restaurants.

In the afternoon Nishi said he would like to show us Tokyo at night if we were not too tired, and we said that would be wonderful. He also asked if we would eat raw fish as he could take us to a local restaurant that tourists were unlikely ever to use, and which we might find very interesting. We agreed to go back to the hotel lounge for a rest and some refreshments before going out again, and not to stay out late as it had been a tiring day and they had a long journey back home.

We left just before 6 pm as the sun was setting. At night Tokyo was a riot of colour, with many buildings, and particularly those at major road intersections, completely covered in neon lights. It was very busy, with lots of people in the streets and in the shops. In contrast to this the restaurant we went to was in a tiny street, more an alley, and was itself minute, only having a handful of tables plus a few seats at the bar. We ate Sashimi, which was raw fish on its own, and Sushi, which was fish on top of a small block of rice. There was a wide variety of food with not just raw fish; some was cooked such as prawn or unagi (eel) and some more vegetable based. Just an amazing experience. As promised we finished early and Charlie and I had a final beer in the hotel bar before going to bed.

The next day we were going to Tokyo Disneyland and were being met at the hotel by two of the TMBS staff who were going to take us there, a girl and a guy. Neither Charlie nor I had been to a Disneyland before, and when organising the trip, I had asked if it was possible for us to go there on the Sunday, as I had heard that Tokyo Disneyland was going to open before our visit.

We met Keiko and Takashi in the lobby. We had been introduced to them on our tour round the office so knew they were the ones going with us. They had explained that they had been selected as they spoke the best English.

'It is a great honour for us to come with you today,' Keiko said on the journey there.

'It's very good of you to give up your Sunday,' I replied. 'We were expecting to make our own way there, I'm sorry you have to spend the day with us.'

'We are very glad to,' said Takashi cheerfully. 'Disneyland has only just opened and it is impossible to get tickets.'

'The company had a lot of trouble to get the tickets,' said Keiko. 'None were available for weeks, they were sold out far in advance.'

'I didn't realise that, when did it open?' I asked.

'Only nine days ago,' replied Keiko, 'but of course as you had asked if it was possible for you to go while you were here, the company would have been embarrassed if they had not been able to arrange it. I think they had to pay quite a lot of money.'

'So you can see why we are so happy to be with you today,' said Takashi. 'Going to Disneyland only one week after it has opened, our colleagues, family and friends are so envious.'

'I feel very embarrassed now,' I replied, 'to know that I have put your management to such bother and expense, they must be annoyed with me.'

'No, you should not be concerned,' answered Takashi. 'Nishi knows you well and said that you would not have asked for this if you had been aware of the situation, so it is not a problem.'

We had a very enjoyable time and the weather was excellent, but at the end of the day it was only Disneyland and I wished I had waited for a subsequent trip to Tokyo to have the thought about visiting it.

On Monday and Tuesday we had various meetings with different teams to look at the potential in the Tokyo market, see what the competitors were doing and try to determine what sales approach we felt was required, and what was needed to achieve this. As we had already experienced from our dealings in Europe with TMBS and at Japanese bank branches, there were significant cultural differences between the Japanese approach to business and those of a Western company. These did bring with them various challenges in trying to reconcile what Charlie and I felt TMBS should be doing and what they felt comfortable with. Some of the differences did exist purely because of culture and we had to live with them, even if we found them frustrating. Others, however, seemed to be driven by nervousness at losing face in front of prospects, due to a lack of detailed knowledge of our products and the business area they addressed. It made it easier that we both knew Nishi well, as he was far more open than would have been the case if we not had the prior relationship with him, and it helped that this had been in London and not Tokyo. We knew we would have such challenges and overall the two days were successful, even on the areas were we didn't agree; at least these were now clearly identified and on the table to progress.

As mentioned I had a very good relationship with Nishi. He had a very nice personality and was generally very relaxed, always explaining to me the 'Japanese way' if a situation arose that required this. Because of this and the fact that my nature meant that sometimes I would wind people up for a bit of fun, I did at times set him up. One example would be when attending a formal meeting. Occasionally when going into the room, before the hosts had arrived, I would make for one of the armchairs, knowing full well we should sit on the sofa.

'Barnes-san, you must not sit there,' he would worriedly say in a loud whisper, 'you must sit on the sofa.'

'Are you sure Nishi' I would respond. 'The armchairs look much more comfortable.'

'No Barnes-san, you have forgotten,' he would politely explain again, 'we are the visitors, we must sit on the sofa.'

Another opportunity to see how he would react occurred when he was taking Charlie and me to the office one morning. Our route took us past the Imperial Palace, the Emperor's residence. The Palace had grounds around it that were open to the road with many smallish trees. I knew the Japanese liked these to grow in interesting shapes, so there were a variety of strong wooden stakes and wire cables being used to force the trees to grow in different directions.

'Nishi, what a shame,' I said to him as we passed an area with these trees.

'What is a shame Barnes-san?' he queried.

'All those trees, look, they are deformed,' I said, pointing. 'It's very sad.'

'Oh no Barnes-san, they are beautiful,' he responded.

'But Nishi, you can see they are deformed, look, the gardeners are using wood and cables to try and make them grow straight,' I naughtily said, keeping the wind-up going.

'Oh no, those are to help them to grow into interesting shapes, that is how we get them to look so nice,' he replied, in no way realising that I wasn't being serious.

'Well they look very odd to me,' I said, shaking my head slowly.

He then said the words he always used in such situations with me: 'That is our way, Barnes-san.'

I had managed to keep a straight face through the exchange but then realised that Charlie had turned to face the other way so Nishi would not see that he was struggling to stop himself from laughing.

On the Monday night we had been invited out with some of the senior managers for a formal dinner and then to go singing - karaoke. The restaurant was obviously very upmarket (one of the guys said to me it was velly, velly expensive) and we sat on Tatami mats again and had a lovely meal, although as before there was the odd dish that didn't suit a Western palate, including some revolting slime in a soup.

For the karaoke (which translates as 'empty orchestra') we went to a tiny nightclub, with a total of perhaps twenty people and a small stage at the end. This was my first experience of karaoke, as it was not that well known in the 80s outside Japan. We were given Japanese Suntory Whisky, which was perfectly ok, and then the singing began. There was a machine on the stage were you could select your musical soundtrack and then, solo, you would sing the words. I refused to go up and sing but they kept pressuring me and finally, as they had given me some English song sheets, I decided to go and sing *Country Roads*. This seemed to be a great success and when I finished there was loud applause.

Talking to one of the managers about karaoke, he said that it had an important role in business life. Apparently it wasn't done to bring up certain subjects while at work, for instance to tell your boss that you were unhappy, but at a karaoke evening (they were regularly organised by a manager for his staff) these rules did not apply, and you could discuss any subject.

The next morning I had said I would join the staff at 8 am for the company singing. This was very common across Japan with everyone standing up at the start of the day and singing the company song. I had asked Nishi if it would go down well if I was there and he said it would. Charlie didn't want any part of it so I went on my own by taxi, using a map with Japanese characters that Nishi had drawn to show to the taxi driver. The reason that getting to specific locations in Tokyo was so hard was that there were no street addresses, and where a number was given indicating a block of land, these numbers had been assigned in order of registration. Therefore the fact that you might be at a block number one less than the block you wanted gave no help as to where it might be. For this reason directions to a location would be linked to visual landmarks and many businesses would have maps on their literature and business cards.

Once you had been to a certain location the easiest thing was to identify the nearest landmark that a taxi driver would know and get him to take you there. There were 3D maps available with drawings of landmarks on them at the locations where they were. These were very useful once you had marked on the map exactly where the office or location was you wanted to get to.

The Japanese in general were very willing to help if you needed it, and the city was totally safe, so you did not need to worry at all on this front if you were out exploring. I had been told that while all Japanese learnt English at school, as they had no opportunity to use spoken English, they lacked confidence, which could manifest itself in them responding as if they didn't understand anything you said. The way round this was to write down what you were asking and show it to them; the majority of the younger people would be able to read it and assist you.

Anyway, I was with Nishi and his department well before 8 am and sure enough at that time a voice came over the Tannoy system, everyone stood up and as the music started they sang the TMBS song. This went something along the lines of 'we will all work hard to make the company a success, we will help our colleagues and be cheerful and friendly'. What I had not appreciated was that there then followed a mass workout – nothing too strenuous but exercise all the same, designed apparently to get you in the right frame of mind to start work. Of course I joined in to show how well assimilated I was becoming to the Japanese way of working.

After this Nishi and I sat down to run through what we would be discussing. These were our final meetings as Charlie and I were flying back the next day. The schedule had us free for the afternoon, which was nice, but I said to Nishi that we would obviously carry on into the afternoon if needed.

'That's very good of you Barnes-san,' Nishi said, 'but I will not be in the office this afternoon and I would prefer to be at any meetings you have, so we must make sure we finish on time.'

'That's ok Nishi, we've taken up so much of your time already you must have lots of work to catch up with,' I replied.

'I do have a lot Barnes-san, but this afternoon I have a difficult task to do that I am not looking forward to,' he said, looking rather downcast.

'I'm sorry to hear that Nishi, are you able to tell me what it is?' I enquired.

'Do you recall one of my staff, Hiroshi, who has been in some of the meetings?' he said. I nodded, recalling a young software engineer who seemed very bright.

'Well, I have a problem as he has been turning up late for work and often is not very smartly dressed,' Nishi explained.

'I appreciate you would rather not to have to discuss these things with him, but why do you say it is difficult?' I enquired.

'Oh this is not London Barnes-san, it is not him I must speak to but his mother in law.'

'His mother in law? Why do you need to talk to his mother in law?' I queried, fascinated.

'Because it is his wife's responsibility to make sure he leaves the house on time and is smartly dressed,' he explained, 'therefore she is not doing her job properly, and I must tell her mother about this so she can go and talk to her daughter and ensure she corrects matters.'

'Wow Nishi, I'm amazed, no wonder you are not happy to have to do that!' I said with feeling. He nodded.

With that final insight into Japanese life we had the remainder of our meetings, went around the office to say goodbye to all those we had met, and headed back to our hotel.

Having that last afternoon and evening to ourselves was a real bonus. Charlie and I were of course extremely grateful for the tremendous way we had been looked after, but it was very pleasant to now be on our own. We could properly get to grips with the layout of Tokyo and browse at our own pace through the streets and shops. We went back to the Akihabara district, where Nishi and his wife had taken us, with many shops both large and small selling a vast array of electronic goods, many of which would never be available in the West. We also found there the latest versions of some items that would not be released in Europe for weeks if not months, such as handheld games, watches and cameras.

I was extraordinarily lucky with my first visit to Japan. I had packed an incredible amount into the few days I was there. In addition to the tourist-related activities I had been given a real appreciation of the personal and business life of the average person and it had been fascinating.

I couldn't wait to go back – which I did, just under a month later.

Chapter 3

Settling in

I left Tokyo to go back to Hong Kong on Wednesday 27th April. That Saturday was my last day at the apartment on the Peak and I was moving to a very different place on the harbour front of Hong Kong Island.

Elizabeth House ('Elee za bar die har' for the taxi drivers) was a residential building with three towers (A, B and C) of 28 floors each with shops, offices and restaurants beneath. It was situated in Causeway Bay, a short distance eastwards from the central district, on the land side of the road that ran along the harbour front, facing Kowloon and with the Royal Hong Kong Yacht Club right in front. The yacht club was built in the late 1930s on Kellett Island, a very small island some way into the harbour. This had been the location for the old Naval Powder Magazine, but by the time I was there you could not trace the island at all as landfill had moved out to surround it and the first Cross Harbour Tunnel, completed in 1972, exited right by the yacht club. Luckily there were no major buildings on the landfill so my view was not spoiled, which as my apartment was on the 18th floor of Block C was excellent. As Causeway Bay jutted out somewhat I could also look left from my windows and see all the way up the harbour to the west.

As predicted by the agents I had been unable to find something like

Carolina Gardens again and Flat C8 Elizabeth House was a normal two-bedroomed furnished flat. The location and views however made up for losing the opulence of the peak, and it was lovely to be able to walk out of the door and be in the heart of the vibrant Causeway Bay district, with loads of taxis available to hail if I wanted to go further afield.

Moving in, I found something that needed to be addressed immediately. On opening the door to the kitchen there was a sudden movement across the whole floor and work surface areas - large cockroaches, at least a dozen of them! They vanished in a flash and on closer inspection, to see where they had gone, I realised there were small holes in various places that they had disappeared into.

Truly horrible, but I had been warned about this. The remedy was to buy a powerful insect spray called Baygon, so off I went in search of some. I started at a little local shop around the corner that had a tiny floor area but with every part of the walls covered with shelves going up really high. A wizened old Chinese man was in attendance and it was immediately obvious that he didn't understand a word of English. I was looking around for his bug spray section to point to the Baygon when he suddenly exclaimed, grabbed his ladder, went up about six feet and brought down - a tin of polish! I shook my head and carried on looking. After he had done the same thing a couple more times, with equally incorrect products, I worked out what was happening. He was looking at my eyes, and if they paused he would make a guess at what I was looking at and bring that to me. Anyway, having failed to spot any Baygon I gave up and went in search of it elsewhere.

Having found it in another shop I started vigorously spraying all the rooms with the green and red aerosol, anywhere I felt a cockroach might be able to enter or exit. The idea was that they would pick the poison up on their bodies so it could do its work. Having almost emptied the large can in a short space of time I suddenly realised I felt faint and was very breathless - clearly I had been rather cavalier and inhaled quite a lot myself!

I left the flat, found a bar close by and helped my recuperation with a couple of local San Miguel beers. When I returned the spray had settled and sure enough, within the next few days, the cockroaches were gone.

While I had been in Tokyo the weather had warmed up considerably and was now quite unpleasant at 29°C and over 90% humidity. I was still wearing my heavy UK suits and decided it was time to buy some lightweight ones, especially as the weather was only going to get worse as summer properly established itself. Hong Kong was not the place for someone of my size (6ft 2ins) to buy off the peg, so one lunchtime I wandered around a nearby shopping centre and popped into a tailor. I had never bought a made-to-measure suit before and was interested in how it would go.

'Can I help you?' asked one of the tailors in the shop.

'Yes please, I am interested in a suit in a lightweight material,' I answered. 'How much would one cost?'

'How much you want to spend?' he responded enquiringly.

This rather floored me as I had not considered that, of course, different cloths would have different prices, regardless of the labour element. And complicating matters, many prices in Hong Kong were subject to negotiation, with the trader trying to gauge the maximum he could extract from you. I realised I should have asked around first to get some input.

'I don't know' I replied, and after some quick thinking, 'you're the first shop I've come into so give me an idea for a good but not too expensive suit.'

'I'd better measure you first so I know how much cloth, then I'll show you some material' he answered, and took his tape measure from around his neck.

'Wah, velly tall man!' he exclaimed as he measured my height.

'Wah, velly big man!' as he measured my waist.

'You must eat too much, I will need lots of cloth,' he stated, shaking his head from side to side as he measured my chest, obviously establishing a position to justify his initial price.

He completed the other measurements, making various noises as he went along to imply how excessive every part of my anatomy was.

Well, despite the amount of cloth supposedly required, and with him complaining that he would not make any money out of me, after selecting a material about half way in the price range the cost seemed reasonable as a starting point. So, after the inevitable bargaining, during which I agreed to an extra suit and six shirts (which I had been thinking of getting anyway), a deal was struck. I went back a couple of days later for a fitting and the day after I picked them up.

As well as the lightweight suits to help in the heat, I had been advised to find routes from office to office that kept you in air conditioning, and it was surprising how many could be found given the proximity of the buildings in the central district, and the number of underground shopping arcades and linking corridors there were. A typical route would have me leave an office building and take a twenty-yard walk outside to the one next door. There you would go up to the first floor, where an air-conditioned bridge linked you to the next building. Down to the basement shopping area and an underground passage which took you to a hotel, where it was up to the mezzanine level, which looked over the lobby and had tables for drinks. Weaving between these you arrived at another air-conditioned aerial walkway to the next building, and so on.

In addition to my new-found status as the owner of made-to-measure suits and shirts, a short while later I had another pointer to the way I was viewed as an expatriate. Arriving at the office one morning, I found sitting on my desk with the other post a large brown cardboard box about an inch thick. Inside there was a copy of a very glossy magazine called 'The Peak' with a welcoming letter from the editor suggesting I take out a subscription. And in addition to the magazine and letter was a quarter bottle of Courvoisier XO Cognac! This was serious stuff, Courvoisier XO was expensive cognac and it was a good sized bottle, not a miniature. In fact I was so taken by the gift that I still have it, unopened.

The first article I looked at in the magazine brought me down to Earth with a bump, and showed that I was clearly not the target audience. It was about cooking for a dinner party, with recipes for a three-course meal. After the preamble, the instructions started off with 'While the first maid is doing .... get the second maid preparing the .... The magazine was assuming that its readership had not just one maid but two! And my latest flat didn't even have maid's quarters. I didn't take out a subscription!

I had by now found a permanent apartment I liked that I would have access to from 19th May, and I would need to move to it by 1st June when my current rent finished. San Francisco Towers was a new development of two 20-storey blocks in Happy Valley. The 1st to 10th floors were configured with three bedrooms, while the 11th and above had two bedrooms, but the same floor area. The apartments were of a good quality although smaller than I had hoped for, and as I was looking at the time they were released I had the pick of all of them. Initially I was going for one on the top floor as I would have use of the roof, but I was advised that this would be very hot and I was better to go one floor below. So Apartment 1A, 19th Floor became my Hong Kong home for the next four years.

Happy Valley was an area further east from where I was living at Causeway Bay but not far from the Central District, the cross-harbour tunnel and the road over to the south side of the island. It was also the location for the racecourse and in fact from my balcony you could see the home straight. Its name in Cantonese was Par Mar Day, which translates as Horse Race Ground because of the racetrack. The English name was given to the area due to the large number of cemeteries there, Happy Valley being a common euphemism for cemeteries in the mid 1800s. In fact there were six: Jewish, Hong Kong (formerly Colonial), Parsee, Hindu, St. Michael's Catholic and the Muslim Cemetery. It was originally very marshy and was not settled due to the high incidence of disease, later identified as malaria due to the mosquitoes. A British military camp had been set up there in 1840 which was closed down after a short while because of the malaria problem, although at the time it was not known what the fever was. In the mid 1800s it was realised that the flat valley was ideal for horse racing and it was cleared, drained and the racetrack established.

It was a pretty good area to be based in. In addition to the easy access to work and other parts of Hong Kong, there was a market opposite me and a reasonable selection of shops and restaurants. The tram did a loop around the racetrack, passing very close, and this was a great way to get into town, the old trams being one of the sights of Hong Kong. The racing was held on Wednesday and Saturdays, and while this did result in a lot of congestion and people milling around, if you planned for it there wasn't a problem.

Getting access to the apartment on the 19th May and moving in 1st June sounded fine in principle, but in practice it was a challenge. There was not a stick of furniture in the place, and I was leaving Hong Kong on the 23rd May to go to Bangkok and Tokyo and would not be back until the 28th. I was then going to be away again from the 6th to the 8th and 12th to 30th June, which included being in London for a planning meeting taking place on my birthday, June 20th. It was clearly going to take some time before I would have the flat sorted, but I had to make it habitable very quickly.

One blessing was that I had discovered Wing On, a department store in the central district that had the great benefit of a car park in the building. This made it easy to drive from the office, buy and load the car and then go to the flat. My first priority was to get a bed and bedding so I would at least be able to sleep at the flat on the 1st June. I also bought an air conditioner for the lounge and one for my bedroom. The flat did at least come with a cooker in the kitchen, so I bought a fridge and basic kitchen items and plates and cutlery. I also had to arrange all the paperwork for the electricity and gas and get a telephone installed. Thankfully Hong Kong had a service orientated culture and getting things done at short notice was a great deal easier than it would have been in many other places in the world.

This was in fact the third place I had to equip in only four years. In 1979 I had bought my house, a new build which needed kitting out from scratch. Then in 1980 I was given a job in Brussels, rented out the house fully furnished and started all over again; although at least the Belgium flat came with carpets and some basic furniture. So by 1982 I already had two of most things, and as I didn't bring anything out to Hong Kong, when I finally went back to the UK in 1987 I had three of everything, ironing boards, cutlery, crockery, glasses, bedding etc. etc.!

Wing On were able to deliver the big items quickly, and I was lucky that we had an office junior who was able to camp out at the apartment to take all the deliveries and let the various workmen in. I had far too much on to do this. One day he called me from the security guards' office (interestingly all local calls in Hong Kong were included in the monthly line rental) to say there was a problem with the fridge. Apparently it would not fit through the door! I could not understand this as I had bought a large US fridge/freezer to cope with the heat and humidity, and had therefore taken the precaution of measuring the door to ensure it would get through. There was nothing for it but to drop what I was doing and get over there.

When I arrived, there was the fridge sitting in the lounge area. It had gone through the front door but the kitchen door was narrower - I had stupidly not thought about measuring that as well. There wasn't much in it, no more than an inch. I had no intention of living there with the fridge in the lounge and decided the only way was to remove the door surround, and then replace it once the fridge was in - not too much of an issue. I contacted the builders we used at work and they said they would go over the next day and do it and sure enough they left a message for me the next afternoon to say 'job done'.

That day after work I popped over to Wing On for some further basics and on walking into the flat what did I see - yes the fridge was now in the kitchen, but instead of removing and replacing the door surround they had just roughly chiselled out chunks of the frame on one side and these bits were littered all-round the door with no attempt at repair. To make matters worse I had a meeting arranged with the landlord the next day at 6 pm to go through various things that needed fixing, as being brand new there were snagging items to sort out. And given I was in Macau for the weekend and flying to Thailand on the

Monday this could not be rescheduled.

First thing the next morning I called the builders and spoke to the manager, Mr. Yip.

'Ah good morning Mr Barnes, I hope you happy with work at apartment' he said, which showed he had no knowledge of what his workmen had done. 'Very rush rush job, Mr Barnes, but for important customer like you not a problem' he continued in a very subservient manner. 'Only too happy to be of service.'

'Well Mr Yip, that's why I'm calling you' I said very politely, 'would you say the job is finished or is there something still to do?'

'No all done, very rush rush as you wanted, look forward to more work at office for you as soon as you have some' he said.

'So the fact that your workmen have destroyed the door surround by chiselling big pieces out to get the fridge in, rather than removing and replacing the frame as we discussed, and then just left it like that is what you consider a good job is it Mr Yip?' I queried.

'Wah, what you say, really?' he exclaimed. 'So sorry, so sorry, my man must have misunderstood, we will fix straight away and I will go myself to make sure all OK.'

I explained the problem with the landlord arriving at 6 pm that evening, and he promised faithfully that it would be repaired so well that the landlord would never know. I didn't hear back from him and only managed to get to the flat five minutes before the landlord, hoping I wouldn't find it in the same state I left it. But Mr Yip had done his stuff and apart from the smell of fresh paint, which didn't seem to concern the landlord, all was in order and my meeting with him was fine.

The trip to Macau that weekend, when I could have done with staying in Hong Kong, was due to an old friend from my time in Brussels staying with me. Barbara had arrived on 2nd May and was flying out the same day I was, on the 23rd. I had promised her we would go to Macau while she was here, as I wanted to visit a couple who now lived there who used to work for the company, and this was the only weekend I could do it with her. Macau was a Portuguese-administered area on the West side of the Pearl River estuary about forty miles from Hong Kong and could be reached easily by ferries, jetfoils or hydrofoils. It consisted of a densely populated peninsula with a border crossing to China and two islands to the South. The first island, Taipa, was joined to the mainland by a long bridge and the second, Coloane, was joined to Taipa by a causeway.

We had a wonderful time there. It was so different from Hong Kong, with the Portuguese history and culture giving it a very different feel. Rhyddian and Angela made us very welcome and on the Saturday night we had a meal at Pinocchio's restaurant, a Macau institution. Excellent food, and as there were eight of us we ordered a large selection including veal, quail, fresh sardines, curried crab, the largest prawns I'd ever seen and bacalhoa (salt cod). All were washed down with Portuguese Vinho Verde wine and accompanied by hordes of mosquitoes, as the restaurant was rather basic. I didn't have a problem with the mosquitoes as luckily they never bit me, but poor Barbara had a dress on and was getting plenty of attention.

Outside the restaurant you had to run a gauntlet of old and very unprepossessing male and female beggars holding tin mugs up. I had been told there was no social security in Macau so I was quite willing to give them some money. We then went to the Lisboa hotel, another Macau institution, where we drank Portuguese brandy until 2 am, after which Barbara and I gave up and went to bed. Rhyddian and a friend of his carried on until 5 a.m. and when we all met up for lunch on the Sunday neither of their wives were speaking to them, and they looked dreadful - just a normal weekend in Macau we were told!

On the Monday evening I flew to Bangkok, the first time I had been there, and in fact the first time anyone from the company had been there on business. The reason for the trip was that the Hong Kong branch of a Thai bank was interested in our system and had requested me to visit their head office and establish contact. I was staying for two days as in addition to my meeting with the bank, IBM (on whose computers our system ran), wanted to introduce me to some other possible customers. On arrival there was a very apologetic message from IBM saying that due to the short notice the people they had wanted me to meet with were not available, so apart from the one meeting I had setup and one with IBM at 9 am, the rest of the time was mine. Wonderful - I had not expected to be able to do any of the tourist stuff as my schedule meant I was unable to add on any holiday. What made the stay particularly pleasant was that I had booked into the Oriental Hotel, at that time generally considered to be the best hotel in the world. I knew the company would give me grief if they knew I was staying somewhere so expensive, but decided I could handle this as in future I would use a cheaper hotel, but fancied trying out such a legendary place. The original building, built in 1879, was still standing but housed the top end suites and I stayed in a newer block, the River Wing. Very nice it was too and you could see why it had such a good reputation. But while the room was a good size and very well equipped, and the service excellent, it wasn't so special that I was going to be too disappointed if I didn't stay there again.

From Bangkok I had a rushed couple of days in Tokyo, getting back to Hong Kong on the Saturday evening. I moved into the Happy Valley apartment four days later as planned but it was very much camping out, as there was no furniture apart from the bed and a couple of foldable directors' chairs. But as I was so busy I was only sleeping there, so it didn't matter. I did have a worrying event on the first evening though. I had moved in that morning but did not get back until about 11 pm to find - lifts not working! Well, I was on the 19th floor and walking up all those stairs in the heat and humidity of Hong Kong in June was terrible. I had never considered this in getting somewhere so high up and had visions of unreliable lifts and having to do this on a regular basis. Thankfully they were never out of action again.

I had to make another short trip to Tokyo for a couple of important meetings the next week, getting back two days before flying out at 10.30 pm for my three week trip to London for the company planning meeting. The meeting, a couple of days in the London office and a course I was attending only took a week and a half of this time, but I took some holiday while back in the UK and had also decided to stay for a couple of nights in Bahrain on the way, as the flight stopped there on its way to London. The company had a small office in Bahrain and the local manager, Tim, was good company, so I decided that although I had no real business reason to visit the office, it was easily justified.

Tim was as good a host as I expected and I also enjoyed catching up with some of the staff I knew. There was one special moment while I was there when Tim had taken me to see the 'Sheikh's Beach', the Sheikh in this case being the ruler of Bahrain, whose title was Emir (meaning chieftain or commander). This beach was next to the Emir's palace. He was the absolute ruler of Bahrain and, as Tim explained, he was very pro-Western and enjoyed the sight of attractive girls. The beach was off limits to everyone except westerners, and it attracted a fair number of young girls in bathing costumes.

We were walking along the path to the beach when Tim pointed out an Arab man ahead of us. 'Look, that's the Emir himself,' he said. 'Do you know, if he decided he didn't like you he could have you locked up for life and no one could do anything about it.'

I decided to take a low profile as we walked past, but as we came up level with him he turned to us. 'Good afternoon' he said, and we, of course, stopped and turned to reply to him.

'Good afternoon to you as well sir,' Tim said in his best British accent. 'I'm just showing my colleague your beach. He is visiting on his way to London.'

'So you are British,' the Emir replied. 'You are very welcome here. As you will appreciate, I have been to London many times, but it is not as good to visit now as it used to be.'

'I'm sorry about that,' I sympathised, deciding I should involve myself in the conversation. 'What has become worse?'

'There are too many Arabs in London now,' he replied. 'When I first started going there I was respected as an Arab, I was proud to walk around, but now people look down on us. I have told your Queen about this. She is sympathetic but says she cannot differentiate which Arabs are allowed into the UK and which are not, and I can understand in her position.' There was a short pause. 'I would have liked to invite you for tea' he said, 'but unfortunately I have to go to a meeting soon.' He turned to Tim. 'Unfortunately your colleague is leaving, but next time we shall have tea together, and I will invite some other British people.'

Tim told me after we left him that he would quite regularly invite a few of the girls on the beach to join him on his veranda for tea.

The other interesting thing that took place on my visit was that Ramadan started on the 12th June – I had arrived early morning on the 11th. The evening of my arrival we had been for a drink in the hotel bar and all had been normal, but when we went back in the evening on the 12th the bar was hardly lit.

'What's going on, Tim?' I asked. 'I can't see anything.'

'It's because it's Ramadan from today,' he explained 'The Arabs are not supposed to drink alcohol for the whole month, so the management dim the lights so they can't be seen.'

And sure enough, looking around about half the customers were Arabs, all taking up the seating furthest from the entrance.

I arrived back in Hong Kong on Thursday 30th June, and had to fly again on the Sunday morning to Tokyo. I had realised by now that the job was going to involve a very significant amount of travel, and this was going to clearly impact what I could expect to do outside of work, and complicate my personal life to a considerable extent. Getting my flat properly furnished and equipped was one of those activities that would suffer, and in fact it would take me until the end of September to be able to say it was finished, four months after I had moved in!

Chapter 4

Life in the office

Our office was on the 8th floor of Hutchison House, a 22-storey building completed in the mid 1970s on the eastern edge of the central business district close to the waterfront. For expatriates its greatest claim to fame was that on the ground floor was the Bull & Bear English pub. This was decorated in mock Tudor style including exposed faux black beams with cream infill and dark wood throughout. It was the most popular place of its type and was usually pretty busy with both foreigners and locals, and it had the added benefit for me of access to it from the lift lobby of Hutchison House.

I had just over twenty locals and two expatriates working for me and we were housed in six rooms at the corner of the building that looked towards Central. Two of the rooms had desks in them despite having no windows, Hong Kong not bothering about these things. A key part of my brief was to significantly grow the business, including putting in place a sales force to make this happen. The company also wanted to increase the number of technical staff to be able to take on work from elsewhere, as staff in Hong Kong had proved themselves very productive, with excellent quality. There was not a spare seat in the current office so one of my urgent actions was to find and equip new office space – another not insignificant task to add to my initial workload!

On starting at the office I had been concerned as to how I would remember who was who as all the Chinese staff looked alike to me, similar height and, of course, everyone had black hair. Within two or three days however I could recognise some of the more distinctive ones, and less than a month later I found it hard to believe that I could ever have thought they looked the same; by then they were all completely different to me. All the staff had Western names that were used in the office.

Hong Kong Chinese did not get these names when they were born, but selected them for themselves when they were old enough, typically before becoming teenagers. The vast majority were straightforward, but odd names included those that were old fashioned and no longer used in the West, a Cinderella (no surprise that she picked it from the children's story), who was one of my customers, and an interesting one in our Singapore office was an Aloysius. This name had, apparently, been suggested to him by a relative who had seen it in *Brideshead Revisited*, the book by Evelyn Waugh. But as no one knew the correct way to say it he grew up with it being pronounced phonetically, and stayed with this even after being advised of the correct way to say it.

Offices in Hong Kong were open on Saturday mornings as well as Monday to Friday, but we had instituted a rota so staff did not work every Saturday. On my first Saturday in the office however I was surprised to find a number of people at their desks who were not down to come in. I was told that as virtually everyone lived in cramped and noisy apartments with their families, they would come into the office if they wanted quiet, to study for exams for instance, which many of them were doing. In terms of gaining qualifications I did find after a time that many Chinese seemed to go over the top with these, perhaps because of the relative insecurity of their status as Hong Kong residents, without full British Citizenship. When interviewing people they would often make a big thing of taking me through all their qualifications in detail, whereas I was more interested in their experience, potential and how they came across - they would not be seeing me if they were not educated well enough for us.

This insecurity was understandable given their situation, and anyone who was in a position to be able to was looking for ways to get a foreign passport. Canada and Australia were favourite destinations, but interestingly, when I spoke to staff or other people I met who had managed to get visas to work in another country, they all said they would come back to Hong Kong once they had gained the passport. They loved their life in Hong Kong; it was making sure they had a bolt hole if needed that was forcing them to go abroad.

I would go into the office most Saturday mornings for two or three hours. It was more relaxed than during the week, so I could have a chat with those who were in and get a few items off my 'to do' list. It was also common for me to arrange to meet people for lunch, as most of those I knew also worked Saturday mornings, and it was simple to meet up at one of the restaurants in the central district.

The most common lunch was the Chinese 'Yum Cha' – literally meaning 'drink tea'. This consisted of dim sum, a wide range of small steamed or fried dishes, which on a busy Saturday in Central would not be ordered from a menu but chosen from trays carried round or pushed on trolleys by the waitresses. You just stopped them to see what dishes they had and they placed on your table those you wanted. The normal drink was Chinese tea, and as your teapot emptied a waitress with a large jug of hot water would be walking round to fill them. To show you wanted more hot water you lifted the lid from the teapot and moved it back to rest half on the opening and half on the handle. I was told a quaint story as to why this sign was adopted. A 'long, long' time ago, so the story ran, the waitresses used just to lift up the lids themselves and pour the scalding water in. But one day an old man had caught a little bird outside a tea-house, and not having a cage, he picked up an empty tea pot as he went in and put the bird in there and then sat at a table. And yes, the waitress killed the bird by pouring boiling water on it. Well it made a good story even if no one nowadays put birds into restaurant teapots. Strangely, this was only done in Hong Kong. Elsewhere in the world when I was in a Chinese restaurant and mentioned this I was met with vacant stares, as if I was an idiot.

Within three weeks of starting in Hong Kong the office move topic went to the top of my priority list. The office next to us was being vacated by Hill Samuel, the British Merchant Bank, and was available. I went to view it and while it was a bit too small on its own (2,800 square feet), if we took it in addition to our current office (2,000 square feet) there was more than enough space, and it would make the whole issue of getting a larger office much easier, not least in keeping our current address.

I selected three design companies to give me outline ideas and estimates. Costwise they were very similar and I therefore selected the one I felt was easiest to deal with. Interestingly these also had their own builders who would be able to do much of the work required, thereby reducing the situation where one company would blame the other if problems arose.

London gave me a budget that wasn't as much as I had asked for, but I knew there would be ways to work within it so I went ahead. The designer had told me that moving or putting in partitions and doors was not expensive, but anything involving changing the lighting or air-con was. This helped me with one of the first challenges I had. Being a merchant bank the local manager of Hill Samuel had a lovely large office, and I wanted it for myself. It was however much too grand for a twenty-nine year old software house branch manager. But, given my limited budget, I decided I could argue that I hadn't been able to reduce its size due to the cost of relocating the lighting and air-con. The important thing was to hide this situation until it was a 'fait accompli' - I knew well enough that if additional money was needed to make sure I had a smaller office it would be found!

My fit-out budget had been based on buying in all the desks and other furniture required, however the designers said that, being Hong Kong, their carpenters could build these on site at a lower cost. Each item would be more minimalist and basic in design, but that suited us as an IT business - nice clean lines. The newly built furniture, being of cheap materials, would all need painting, and this helped the decision on the colour scheme, which I chose as grey with white walls and a charcoal carpet. By painting all the existing furniture the same grey it would fit in and could be reused. Hill Samuel had left very nice built-in wooden cabinets and a very large conference table, and again these were painted to match, saving more money. I even had a couple of two-seater sofas that had been left in the manager's office re-covered in charcoal grey cloth to match the scheme, for a rock-bottom price.

I was well pleased with the result, which was very smart and impressive. I had my super office, which did raise eyebrows and comments when anyone senior was in town. The designers did however ask a favour, that I keep quiet about the low cost, as it would cause them problems in future if anyone thought they could get this amount of space fitted out for what we had paid.

Just after we had taken possession of the new offices I caused a couple of upsets over two very minor items. The first was that the manager of the technical group, Winnie, a very capable person whom I had a lot of time for, said her team had asked if they could have an electric pencil sharpener. In those days programmers did not sit at their own computer screens but would write new programmes and show changes to existing ones on paper forms and printouts in pencil, so they were used a lot. I couldn't see the point of one central sharpener so I told her it made no sense to me, and that I felt it better if they just carried on using their individual sharpeners.

The other was the subject of tea and coffee in the office. We had our own small kitchen and I had inherited a system that was based around an enormous old electric kettle that took forever to boil, especially as the procedure seemed to be to fill it to the very top regardless of how much water was required. After a number of instances when I asked guests if they wanted a drink to find the meeting had almost ended before any tea or coffee arrived, I decided something had to be done. As the blame each time was laid at the door of the slow kettle, I bought in a machine with continually boiling water, and chucked out the kettle. I soon found out that I had upset quite a number of the staff, firstly over being considered exceptionally mean in regard to the pencil sharpener, and secondly, for changing a core part of the culture in respect of their venerable kettle, which I expect was based on having given them a good reason to gather and chat in the kitchen while waiting for it to boil.

The staff were anything but lazy so their time spent chatting was not an issue to me, but we were certainly not going back to the geriatric kettle days. However I gave way on the electric sharpener, realising I should have agreed in the first place, and although a small thing, my willingness to do this seemed to settle matters.

From my new office I had a view eastwards, most of it blocked by the Murray Road multi-storey car park (very handy though, as that was where I parked). This was also the location of the ICAC (Independent Commission Against Corruption). This special body had been setup in 1974 to tackle the endemic corruption which at that time existed in most areas of Hong Kong life, and it reported directly to the Governor. Bribes (called 'tea money') were paid for everything from getting a telephone installed through to very serious cases involving the police and government officials. The event that triggered its creation was a senior expatriate policeman (Peter Godber) fleeing from Hong Kong just before his retirement after it came to light that he had US$600,000 in cash in multiple bank accounts, more than six times his total income from the police force. The scale of the corruption that existed then was evidenced by the ICAC's first Annual Report, which stated that it had received 3000 corruption complaints in the first ten months of operation and 108 persons had been prosecuted, of whom 56 were government officers. Three years later in 1977 the ICAC's single biggest operation took place, when 87 police officers were arrested on suspicion of taking bribes related to heroin supply at a fruit market in West Kowloon. The potential to make money was also shown in the late 1970s when a relatively lowly detective sergeant called Lui Lok was forced to retire early after he could not explain his extensive assets, and was eventually fined HK$16 million. By the time I was in Hong Kong corruption was, thankfully, nothing like this, but it continued to exist of course and the ICAC was still active. I would regularly see people jogging around the roof top of the car park, and was told that these were prisoners taking exercise, as they apparently had a number of solitary confinement cells there.

With the new office I also had to make provision for one of the quirks of working in a Chinese environment - Feng Shui. Literally this translates as 'wind water', and is to do with making sure a building is constructed in a location and in a way which ensures harmony with the many elements that are in play from a Feng Shui viewpoint and that your office layout also follows correct principles. If you have good Fung Shui energy, positive benefits will result, but if it is bad the opposite will be the case. No matter what I might have thought of this as a westerner, the locals really believed in it.

I had already heard about this in the context of Kowloon, the part of the mainland facing Hong Kong Island. Kowloon translates as 'nine dragons', as there were nine hills around it (in some tellings it's eight hills plus the Emperor, who was considered a dragon) and the Chinese believe that each hill has a dragon living in it. Therefore if you were going to build something on one of the hills, it was important to make sure you didn't build where the dragon's head was, as this would irritate him and give you very bad Feng Shui.

I was having lunch one day about this time with Mike, a senior manager at IBM who had worked in Hong Kong for a long time, and I asked him about it. 'Feng Shui' he replied, 'you must make sure you have this covered Bernard, get a Fung Shui master in and follow any advice he gives - that way the staff will know everything is OK.'

'Hmm, I've heard they're quite expensive and I can't see London being happy with seeing a bill for this,' I responded.

'Nevertheless you have to do it - even if you pay for it yourself,' he said very seriously. 'I've had problems myself over this. I moved my sales team to a new office a couple of years ago and they told me it didn't have good Feng Shui as we faced the corner of another tall building. Apparently the negative energy leaves a building via the corners so it was coming straight into our new office.'

'But doesn't that make an office like that unlettable in Hong Kong?'

'Luckily Feng Shui is pragmatic. I brought in a Feng Shui man and he suggested a couple of things involving plants and shiny pots that were easy to do, which would supposedly bounce the bad energy away.'

'Oh good,' I answered, 'so at least if there are issues for me they can be sorted.'

'Yes, but get it done quickly. I left it about a month as I was busy and then went on a trip, and I suddenly realised our sales opportunities were going nowhere. These are bright, Westernised guys but they really believe this stuff and it affected their ability to do their jobs. I did what he advised, and you wouldn't believe it, the atmosphere amongst the team changed overnight, and they were back to their normal energetic, positive selves.'

'Well, thanks Mike,' I responded. 'Clearly a case of when in Rome.'

So I brought in a Feng Shui man. The staff and I were fascinated as he went around the office checking everything out with a very complicated compass-type instrument. When he had finished he explained that our office location was good as one side faced Harcourt Road, a one-way street coming towards us from the central business district and this 'brought lots of potential business towards us'. Our address was good as well, as we were 818 Hutchison House. I already knew that eight was a very lucky number as its Chinese pronunciation was very similar to that for wealth and prosperity, and we had two eights in our address; however he went on, it was slightly reduced because the 1 in the number could mean wealthy once only, but having two eights would counter much of that.

All good so far. The only negative was in relation to a small room we had in the new part of the office, where there was apparently some bad energy hitting us. He told me to put three gold-coloured pots on the windowsill to nullify the effect of this. I asked Winnie to find the type of pots that would be considered the correct ones by the staff. So that was another interesting experience to add to the collection I was building up.

A vital person in my business and personal life was my secretary, Margaret. Apart from all the normal secretarial duties she provided a wealth of local knowledge and, of course, her language skills. My cleaner ('amah') at the flat didn't speak a word of English, and most of the tradespeople who were needed to sort out various matters also spoke little or no English. She would get people in to do the work and make sure that they understood what had to be done, translating between us if needed.

Margaret had a number of strengths, but shorthand wasn't one of them. I tended to write letters longhand and then get her to type them. This was because my letters were relatively few and simple, with most requiring some deliberation and reworking before I was happy with them. Another reason was that I wrote a lot of letters when on planes or in hotel rooms, and these she typed when I was back in the office. One day I did have a number of simple ones I could just rattle off, and had time to do them in the office. Margaret duly came in with her shorthand pad and I dictated. Off she went and the typed letters were shortly back on my desk, but something very odd had happened in the process; while each letter was basically as I had dictated it, there were various odd additions and changes. Margaret's spoken English was excellent and looking at the letters I felt the problems weren't just down to a poor grasp of shorthand. I decided that the likely reason was that during the process of going from my spoken English through shorthand and back to typed English, Cantonese was somewhere coming into play, that being Margaret's mother tongue. Anyway, I decided it was best to give dictation a miss in future.

Margaret had a rather complicated personal life, as she was separated from her Chinese husband, but their son, who was about six years old, lived with her. She had an English journalist boyfriend, Nigel, who was working in Hong Kong, and their relationship was serious enough that they were considering getting married. She didn't however want to live in England, which was clearly were Nigel planned to end up. Her reluctance to move there was reinforced when Nigel, very stupidly, took her to the UK for her one and only visit in the middle of winter, instead of a better time of year. To make matters worse they spent the whole time at the home of his mother, who lived, if I remember, in Broadstairs or somewhere similar, and he didn't take her anywhere interesting the whole time they were there. I fully sympathised with her when she told me how dire the trip had been. Broadstairs, being a coastal town, was completely dead in December, the weather was miserable and made worse by storms coming in from the sea; the whole town was grey and unwelcoming and life at Nigel's mothers sounded as dull as dish water for a Chinese girl used to vibrant Hong Kong.

Margaret therefore realised that she had to consider other options and decided on going to Canada. This was for two reasons; her mother lived there, and she wanted to get a Canadian passport. She wasn't prepared to leave her son, but taking him to Canada required the consent of her husband, which he wouldn't give. She would regularly come into my office and bring me up to date on the latest situation with regard to trying to get her son to Canada despite the husband's refusals, and on where she was with Nigel. It was rather depressing for me to have to listen to this as I couldn't see any positive outcome or offer any advice that would make her feel better.

The worst moment was when she asked me for a private talk and said she wanted to involve lawyers to help her get her son to Canada. She said she didn't have the money for this, but as she had worked at the company quite a long time could I get approval to lend her the money and she would pay it back out of her salary. I told her I'd have to think about it. This was a tough one as I wanted to help her, but knew London would take a lot of convincing to even consider something like this, and would most likely say no. I wondered whether I should lend her the money myself, but as I thought about it I realised that the answer was really about her ability to pay off what was quite a large amount of money. I was pretty sure, from what she had told me previously, that her finances were very tight each month as it was. Therefore she would struggle to repay any money, and involving expensive legal help was going to be a slippery slope in respect of more and more costs.

I explained this to her as the reason I had to decline and, thankfully, while disappointed, she could see the logic and accepted that I had made the correct decision from the company's viewpoint. Happily therefore this didn't cause issues with our working relationship, which continued to be excellent right up to when I left Hong Kong.

A couple of months after I had arrived I decided to have a staff get-together one evening. I booked a function room at a club next door to the office, and after a presentation from myself as to what the plans were for Hong Kong, and how we were progressing, we had some drinks and then a sit-down meal. This taught me a couple more things about the differences between working with Chinese and Western staff. Firstly, at the meal, I noticed that a cheese plate I had selected as one of the courses was almost universally left uneaten. Asking why, I was told that Chinese people were not keen on cheese, and historically had eaten virtually no dairy products. Apparently this was gradually changing, but for most of them cheese was still a step too far. I resolved to make sure that in future I would get Margaret's input on my menu selections, and in fact later discovered that lamb was also a food not too most local people's taste. Then later, when I looked at the drinks bill, it was 90% orange juice. In fact you could spot the expatriates who were there by the alcoholic drinks – I had been on wine, another had been on gin & tonic and the third was drinking beer. Margaret explained that while most Chinese people did drink alcohol, it needed to be in situations where they felt comfortable, and a company dinner with the boss was not one of those.

The Hong Kong office was not just a branch but a location that was used as part of the global financial structure the company had in place, and they kept a large part of their cash there. Therefore a Hong Kong company had been incorporated, and as the most senior locally based manager I was appointed Managing Director to allow London to operate the company. Of course I was the MD in name only as the Hong Kong entity needed to have one together with a Board of Directors, meetings and board minutes to be able to operate.

I was also a signatory on the company's bank account, and as only one signature on a cheque was required this made it easy to pay the bills. In their wisdom London had set up a control in that there was a maximum amount each cheque could be written out for. There was however no limit to how many cheques I could write out (even to a single payee), or to how many chequebooks I could request, so it wasn't really an effective measure. As the amount per cheque was set quite low any large bill required multiple cheques, the payroll for instance requiring me to write out five cheques each month to the company that handled it!

Having finalised all the paperwork regarding adding myself to the Hong Kong company, it struck me that it would be good if I could have the more impressive title of Managing Director on my card rather than General Manager, which I was using so far. Given I had this title legally I decided that was enough justification. Status was very important in Asia and I also felt that if I looked for or was approached about roles outside the company this title would be beneficial. Best not to ask, I decided, so I just went ahead and had new business cards printed.

Margaret suggested that I should use this opportunity to have the Chinese language equivalent of my name on the other side of my card - a common practice in Asia. But this meant I needed a Chinese one, so she sat together with a couple of the managers to come up with something suitable. They selected three characters which were written vertically with, top down, my name being pronounced BA BUN LAP. The translation of the BA was 'white', and the LAP 'outstanding'. The BUN in the middle apparently had a different meaning whether there was peace or war at the time. In peacetime it was 'lot of knowledge' and if at war 'fighting'.

Talking about status I had noticed that quite junior girls in the office had Louis Vuitton bags and expensive watches by such brands as Cartier or Rolex. I had thought they were fakes as these were quite easy to come by. Apparently this was not the case; I was told that this was part of the culture for those who worked in the sort of companies that had offices in the central district. When they started their first jobs, however lowly, they would save to buy these luxury items, as having them meant a great deal. I then realised that everywhere you looked there were designer labels and logos. As someone who had grown up in middle class North London I didn't have the least interest in designer goods, but this changed gradually while I was in Hong Kong, given the incessant exposure from advertising and what people I met were wearing.

Chapter 5

Oxelotel II

On Saturday 9th July 1983, with just over four months of living in Hong Kong under my belt, I was browsing through the *South China Morning Post* classifieds for anything for my flat when I saw an advert for something altogether more interesting: 'One fifth share in 40-foot Chinese pleasure junk, berthed Aberdeen, full time boat boy - HK$15,000'. This was about £1,100, which while quite a lot of money in 1983 was easily affordable, and the idea of being part owner of a junk definitely appealed. There was a box number, so I quickly wrote a letter and popped out there and then to post it.

A couple of days later, sitting on my desk with the other post was a purple envelope addressed in green ink to myself. Very strange, I thought as I opened it. Inside was a reply from the owner of the one fifth share, also in green ink on purple paper. He confirmed that his share was still available, gave me a few more details of the junk and included his contact number, which I immediately rang.

Jack Hand was a government employee who was leaving Hong Kong, hence the sale. We arranged to meet that Saturday so I could look over the boat and get more information. As noted in the advert it was moored in the Aberdeen typhoon shelter, which was a harbour on the south side of the island. The meeting place was the jetty of the

Aberdeen Boat Club, also in the typhoon shelter. I couldn't wait for the weekend to arrive, not only to see the junk, but to find out what type of person used such an extrovert colour scheme for his correspondence.

On arriving at the jetty Jack was there waiting for me, and explained that the junk was on a floating mooring and we would therefore have to get a sampan to take us to it. Sampans were water taxis and the small ones, taking about six people, were manually rowed from the rear with a long single oar, usually by women. They were flat bottomed and only operated in the typhoon shelter as they couldn't cope with rough seas. Jack hailed one of them, agreed a price, and I gingerly stepped into the tiny boat, which was bobbing around all over the place, and a few minutes later we arrived at the junk. Its name, prominently painted on its side, was Oxelotel II.

'The Ox', as Jack referred to her, turned out to be twenty years old. Originally a fishing boat, it had been converted into a pleasure junk ten years ago. It was painted dark blue with two long white stripes down the side and had a large wheelhouse running across the width of the boat just about in the centre. From this, looking forward, there was a flat open area covering the cabin which extended halfway to the bow. Rearwards coming off the back of the wheelhouse the whole of the deck was covered with a roof made of some sort of tarpaulin material, but completely open at the sides.

'She's powered by an ex-Kowloon Motor Bus engine,' Jack told me. 'Once they're worn out in the bus they are used for junks, where they don't have to run at any speed to drive the screw.'

'What about the full time boat boy you mentioned?' I asked him.

'Not a boy at all actually, but a lovely old Chinese chap called Ah Kwok,' Jack replied. 'He's sixty-nine but looks eighty plus. If you want to take the junk out he's always available and sorts out everything from fuelling to helming and docking her, oh and he makes a great cup of tea as well.'

'How good is his English?' I asked, as he had already told me that the other four partners and their wives were all English speakers.

'Hardly a word of it, but we don't usually have a problem getting him to understand what we want to do when we're on the boat. He's very well known in the typhoon shelter by the way, as he used to be captain of the Aberdeen fishing fleet.'

'So I'll have to get my secretary involved if I need to contact him?'

'Not needed,' Jack responded. 'Everything's handled through the secretary of one of the other partners, she's the one who deals with Ah Kwok. In terms of running costs, your share is HK$1,500 a month, which covers everything except exceptional items. We had a survey done on her recently and everything's fine, I'll let you have a copy of that.'

'Interesting name,' I said. 'Where does it come from?'

'It predates the current partners. Apparently it's a lizard that can change its colour, and relates to the original owners and the lively parties they had on the junk, compared with their staid banker/government images at work.'

He then walked me round the boat, pointing out various items, and took me down to the cabin, which was just a large open space for storage with a rudimentary kitchen and the toilet. Back on deck he showed me where the engine was and then we sat down and chatted about our backgrounds, and he gave me more information on the other four partners. That wrapped up what we needed to cover at that time, so he hailed another sampan and we went back to the jetty. Once we were both back on dry land he turned to me.

'So, having seen her are you still interested in buying our share?' he queried.

'Definitely,' I replied. 'What a great thing to be involved in while I'm based here.'

'Well if you're free Friday night, all the partners are going out on the junk for a seafood dinner. 'That would give you and them a chance to meet, and I can introduce you to Ah Kwok and we can go from there. I'll give you a call to confirm arrangements.'

'That would be really good,' I replied, and we shook hands.

In the car driving back to my apartment I mused on the possibilities afforded by the Ox, and also on what I thought of Jack Hand, and decided that for someone who wrote in green ink on purple paper, he had turned out to be a totally normal individual from what I could see.

That Friday I met up with everyone on the Aberdeen Boat Club jetty at 7.15 pm. Three of the other owners, together with Jack Hand and his wife, were there, and after the introductions we went to Lamma Island for a seafood dinner. This island, called Pok Liu Chau in Chinese, the third largest in Hong Kong, is just over four miles in length and about a thirty-minute ferry ride from Aberdeen, although at the six knots the Ox travelled it took us a fair bit longer than that. The journey also traversed a major shipping lane and I was told that as Ah Kwok's vision, particularly at night, wasn't wonderful, one of those on board was always nominated as a lookout. With massive container ships going up and down the channel, as well as lots of smaller stuff, this made sense.

Lamma was undeveloped and had a laid back style. Quite a number of expatriates, attracted by the cheaper rents and the low key lifestyle lived there. The vast majority of the residents were in the north and east of the island with very few living in the southern half, as with no roads getting there required hiking or private boats. The island also had the only breeding place for green turtles in Hong Kong, and one of the few in Asia. The beach the turtles used was at Sham Wan Bay in the south-east of the island, which was also an archaeological site where a Bronze Age settlement had been discovered.

Lamma was well known for its seafood restaurants, centred on two of the villages. Private boats would go there in the evenings and at weekends to eat in them, but they were also accessible by ferries. The one we went too rejoiced in the name of the Lamma Hilton, but any ideas that it might be related to the hotel chain were dispensed with on arrival - it was very basic. The food though was outstanding, and with such a big group we were able to order a wide variety of dishes including whole fish, which were expensive as they were kept alive in tanks.

It transpired that the owners had ten children between them, and one of the wives was pregnant. They explained that the way it worked was that on Friday evenings the junk did what we were doing tonight, going to Lamma for a meal, and as there were no children, guests were welcome. Saturday was an owners' and guests' day but Sunday was only for owners as the boat was usually pretty full given the large number of children; however this rule was relaxed for non-Hong Kong residents. During the week there was a first come first served booking arrangement.

Apparently there were other people interested in the junk, and a decision would be made next week as to who would get first refusal. This deflated me a bit because as the remaining four owners all had families, I wondered if they might not be keen on a single guy.

Just after 10 pm when we had finished eating, we went back on the junk and motored round to a small quiet bay where we drank coffee and chatted, and some people went swimming off the boat. What an excellent way to spend an evening, so different to the normal hustle and bustle of Hong Kong.

Well I didn't have to wait long to find out the situation. Jack called me the very next day and said everyone had agreed that they were happy for me to buy his share. It transpired that my concerns as to being single were misguided, and in fact this made me more attractive. Given how many children could be on the boat, especially on Sundays, someone without any was considered preferable.

I managed four trips out on the Ox in the next month before going for a week's holiday on the 8th September. While I was away Typhoon Ellen hit Hong Kong, causing major damage, and while my flat escaped untouched unfortunately the junk did not. The boats in the typhoon shelter suffered badly. The Ox came off better than many but the large wheelhouse was completely blown off, all the guard rails were torn from one side and there was other more minor damage. I remember talking to one of the other partners about the force required to rip the whole wheelhouse off. He then made a good point about just how much damage it would have caused to other boats, as it was blown through the typhoon shelter by the hurricane force winds. The estimate for the repairs was £3,000, but thankfully the insurance covered that. The Ox was out of action for over two months, being ready again in mid-November. This unfortunately covered a three-week period my sister Marion and her boyfriend were in Hong Kong, so while they saw the junk on the slipway being repaired, they never made it out on the water in her.

Despite Jack's explanation of the Oxelotel name I was never able to find any lizard (or other animal) called that. The closest I came across was an Axolotl, a very strange type of salamander found in only two lakes in Mexico. Salamanders spend their early years living as larvae in water, and as they reach adulthood grow in size and transform into a land-dwelling animal. Axolotls do not, but reach maturity still living in water and keeping their gills, webbed feet and other aquatic differences. But if a situation occurs where they get reasonable amounts of iodine (including being given it in a laboratory), then they will quite quickly change to the larger land-based salamander form as the iodine stimulates the thyroid, which triggers this metamorphosis. Given this I wondered if the name (despite being spelt differently) was chosen not due to a colour change, but represented the idea that the owners had reached adulthood without properly 'growing up'.

A trip on the junk brought with it the interesting experience of the Aberdeen typhoon shelter itself, the largest in Hong Kong. When I had someone coming out on the Ox who had not been there before, I would often arrive early with them and pay the sampan extra to take us for a tour. The typhoon shelter was a C-shaped stretch of water between Hong Kong Island and the small Ap Lei Chau Island, and it was split roughly in two by the bridge that joins them to form the west and south shelters. At each end there were breakwaters which had been constructed in the 1960s. Also known as Aberdeen Harbour, it was one of nine harbours in Hong Kong.

Aberdeen harbour was where the early European sailors landed, the first of whom would have been Portuguese in the 1500s, and it is from Aberdeen that one of the contenders as to how Hong Kong gained its name comes. There are various views on this, and my favourite is attributed to a misunderstanding by these sailors. At that time there was a small village there called Heung Kong, which can be seen on maps from the Ming dynasty (1368–1644). This translates as 'fragrant harbour', and it was so named as incense from sandalwood trees was stored here before being shipped elsewhere in China. These early sailors didn't realise that the name Heung Kong referred only to the village but thought it was the name of the whole island.

The shelter was home to the 'boat people'. They were nothing to do with the Vietnamese refugees but consisted of two Chinese clans, the Tanka and the Hoklo. They traditionally spent their life on their boats from birth to death, very rarely going on land and, in the case of the Tanka, historically being banned from doing so. Recognisable by their large brimmed hats, in the 1960s and 1970s there were tens of thousands living in the shelter in thousands of boats, but gradually the numbers were dwindling as they moved to easier land-based jobs and more comfortable apartments. While nowhere near as dense as you could see in old pictures, the boats were still packed tightly together and as the sampan went around you could see so much going on: cooking, washing, mending nets, children playing and social activities such as the game of mah jong.

The Tanka, also called 'gypsies of the sea', can be traced back to the Tang Dynasty (c. 600 - 900 BC) and some historians believe they were Chinese fishermen who decided to live on their boats to avoid civil unrest and fighting on the mainland. Other researchers believe they may be a distinct ethnic group in their own right. Historically they were considered outcasts and of the lowest class, and were not allowed to mix with or marry land-based Chinese. Their image was not helped by Tanka prostitutes. While land-based Chinese prostitutes in the early years of Western contact considered European men strange and would not deal with them, Tanka prostitutes had no such concerns, and this lowered their status even further. In fact so badly were Tanka women considered because of this that in areas with Tanka communities it was not uncommon, when surveys were done on prostitute numbers, to count every single Tanka female as a prostitute. The name Tanka, literally meaning 'floating', is not one that they use themselves, but it is derogatory and was coined by land-based Cantonese speakers. The names the Tanka give themselves translate as 'people of the water', 'boat dwellers', 'lives on the waters' and similar.

The Hoklo however were viewed differently. Also known as Hokkien, their traditional ancestral homes were in Fujian province in China. They spread all over South East Asia; in fact 70% of Taiwanese people are believed to be descended from the Hoklo. Those in Hong Kong most probably took to living on boats and fishing due to difficulties with living off the land in the Fujian area. Therefore while the Hoklo in Hong Kong are also considered 'boat people', they did not have the historic issues of being seen as outcasts or of low class, as the Tanka were.

Aberdeen was also particularly well known for its giant floating restaurants, the Jumbo and the Tai Pak. These were firmly on the tourist trail and made wonderful photographic material, particularly at night, when they were very brightly lit up. They were modelled on Chinese imperial palace lines, being very ornate and colourful. The Tai Pak was much smaller than the Jumbo, seating about four hundred, while the latter could take over two thousand. They had their own jetties in the typhoon shelter from which a shuttle boat would take customers to and from them.

I had been told that the first of the restaurant boats dated back to the 1920s and served the families living in the typhoon shelter, and they were the venue for many of the weddings between the boat people. The floating restaurants as they were by the time I was in Hong Kong dated back to just after the Second World War when two, the Tai Pak and the Sea Palace, were opened. These were both replaced by bigger versions as their popularity grew, with the original Tai Pak being towed to a bay on the mainland in the 1960s, where it traded until this bay was reclaimed for building.

The Jumbo started life in 1971 but in October of that year, before it was opened, there was a terrible fire which killed 34 people and completely destroyed it. The rebuilt Jumbo finally opened in 1976. If you went round the back of it by boat, you could see that the kitchens were on a separate floating section, presumably so that if a fire did break out again they could be towed away from the main structure.

The Ox was a traditionally built junk with a high stern which sloped down to the front of the boat. She had no keel and therefore in certain wind and wave conditions would wallow from side to side uncomfortably, and I believed this was a design flaw. This was not the case though, and on a trip on the boat one of the guests, who taught at the university in Hong Kong, mentioned he was interested in the history of junks and gave me some background to them.

Apparently the lack of a keel was deliberate as it allowed them to enter shallow waters; but if it was a sea-going junk then it would have something called a sternpost rudder which could be lowered into the water, and this operated as both a keel and a rudder.

He explained that the first record of junks goes back to the second century BC, but during the Song Dynasty (960–1279) documents show that the early design was improved in a number of ways. These included multiple compartments accessed by separate hatches and ladders to give strength and provide watertight compartments to cope with typhoons, the sternpost rudder to aid steering and stability, and wooden battens in the sails which made them more easily controlled and increased speed. The design had proven itself as they regularly undertook extensive ocean voyages successfully.

Junks could be enormous and in the Middle Ages there are reliable accounts of a single junk being able to carry a thousand men with six hundred being sailors and four hundred men-at-arms. The largest ever junks were used by the Chinese Admiral Zheng He in the early 1400s when he undertook a number of voyages to Asia, the Middle East and East Africa. These 'treasure ships' were massive and, while the purported dimensions of over 130 metres (420 feet) long and 55 metres (180 feet) wide with nine masts may be overstated, even the smallest estimate by experts of 70 metres (230 feet) in length put them at the same size as the largest ships in Europe some two hundred years later.

Interestingly the name 'junk' is not linked to what they were called in Chinese, but originates in the Javanese word 'djong' meaning ship or large boat, with the English word derived via the Portuguese 'junco' and Dutch 'jonk'.

My involvement with the Ox didn't just deliver the opportunity for interesting day or evening boat trips but, unexpectedly, had a major influence on my social life away from her. The other owners turned out to be very friendly and sociable and we all got on extremely well. This resulted in invitations to a variety of events including dinner and birthday parties, barbecues, meals out, trips on the company boats of the other partners (all bigger companies had their own corporate junk or pleasure boat) and Rotary social activities, as a couple of the men were members. And, of course, with these activities and trips out on the Ox I met many other people. Through Bob, one of the owners, I also had access to video tapes of the latest UK TV programmes. He had a friend who would video programmes of interest and send them out to Bob's secretary and she handled the circulation of them and their posting back to the UK for re-use once finished with.

It was from my experience settling into Hong Kong that I formulated a piece of advice that I was to use in the future when talking to anyone moving to a new location. Obviously you wanted to make a new circle of friends. In my view what you had to do was to work out how you were going to quickly meet around one hundred people. It was a matter of odds. From one hundred people you could expect to find ten you particularly liked, and from those ten you should find three you could become good friends with. The key was to get out and meet the hundred, and this was not that difficult if you applied yourself to it, given the different clubs and organisations that existed. Joining a club wasn't necessarily because you were interested in what it did, it was a way to meet people, and having met the members you could always stop being active or resign if it wasn't for you.

In the course of a year the Ox would visit a variety of places that were in reach of Aberdeen harbour, although her slow speed did require time to get to some of the further ones. Lamma Island, as already mentioned, was a short trip and good for seafood meals and relaxing in one of the bays, anchored a swimmable distance from the beach. About two hours away to the north-west was Lantau Island (where friends of one of the partners lived and we would sometimes have lunch at their house), and an hour and twenty minutes south-east was Po Toi Island, another seafood meal location. There were a range of other options from bigger inhabited islands such as Cheung Chau to those that were not much more than barren rocks, but had a usable beach. In terms of Hong Kong Island itself one place we went to on occasion was Stanley, on the south side of Hong Kong Island. Stanley was quite developed with a market, shops and restaurants, and gave the option of exchanging the relative peace of being on the boat with going to town on the small tender we had.

Stanley was the location for the annual Hong Kong Dragon Boat Racing contest, held in May or June. Dragon boat racing goes back over two thousand years and has its roots in village competitions across Southern China. Since the mid 1970s it had expanded from its Chinese religious and folklore background to become an international sport, and Dragon Boat Day in Hong Kong was a big event.

A dragon boat normally had a crew of 22, consisting of twenty paddlers in pairs, one drummer and one sweep (who steers the boat) standing at the rear, however they can vary in size, being smaller or much larger than this. They have decorative Chinese dragon heads and tails at each end, hence their name.

One year we took the Ox to watch the racing. This was a much better way to see it than from the shore, where the beach was jam-packed with people, with the attendant challenges in getting to and from Stanley by road with so many others. There were a lot of other junks and pleasure craft there and they all moored in a line, parallel to the beach but far enough back to give plenty of room for the racing. This meant that the shore line and the row of boats marked out the course of the race, and we had great views, sitting in comfort with plentiful supplies of drink and food to hand.

In the process of tying up to the boat next to us Ah Kwok managed to get the propeller fouled by someone else's anchor rope. This meant three of us having to get into the water to free it. In the process I tripped and went headfirst into the cabin roof. There was lots of blood and I was excused duties and made to sit with an ice pack on my head. To disinfect the wound one of the wives put Mercurochrome on the cut. I had never seen this stuff before but it was bright red and she put so much on it ran through my hair. I then discovered that it doesn't wash off. Being fair I had bright red highlights in that part of my hair for a week before it finally disappeared.

It was a very hot day with no wind at all, so at 12.30, when there was a half-time break in the racing, we decided to move to a quiet bay for lunch, a swim and windsurfing. As we were on our way the weather worsened considerably and there was a rather concerning part of the journey as we rounded a headland. The Ox didn't like the conditions at all and was rolling from side to side like mad, and we were all quite uncomfortable. Finally we entered the quieter water of the bay, but by the time we had anchored the heavens had opened and it poured for the rest of the day.

I gave up my share in the junk in March 1985, at the same time as the other partners, a year and three quarters after I had seen the advert. What precipitated this was an electrical fire on her. No one was on board at the time and there was £3,000 worth of damage. While the insurance covered this, one of the partners canvassed the others to see if we would consider selling our shares. His company wanted to get a boat of their own and he said they were happy to take the Ox over. They would want to do quite a lot of work on her and this could be done at the same time as repairing the fire damage. We all decided that we would take him up on his offer. In my case I was so busy I hardly went out on the junk, so the monthly cost wasn't justified, and this was a very easy way to say goodbye to her.

Chapter 6

September 1983, Black Saturday and the fallout from 1997

With six months under my belt, September 1983 saw me in good shape in most key areas: my flat was just about fully kitted out, the new offices were underway and would be ready to move into very soon, I had made friends and was enjoying a good social life, and I was now on top of the major elements of the job. But of course there is often something 'waiting in the wings' to trip you up. For me, that September, it was the 1997 negotiations between the UK and China on who would control Hong Kong when that date was reached.

The background to this was what the Chinese called the 'unequal treaties', which they refused to recognise, as from their perspective they had been signed in the 1800s by force, given Britain's powerful military capability in the region at that time. The first of these, The Treaty of Nanking, signed in 1842, ceded Hong Kong Island to Britain in perpetuity. The second, The Convention of Peking, signed in 1860, ceded the Kowloon Peninsula to Britain, also in perpetuity. The third, signed in 1898, was a 99-year lease on the New Territories which expired on June 30th 1997. The New Territories comprised a large amount of the mainland adjoining Kowloon and around two hundred islands.

Regardless of the views as to the legality of these treaties, the critical issue was that in 1997 the Chinese would get the New Territories back when the lease ran out. They made up about 90% of the land area of Hong Kong and for a number of reasons (including food production, infrastructure and what would happen to those living there), Hong Kong Island and Kowloon could not operate without them. This issue had, of course, been hanging over the colony for many years, but in September 1982 it came into stark focus when, with the date getting closer, Margaret Thatcher, the British Prime Minister, visited Peking to open discussions on post-1997 Hong Kong. With it being clear that China wanted Hong Kong back, and realisation that the major risks this implied would be firmed up in the not too distant future, confidence started to weaken considerably. This increased significantly the number of people looking to move their assets abroad and progress getting foreign passports.

Between October 1982 and February 1983 a number of talks were held which were unsuccessful in moving the situation forward. This was due to both sides remaining firm on their positions. In essence Britain considered that the treaties were valid and they had continuing sovereignty over Hong Kong and Kowloon, while the Chinese disagreed and said it was they who had always retained sovereignty, but had allowed Britain to administer both as they occupied them.

Given the very weak negotiating position the British were in due to the definite loss of the New Territories, and the intransigence of the Chinese, the British Government realised that the only way to move forward was to soften their position. In March 1983 Margaret Thatcher wrote in a letter to the Chinese Premier Zhao Ziyang that the British would accept the Chinese having sovereignty, as long as a number of conditions could be achieved which would ensure 'the future prosperity and stability of Hong Kong'. This had the desired result and between July 12th and September 23rd four more rounds of talks were held.

In the middle of these talks I had a holiday. I had been working flat out for six months and needed a break, just to chill out on a beach or something similar. I decided to spend a week on Phuket Island in

Thailand. At that time Phuket was not the major tourist destination it was to become (which started with Club Med opening a resort there in 1985). There was one main holiday area at Patong Beach, with most of the bars and restaurants, but the accommodation was nothing to write home about, although fairly cheap. Luckily there was one decent hotel on the island, the Phuket Island Resort, which was a taxi ride away out of town. It consisted of a low rise main building and a number of villas dotted around the grounds which led down to the sea. I fancied a bit of luxury, so I booked into it.

I was originally going to fly on Friday 9th September. Unfortunately by Wednesday 7th it was clear that a major typhoon (Ellen) was going to come very close to Hong Kong on the Friday and therefore all flights would be cancelled. I thought about rescheduling the holiday, as I quite fancied being in Hong Kong when a typhoon struck to experience it. Looking at my diary though, I realised that if I did not go now, it would be weeks before I could rebook it, due to my commitments. I decided I needed the break more than I needed to experience a typhoon, and thankfully I was able to change my flight and reservation at the hotel to the day before, and flew out on the Thursday.

There were no international flights to Phuket in 1983, you had to go to Bangkok and then take a domestic flight. I had a two-hour connection between landing in Bangkok and my flight departure and as it was lunch time I decided to have a meal. The airport was pretty basic but I found a Thai restaurant, although its decor and ambience left much to be desired. On the menu was a 'Jungle Curry', which sounded interesting. The waiter arrived.

'I'll have the Jungle Curry please and a Singha beer,' I said to him.

'Too hot for you' was his brusque reply, 'you order something else.'

Now I liked spicy curries so I replied 'It's OK, I like hot curries, I'll have the Jungle Curry.'

'You not be able to eat, much too hot for you,' he said again, 'order something else from menu.'

I was a bit annoyed by this but decided to stay calm and polite, as was the way in Asia.

'Thank you for warning me about the heat, but I like spicy food very much and I definitely want the Jungle Curry.'

'OK it's up to you,' he said, shrugging, and went off to the kitchen.

It then struck me that I might well have made a major blunder. Given it was Thailand, I was quite sure the standard Jungle Curry would be very hot, even though it was an airport restaurant, hence his warning. But given I had rejected his advice twice, what if he decided to teach me a lesson, and was at this very moment telling the chef to boost the heat to incredible levels? Nothing I could do now but wait.

A nice cold Singha beer arrived and five minutes later the curry. The first thing that I noticed was that there were a lot of crumbled dried leaves on the top of the curry. I wondered if in addition to the extra heat, they had gone out the back and picked up a handful of dried leaves to make my humiliation complete.

In trepidation I tried the curry. With relief I found that while extremely hot, it was not hotter than I was happy eating and I polished it all off.

The flight down to Phuket was uneventful, but the arrival was not. There was a powerful storm over Phuket as we came into land. With the plane being blown all over the place and rocking violently from side to side the pilot made two abortive attempts to land, giving up almost as he was on the runway each time, before diverting to Hat Yai about two hundred and fifty miles away. Now I was not a particularly nervous flyer, but I had never had a last-minute aborted landing before, let alone two in a row, and the two approaches we made were quite frightening. Thankfully about two hours later we finally landed at Phuket in calm conditions.

On arrival the strong winds had abated, but it continued to pour with rain. This was no surprise as it was the monsoon season, and I knew that September was the worst month in the year for weather. On average it rained on 21 days in that month and had the lowest temperatures of the year. Of course this was the reason I had not experienced any trouble in changing my travel plans at the last moment. It was not all bad news though, as normally after a bout of rain the sun would come out. In fact the average amount of sunshine per day in September was seven hours, which, as we were near the equator with only about twelve hours of daylight, wasn't bad. And the lowest temperature was a relative thing – at an average 27C it was warm enough for me.

Unfortunately the rain continued all through the first night, all the next day and all that evening. By bedtime Friday night I was having serious doubts about the 'average' weather I had been led to expect. My faith was rewarded on the Saturday, which was delightful, dry and sunny. I had booked a day trip to Phang-Nga. This was a coastal area, full of mangrove swamps with amazing limestone outcrops rising up high to form small islands. The area had become well known as it was one of the key locations in the Bond film *The Man With The Golden Gun*. When I found out it was a three-hour trip from Phuket this had been one of the reasons I decided to go there.

We had a cramped coach ride for about 40 miles and then took a long-tailed speed boat through the mangrove swamps to the islands, via a seafood lunch at a Gypsy village built in the swamps completely on stilts. The highlight was stopping at 'James Bond Island', where the filming had taken place. This was surprisingly uncommercialised, only having a couple of boats drawn up on the beach with Thai goods for sale.

On Sunday I went to the main beach on the island. Patong Beach was just over a mile long and had thatched huts for cheap accommodation (with prices from £1.30 a night!), thatched huts for bars and thatched huts for seafood restaurants. It did however boast an excellent Austrian/German bar which also served Bratwurst, the German grilled sausage, and very good they were too.

I had arranged to go fishing the next day with one of the boats on the beach. I turned up at 9 am as agreed to find the boat ready but no rod and line, the fisherman having clearly said he had the gear to get my booking, but he had then not been able to get his hands on any. While I was hanging around mulling what else to do, a German couple I had become friendly with on the Phang-Nga trip rolled up in a rented car. Having heard about my failed fishing trip they said they were going to drive around the island and I was welcome to join them. So I hopped in and had an interesting day, much better than lazing around at a beach bar, which had been the best idea I had come up with prior to their arrival.

That night I went into the bar of the hotel and started chatting to a young American guy who was also staying there. Jim was the same age as me, working in Saudi Arabia, and had come to Thailand for the diving. He was on his own for the next couple of days until a friend joined him, when they were heading off to a diving resort. He was going snorkeling around the reefs the next day and invited me along. We had a great time, with no other boats in sight and fantastic coral and reef fish.

We agreed to go into Phuket Town that evening for dinner. After the meal we walked around a bit and then went into a bar. Half way through our first drink we decided to see if we could get anywhere with a couple of attractive Asian girls sitting at another table, who seemed to be on their own. We thought they might well be hookers, but as there were two of them there was a reasonable possibility that they were locals or on holiday, and there was only one way to find out. They were happy for us to join them and, as they spoke good English, there were no communication problems.

After perhaps twenty minutes or so a shocking realisation struck me – they both had Adam's apples. They were guys! I was well aware that Thailand was famous for its 'katoeys' – transvestites, also called 'lady boys', and that many were almost impossible to differentiate from real girls they were so well turned out, especially if they had been 'enhanced' by hormones or surgery. I looked again but there was no doubt. It was really disappointing as they were both very attractive, and we had been getting on so well.

I was wondering what to do next when luckily they both went to the toilets together.

'Jim, bad news I'm afraid, I've just realised they are transvestites,' I said to him.

'You're kidding!' he replied. 'No way, they're much too feminine for that.'

'Have a look when they get back,' I said to him, 'I agree they look great, but they both have Adam's apples, so that's a giveaway. I think we should say our goodbyes as soon as they come back and find another bar, if we talk to them for too much longer it might be hard to shake them off.'

'I still find it hard to believe. I'm not doubting you, but let me see what I think once they're back.'

The 'girls' soon arrived and after a few moments Jim turned to me.

'They look real to me Bernard,' he whispered, 'really sexy. I think I'll see how I get on and take the risk.'

'Fair enough,' I whispered back to him, 'but will you be ok if I make my excuses and leave?'

'No that's fine. You Brits, you're too cautious.'

'Better safe than sorry,' I replied.

I made some excuse about an early start and said goodnight. It was a lovely evening so I wandered around town for about 20 minutes. Not having seen any other bar I fancied, I decided to go back to the hotel and hailed a taxi.

Well the hotel had quite a long drive leading up to it, and where the drive met the main road there was a security control with a guard and a barrier. As my taxi pulled up there we were behind another taxi, and as one of the passengers in it turned to talk to the guard, I saw it was Jim. And sitting next to him surprise, surprise was one of the girls. The guard waved both taxis through and his turned off the drive, as he was staying in one of the villas in the grounds, while mine carried on to the main building. Jim had not realised I was behind him, and I wondered as I went to bed how he was getting on in his villa!

We hadn't arranged to see each other the next day as he was meeting his mate at the airport and then they were going straight off to the dive resort. At 10 am, however, my phone rang, and it was Jim asking if I wanted to meet up for breakfast.

'So how did you get on last night?' I asked him when we met, not mentioning having seen him in the taxi.

'Oh, complete washout,' he replied. 'You were quite correct about them being lady boys, I realised five minutes after you had left. I walked around a bit looking for you but then came back here.'

It would have been really interesting to find out what had gone on with him last night, but on the basis that he was keeping very quiet about bringing her back to the hotel, it seemed best I shouldn't mention that I had seen them.

Later on in the week I managed to track down a fisherman who did actually have fishing rods and reels and arranged for him to take me out. I had an excellent time. From 10 am to midday we anchored over a large reef in the main channel between Phuket and the mainland. I caught over a dozen fish including grouper and red snapper and a couple of other species I did not know.

He then took me to an island where a friend of his lived, in a little house all on its own in a small bay. His friend was not there but his wife cooked the fish I had caught for lunch for us. She used the smaller ones to make a very tasty fish soup and grilled the bigger ones and served them with fried rice. It was another world completely, sitting under the coconut and banana trees while her young children played all around us.

After lunch we set off in the boat again and went to deep water to try for large fish, but having no luck the boatman said we should go inshore and try for a type of fish where all we would use was a fishing line with the hook on, no weights. This was called drift lining and was fantastic sport on the light rod he gave me, with the fish fighting really hard. When I caught the first one I recognised it as a garfish. These are long and thin and a member of the mackerel family. I caught five before it was 4.30 pm, when we had to go back.

I had a stroke of luck though as we were packing up. The boatman asked me when I was going back to Hong Kong and I said in a couple of days, on Saturday. He queried this and said that tomorrow was Saturday. At first I thought he was the one who was wrong, but on going through the days I had been here and what I had done I realised he was quite correct. Well, I thought, it must have been a good holiday if I had lost a complete day. The only thing in my defence was that the date on my watch was wrong. I might well have missed the flight if it wasn't for him as the hotel gave me no indication I should be checking out and I could easily have gone off for the whole day.

I arrived back at my flat about 11.30 pm on the Saturday to find waiting for me a colleague from the company in London. Sean was on a holiday around Asia and I was letting him stay with me while he was in Hong Kong. He was up for going out despite the late hour, and we made a night of it, getting back at 5 am.

I had another hectic period coming. On Wednesday I was flying to Tokyo and, having been on holiday, had loads to do in the office before I left, and at the same time I was showing Sean Hong Kong. I was arriving back from Tokyo on Sunday and leaving the following Saturday for Singapore for eight days. During the week in between I had loads of people in town including the global sales director on the Thursday and the finance director on Friday, both from London. They each required time in the office to go through business matters and then to be looked after socially in the evening, although at least they were good company to be with, unlike some of the London executives. On the Wednesday I had one of my team over from Tokyo, where he was based, to go through various work matters and to be entertained in the evening, but as he worked for me this was pretty relaxing compared to being with the London visitors. As the Singapore trip included a planning meeting I had a number of papers and presentations to put together for it. There was no way I was going to be able to get these all done in time, and I ended up working from 5 am both mornings of the meeting putting together presentations for that day - talk about 'just in time'!

Arriving back in Hong Kong from my holiday I found the flat untouched, thankfully, by typhoon Ellen. This had turned out to be a very powerful typhoon with hurricane force winds lasting for five hours; eight people had died and 120 were seriously injured. The next day I heard that the Ox had not been so lucky and was quite badly damaged. She would be out of action for perhaps three months, which was a great shame as I'd been looking forward to some trips on her.

After I had surfaced on the Sunday from the 5 am session with Sean, I updated myself with happenings in Hong Kong while I had been on holiday. It was clear that the 1997 negotiations had been going from bad to worse, and having a very negative impact on confidence.

I've covered earlier in this chapter the historic background to the 1997 negotiations and mentioned the four rounds of talks that took place between July 12th and September 23rd.

The worsening of the situation with each of the four rounds of talks is clearly summed up by the official statements made after each of them. After the 1st round (12th and 13th July) the statement was 'useful and constructive', even though indications were that nothing had been accomplished. By the 2nd round (25th and 26th July) it had deteriorated to 'useful' and by the 3rd (2nd and 3rd August) and 4th (22nd and 23rd September) rounds not even this.

The main issue at this time was that although Britain had effectively conceded sovereignty to China it was holding out for the right to administer Hong Kong post 1997, which the Chinese adamantly refused. There had been increasing concern locally as it became clear the talks had hit problems, not helped by a constant barrage of inflammatory propaganda in the Chinese newspapers, which were readily available. The Hong Kong dollar had been weakening for some months, reflecting the concerns and the increasing number of people and companies switching assets from being Hong Kong dollar based to being foreign currency based.

By the time of my return from Phuket on the 19th September the rate had weakened enough due to the bleak outlook that the finance director called me on the Sunday urgently, because the company had most of its spare cash on deposit in Hong Kong dollars.

'I know you're just back from your holiday, but the Board and I are very concerned at the weakening dollar and we're considering switching into sterling,' said Steve. 'I was going to leave it until I saw you next week to discuss it, but I don't think we can wait that long given what's happening.'

'That's a tough one Steve, not sure how good my crystal ball is,' I replied.

'I appreciate that, but we've spoken to our bankers here and they aren't willing to give a view, so I said I said I'd speak to you and get your thoughts from a local perspective.'

'I think the best thing is for me to contact some of our customers here tomorrow for their views and get back to you.'

'Thanks, that would be good,' he replied, and hung up.

I managed to speak to four of my contacts on Monday morning and called Steve back when London opened with my findings. 'The consensus is the same,' I told him. 'The next three to four weeks is going to be rough, but it's not in anyone's interest for the currency to collapse, so something will be done to get it stable again. They believe the sensible option for us is to wait it out if we have no immediate need for any of the money.'

'I'm happy with that,' replied Steve, 'I'll let them know at this end.'

'Mind you,' I continued, 'that was how they felt about the company's money, but a couple of them told me they are however buying gold with their personal savings to ride out the storm. I don't know if you want to factor that into your thinking.'

'No, that doesn't bother me,' he replied.

After we had hung up I gave the money in my own savings account some thought. I did have a fair bit of cash in the bank, which was the money I was putting away to pay my income tax. If the local dollar was going to get weaker and stay weak for some time I thought it would be good to have this in US dollars or sterling to use when I was abroad, otherwise buying things overseas could get much more expensive. Putting my savings into another currency, while sensible, seemed rather dull compared to putting it into gold. Being someone who never had any savings, let alone the requirement for investing, the idea of my holding gold had never crossed my mind. It was exotic though and something very Asian, the Chinese being big on gold as an asset.

So I went out and used my savings to buy Krugerrands, the South African solid gold coin. I was rather concerned about being mugged with all these in my briefcase until I had managed to open a safety deposit box (another first).

I went off to Tokyo, and sure enough it went from bad to worse. The non-event of the ending of the fourth round of talks on Friday 23rd September and what this meant, coupled with rumours that some banks were on the verge of failing, precipitated a massive crisis of confidence. The Hong Kong dollar plummeted from 7.9 to the US dollar on 16th September to 9.6 on the 24th September, thereafter called 'Black Saturday'. There was panic buying of basic goods and imported items and many shops would only accept foreign currency, quoting prices in US dollars. The authorities clearly had to do something very significant to quell the collapse in the dollar and support it going forward. What they did was to announce the next day that they were putting in place a currency stabilisation plan. This took the form of pegging the Hong Kong dollar to the US dollar at 7.8, with the government holding assets to support the currency at this rate. Together with the removal of a tax on interest income which had penalised holding Hong Kong dollars, this had the desired effect, and stability returned to the dollar.

One effect of this was that my Krugerrands were immediately worth less than I had paid for them, as I had bought them when the rate was below 7.8. I should have followed the advice I had given Steve! But 'c'est la vie', I had at least had the experience of owning solid gold. I made a decision: once it was clear the peg was going to hold, I would sell my Krugerrands to get the cash back. I decided though to hold onto one and either sell it for a profit or blow it on an outrageously expensive meal (given it was worth about £260 in 1983) when I was leaving Hong Kong for the last time.

The trouble was that sorting out the stability of the dollar did not resolve the issue of 1997. In December 1983, with an indefensible negotiating position, the Black Saturday debacle and the Chinese Premier playing hardball, the British government capitulated and agreed to negotiations on the basis of Chinese sovereignty and administration. This allowed detailed talks to begin on every aspect of the handover. These lasted until the end of September the next year, when they were finally agreed to, and the 'Sino-British Joint Declaration' was initialled. Even then it took until the end of May 1985, at a ceremony in Peking, for the declaration to officially come into force.

For me and my business aspirations what the whole 1997 issue meant was that, a few months into the job, the bottom fell out of my biggest market – Hong Kong. With the exception of the Japanese banks, who took a very long-term view, no other banks would invest in new computer systems until the dust had settled and the future was very much clearer. If I was to succeed in the next eighteen months or so the bulk of business would have to come from elsewhere in the region.

Chapter 7

Singapore and Manila

The first week in October saw me in Singapore. There were a number of meetings and events I needed to attend while there, but I also decided to add on a couple of days for sightseeing. I therefore stayed for eight days, travelling there on a Saturday and back on the Sunday of the following weekend.

Just about everything to do with Singapore was completely different from Hong Kong, and this started with the airport. Changhi was brand new, having only opened two years previously, and was just under eleven miles from the city centre. The terminal building was bright, spacious, airy and everything worked like clockwork. I was one of the first off the aircraft. It was not too long a walk to immigration, which had enough desks manned that there was no queue, so I was very quickly through, and a few minutes later I was at the baggage area. And unbelievably, given how short a time it had taken me to get there, I saw my bag already on the carousel.

Charlie was good enough to pick me up and as we walked out of the terminal building I was surprised that his car was no more than fifty yards away. The car park was just the other side of the road that served the building. And this was no small regional airport - it handled over two hundred flights a day!

The drive into town to my hotel was equally impressive. Everything was green and colourful. The dual carriageway had very imposing king palms on both sides, and the central island was a mass of small bushes full of brightly coloured flowers. Even the concrete bridges had been covered with climbing plants, so they were attractive as well.

On the first section of the road into town Charlie pointed something interesting out. 'Do you see how dead straight this road is?' he said.

'Yes,' I replied, 'I had been thinking that it was just like a Roman road in the UK, presumably to ensure the shortest possible route.'

'No, that's not the reason. Take a look at the bases of the lamp posts and the central reservation.'

'The lamps seem to have special fittings where the post joins the ground, and the bushes are planted in large metal containers,' I responded.

'That's because this road is an emergency runway. If they need it they can lower the lamp posts to the ground quickly, and they have a team with chainsaws who will cut the palm trees down. And the central planters can be quickly moved out of the way.'

And sure enough after a short time the road changed as we left the airport. While basically the same to look at, it was no longer dead straight. The lamp posts went directly into the ground and the bushes in the central reservation were planted in the earth.

Once dropped off at my hotel I had a couple of hours to relax before meeting up with Charlie and his wife Christine and a couple of other people from the company. He had explained that we would start as tourists by having Singapore Slings at Raffles Hotel before going to Newton Circus, an open air venue, for dinner. Raffles was opened in 1887 and was named after Sir Thomas Stamford Raffles, the founder of Singapore. It was one of the world's 'grande dame' hotels with colonial style architecture, very attractive and, therefore, a tourist attraction. At that time in 1983 it had become rather faded, however, and there were rumours that developers were trying to get it knocked down as it was prime real estate in the centre of the city.

Land was so valuable in this part of Singapore that there had been extensive landfill in front of the hotel. It was on Beach Road and true to its name, when the hotel was built the sea had come up almost to the hotel. However, by the time I was there Beach Road was several hundred yards from the water.

The tourist drink to have here was the Singapore Sling, and the place to have it was the Long Bar at Raffles, where the drink had been created in 1915. It was a plum pink colour and included cherry brandy and mixed fruit juices. Quite how it came to be so world famous was a mystery to me. I was all right with it as I had a cosmopolitan taste in alcohol and a sweet tooth, and if a cocktail had an umbrella in it then I was likely to enjoy it!

Some years later, after a massive refurbishment, the Long Bar was moved upstairs via a back staircase (an inspired idea to generate money from what had previously been a dead area), but at this time it was on the ground floor by one of the gardens and you could have your Sling sitting outside. What amazed me though was the tardiness of the service, especially for Singapore. This was a very expensive drink for what it was, the hotel was struggling financially, but could we get a waiter to come and take our order? It was like getting blood out of a stone. Finally one sauntered casually over and took our order, but when we wanted refills it was just as difficult.

After a couple of rounds and some obligatory photographs we moved onto Newton Circus to eat. This was an open air venue with a large number of hawker stalls selling every type of Asian food imaginable. You found an empty table and then ordered your food from whichever stalls took your fancy. Being a Saturday it was packed with both locals and westerners. One of the dishes to have in Singapore was Chilli Crab, so we ordered a large plate of this as the centrepiece. It was not at all hot, despite the name, and consisted of large crabs in a thick red sauce. It was very messy to eat and was accompanied by both steamed and deep fried bread buns for wiping up the sauce. Charlie couldn't be bothered with the bodies of the crabs so specified only claws. The Chilli Crab man was very happy with this as he charged us for each whole crab and kept the bodies for himself; apparently the Chinese preferred these to the claws.

The other food we had with the crab was pretty standard fare including steamed prawns, noodles, rice and duck. I did however try something for the first time that became a favourite of mine - mutton soup. This was a highly flavoured broth with Indian spices in it, not hot with chilli but packed with taste – absolutely delicious. Christine mentioned that it might be goat as the word mutton could refer to that as well, but that didn't bother me. It tasted like lamb to me. Not having eaten goat at that time if it tasted the same I didn't care, and I had no problem eating goat if that was what it was.

Sunday I had decided to spend on my own looking round the island. Singapore did not boast any 'must see' sights and the real interest was in wandering around the streets. There were a number of different areas including Chinatown, Little India and the Arab quarter, each, as you would expect, very different. In a number of places there were pedestrian-only lanes crammed with small shops and street vendors. One of the specialities on offer was fake goods, especially watches, but one of the tempting items to buy were bootlegged cassette tapes of albums. The sound quality was not the best but when played on normal car stereo or home systems they were reasonable and so much cheaper than the real thing.

The rest of the week passed quickly enough. One highlight was to have a banana leaf curry. There were a number of restaurants serving this, but the one our Singapore staff used most was called Banana Leaf Apolo in Racecourse Road. There hadn't been a racecourse at that location since 1933, but the name remained the same. When you sat down you were given a piece of banana leaf as a plate, and for westerners a spoon and fork, although the Indians ate with their fingers. You ordered your main dishes from the waiter but while waiting for these to turn up different waiters would arrive at your table and serve you what they were bringing round. There would be a choice of rice, white or yellow, a vegetable dish or two, poppadoms and some spicy accompaniments. The menu had a wide choice of dishes, including some enormous prawns in a thick sauce, but the star of the show was of course the fish head curry. When this turned up it was not what I had been expecting, and frankly, I had not been particularly looking forward to it. What arrived was a very large deep white bowl and, in the centre of it, was the most enormous fish head the size of a melon, sitting in a rather thin brown curry sauce. Rather than having to pick little bits of meat off as I had been expecting, the head was so big that it had a large amount of delicious juicy flesh at the neck end, and the cheeks of the fish also provided plenty of meat. It was a great experience, delicious and fun to eat. We washed it down with copious quantities of local Tiger Beer, although in addition to the normal range of drinks they had whole coconuts and large glasses of fresh pineapple juice.

Returning from Singapore I had almost three weeks of relative calm, with only a couple of business trips to Macau in the way of travel – a nice change from being on a plane every week. At the end of this period one of my sisters arrived with her boyfriend. Marion and Adrian were staying for three weeks before heading off for Sri Lanka. I had tried to stay in Hong Kong while they were there but I did need to make a four-day trip to the Philippines during this time.

This was my first trip there, so it was going to be very interesting even though I was only going to be in Manila, the capital city. I had to go that week as the reason I was there was that IBM were having an 'open house' for the banks and financial companies to display the products they had available. The Philippines was not an important market for us as our product was too expensive for the vast majority of the businesses there, but as IBM were making all the arrangements and wanted us to be present it was an easy decision to attend.

Discussing my visit with friends brought up some interesting comments. Manila was a city where you had to use common sense if you were to avoid problems; there was a lot of poverty which, of course, translated to the risk of being ripped off or possibly something more serious such as being mugged. In one of my Asian guide books there was an interesting comparison to Singapore which stated: 'if Singapore is the beginners guide to Asia, then Manila is the advanced course'.

Marion and Adrian had been in town for a week when I left so were up to speed, and I arranged for a friend to take them out on his boat on the Saturday while I was away so they were catered for.

On arriving at Manila the 'advanced course' comment came straight back to me as I left the terminal building. It was incredibly busy and disorganised. I stood on the pavement and looked around for the taxi rank or signs to it but couldn't see either. I walked left and right for a short distance, fighting my way through the massed people, but nothing. A few private cars and vans were going slowly past but no taxis – I decided I was in the wrong place.

I retreated from the melee back into the terminal building to think about what to do next. Luckily while walking around, trying to find someone to ask, I saw a sign for hotel taxis. This led me out of a door a reasonable way from the main entrance and thankfully into an area of relative calm, with a queue for the taxis, which I joined. These were not special hotel taxis but ordinary ones that would only accept hotel destinations, although being the Philippines I was sure if you offered enough extra they would take you anywhere. I had been advised of the fare I should expect to pay and that I should insist on the meter being turned on, as some drivers would try not to use it and quote a stupidly high fixed fare. However even when used you could not rely on the meter, as apparently some had been modified to run at a much higher rate than they should.

You also had to be careful that the driver did not steal your luggage by driving off once you had arrived at the hotel and stepped out of the taxi! The approach therefore was to stay in the taxi until the bellboy had arrived and the driver had to get out to open the boot. You handled paying the driver once your baggage was safe with the bellboy. If the fare was too high you could then dispute it and tell him what you were prepared to pay. If the driver became difficult you would ask him to go to reception with you and it could be sorted out there, which they were never prepared to do.

I had decided to stay at the Manila Hotel, an old style luxury hotel along the lines of Raffles in Singapore, which had opened in 1912. My taxi driver was fine and the fare was in line with what I was expecting, so I was soon ensconced in my room.

In addition to the IBM event I had arranged meetings at the branches of four big US banks, as if interested they were likely to be more amenable to the costs of our software. One of the benefits of the lower cost of living in the Philippines was that it was possible to hire a taxi for the whole day at a reasonable cost, rather than risk hailing one in the street with possible problems. Those to use were proper 'hotel taxis' that were part of a fleet attached to your hotel, although the drivers were not employees. I agreed a price with the front taxi in the rank for two days and two nights.

That first evening I stayed in the hotel, as I had quite a lot of preparation still to do for my meetings, but the second night I thought I would explore Manila. I had decided to eat at a restaurant called The Hobbit House. Its claim to fame was that it only employed dwarves, to emulate the short Hobbits in Tolkien's *Lord Of The Rings*. The restaurant had been started in 1973 by an American and as it was still going 10 years later I felt it must be a reasonable place.

Following this I felt that, being single, I should experience the noted Manila 'sin city' nightlife. Due to the poverty in the Philippines many girls had migrated to Manila to work in the sex trade. There was a lot of money available, as due to this Manila was a favourite US R and R town. The main area where this went on was Ermita which was in the centre, close to the sea and the US Embassy. My trusted taxi driver, who was called Felix, drove me there and mentioned a couple of places where I would not be ripped off and which had 'interesting' stage shows. Walking up the main street I went past lots of bars and pole dancing venues, and poking my head into a couple I found that they were full of really attractive girls. The street itself had no shortage of girls, each one propositioning you as you went past.

I arrived at one of the bars the driver had recommended and went in. It was quite comfortable, well decorated and actually felt quite upmarket. I sat at the bar and ordered a beer. There were around eight poles with a girl in a bikini at each one dancing. It didn't take too long and I had a couple of girls either side of me.

'You American?' the first girl said.

'No I'm from England,' I replied, 'but I work in Hong Kong.'

'English men very nice,' the second one said, 'treat girls very well.'

'I'm glad we have that reputation' I answered. 'Do you get many English people here?'

'Not too many,' she replied. 'Lots of Americans, but some English people live in Manila and come here with their friends.'

'Would you like to buy us a drink?' the first girl chimed up.

'Not at the moment,' I replied. 'Maybe later if I stay here a while.'

I had hoped this reply would get them to move on, but when they did not I decided that as the bar was quiet they had decided I was a better bet to stay with, in the hope that 'maybe later' might actually occur. They both spoke excellent English and rather than maintain a stilted silence I decided to talk to them about their backgrounds. They both had similar stories, that they were from the country, their families had no money, so they had decided to work in the sex trade to help their families, not just putting food on the table but also for education and medical costs. I knew that poor families could not pay for their children to be educated, and that medical treatment and even drugs could be hard to get due to the high cost, so possibly what they were saying was true.

While we were talking the stage show started. This consisted of a single girl, naked, performing the most incredible tricks using her 'anatomy'. I had heard about such displays but never seen one. There was nothing sexy about the show at all - my feelings were simply ones of amazement at what she could do. She performed about a dozen tricks including firing ping pong balls at customers, squirting water as if from a water pistol, opening bottles of beer and cutting slices of a banana. I thought as the show ended what a shame it was that the vast majority of people in the world would never see this. Her skills deserved a wider audience.

After the show she came round the customers looking for tips and I gave her some money. Seeing me get some from my wallet perked the two girls up.

'Will you buy us a drink now?' one of them asked. 'You have been here for a while and seen the show.'

I had already asked the barman the price of a girlie drink, which was reasonable, so I told them I would. Their drinks arrived and they both toasted me.

'When you finish your business,' the first girl said, 'why don't you have some holiday, very beautiful beaches here.'

'I'd love to' I replied, 'but unfortunately I don't have the time and I must get back to Hong Kong.'

'Take some holiday,' the second girl piped up. 'You can take both of us with you and we can make sure you have a lovely time.' She gave me a knowing look.

'No, I really do have to get back,' I replied, 'otherwise I would love to.'

'You a nice guy' said the first girl, 'don't worry about giving us any money, what we will do is you take us on holiday and find hotel you like, and ask the price. Then let us talk to owner and we will get discount. Just let us keep the discount.'

I have to say this was tempting as it didn't feel like you were paying for sex, and both girls were very attractive - and I did have normal male blood in my veins! Unfortunately I really did have to go back, both for business reasons and because Marion and Adrian were in Hong Kong.

'Look, I honestly would love to go away with you both but I can't, I do have to get back to Hong Kong,' I replied.

'I know the problem,' the second girl said, 'you think we may not be good girls, that's why you don't want holiday with us. I tell you what we do, tomorrow you take us to doctor you choose, he checks us out, proves we are good girls.' She paused for a moment for effect, and with a cheerful expression exclaimed, 'Then you take us on holiday.'

Well I had to let them down, but I gave them each a generous tip as they had been great fun, then left the bar to find Felix and go back to the hotel. I have always looked back on that encounter and wondered what I would have done if I had been in a position to take them up on their offer. Would I have actually gone with them if I could have?

The second night I did not fancy a return to the girlie bars and after a simple meal in the hotel coffee shop I asked Felix if he knew a good place for live music. He did, but said the best place was in a rather run-down part of Manila. He assured me I would not have any trouble if I was with him, so I agreed. Sure enough we turned off the main street after a while and it became very run down and dismal, with the street lights not bright and very basic housing. We arrived at a crossroads and he parked up. On one of the corners was a large building, obviously a bar. There were a number of scruffy young boys hanging around who Felix obviously knew and he called one of them over and asked me to give him a small amount of money.

'He will look after the taxi,' he explained to me, 'and you should give him the same amount when we leave.'

On entering the bar it was a pretty basic place, with a number of small tables and a counter at one end. The driver waved to a couple of people he knew and then we sat down.

'The music is upstairs,' he explained, 'but it won't start for a while, so we'll have a drink here first.'

I told him I'd have a local San Miguel beer and gave him some money to get them, he had the same. While he was getting the drinks I looked around the room more carefully and decided that it was a good job I knew Felix well by now, otherwise I would have been concerned as to my safety. I noticed that the stairs that went upstairs were enclosed in a metal cage, with a door at the bottom which had someone manning it. A couple of people came into the bar and went up to the entrance to the stairs. I distinctly saw them hand the guard a small knife, which he put in a cupboard on the wall, and then let them into the cage to go up the stairs.

'Why is there a cage around the stairs?' I asked Felix when he came back. 'I'm sure those guys handed over a knife before going upstairs.'

'It can get very busy when the band is on, and there is bad blood between some of the people who come here,' he explained. 'This bar is owned by the local gang boss and he has said that everyone must be unarmed to make sure there is no serious trouble'.

'But they are not being frisked, so anyone could take a weapon up the stairs.'

'The boss is very powerful so they obey him,' he explained, 'otherwise they would be in big trouble. You will see that some people even hand over guns.'

Sure enough people started to arrive to go upstairs, and Felix said we should go too, in order to get a seat. We took up fresh beers and found a seat. About twenty minutes later a five-piece band arrived.

At a small table near the band sat a drop-dead gorgeous girl, on her own, and impeccably dressed. 'Who is that fantastic girl over there?' I asked Felix. 'Is she with one of the band?'

'No no' he replied, 'she is much too special for them, she is the girlfriend of the gang boss.'

'So I'd better not go over and chat her up then,' I said.

'Absolutely,' was Felix's response. 'You would be in big trouble if you did that.'

Well the band were fantastic, playing a wide range of Western songs, and it was thoroughly enjoyable and sure enough, despite the amount of weaponry in the cupboard downstairs I didn't experience or see any trouble and we made it safely back to the hotel.

I flew back the next day, a Saturday, and gave Felix a good tip at the airport. He had been fantastic and it was good to now know someone like him to use on future trips. This did not look like being too imminent from a business perspective, because as expected the IBM seminar and the meetings I had did not come up with any hot opportunities for business. However from a tourist angle I had an excellent trip, and some great stories to regale Marion and Adrian with when I arrived back at my flat.

Chapter 8

The Greasy Goose, hairy crabs, Round Table and a new car

I had a week back in Hong Kong with my sister before she and Adrian left for Sri Lanka, and the evening before they flew I treated them to one of the gourmet delights of Hong Kong. The 'Greasy Goose' was primarily an open-air restaurant situated under a flyover, quite a long drive into the New Territories. This was not of course its proper name, which was Chinese and difficult to pronounce, and as its nickname implies, it was known for goose, and in particular a dish of fried solidified goose blood! It was an extremely basic venue, and the sort of place ordinary tourists never got to, but well worth experiencing. Despite what might be expected given the English name, the quality of the food was excellent, as was evidenced by the fact that around 90% of the customers were Chinese. I had been introduced to it by one of my programmers who considered himself a bit of a gourmand.

Walking from the car to the tables under the flyover you passed the ramshackle kitchens, and saw over a hundred geese hanging from makeshift rails similar to those found in clothes shops. This was where they had a marinade of soy sauce plus other flavourings poured over them multiple times before being ready for cooking. There were this many geese as the restaurant didn't just provide them for its own tables but, given its reputation, also sold them to shops and other restaurants.

I had made up a party of ten so that we could have a good variety of food. This was not too hard, as I knew a number of people who were willing to go there, given its reputation. The menu had a full selection of food in addition to the geese, including a range of seafood; it was all really well cooked, so we had a great meal.

While we were there some of us experienced one of the other interesting features of the place. The Chinese had a saying that the closer a restaurant toilet was to the kitchens the better the food, and the toilets here were right next to them. This in itself was not a problem, but you then had to factor in that they consisted of two very run-down narrow wooden huts, each just large enough to get into. No Western sit-down toilet here, but instead the type that was flush with the ground and you had to stand on two raised ceramic platforms. Hygiene was not their strong point, added to which it was hard to see much as the lights in each cubicle were very dim, perhaps, given the situation, no bad thing. But what really made them stand out was that there was a narrow path leading up to the cubicles, and running down the middle of the path, with your feet either side of it, was the drainage channel from both, completely open to view! Quite revolting, especially if you had to queue.

One of the girls had gone there, despite my warning, but quickly came back saying she would hold out until we moved on elsewhere. Another, some time later, said she had to go, and on arriving back said it had been the worst experience of its type she had ever had. The open channel disappeared off into the gloom under the flyover and I often wondered where it ended up – but I had no inclination to go and find out!

So the next day I took them to the airport for their 6 pm flight. I had not been home for long when I had to leave for the airport again as, 'one out, one in', I had a friend arriving at 8.15 pm for five days on his way from Australia to the UK. It was nice to be popular but I did often long for a few days actually in Hong Kong, with no social commitments.

While my sister had been in town I had the pleasure of picking up my new car. I had inherited an ageing Mitsubishi Gallant from my predecessor Clive, and while it was totally reliable, it was very '70's Japanese' in its styling, which didn't appeal to me. Charlie had told me when we agreed the terms for the role that I could have a new car, and it was something I had been looking forward to. Given we were in a completely different economic environment to the UK I did not have a set budget for the vehicle; instead I had to justify what I wanted by reference to other cars the company was running for managers of similar seniority to me.

I had fancied a BMW but on researching them it was clear I couldn't justify the price of one of these in Hong Kong. BMWs and Mercedes were real status symbols among the Hong Kong Chinese and they were premium priced to reflect this, whereas Japanese cars, not having the same cachet, were much better value. Honda had recently announced the second version of their Prelude two-door coupe which had first appeared in 1978, and it had just become available in Hong Kong. I didn't fancy the earlier version as it had the old fashioned Japanese styling I disliked, but this latest version was something completely different. It was very European looking, modern and sporty. Honda had an outstanding reputation for quality and this was allied to great reviews of the sporty nature and handling of this model, not that there was any real opportunity to make use of this sort of driving in Hong Kong.

Looking at the alternatives it was a no brainer for me to go for the Prelude, even though it was only a 2+2 and would be a squeeze with four adults in it. Being a Japanese premium model it came with a vast array of goodies including electric sun roof, air conditioning, electric windows, pop up headlights and alloy wheels. Many of the features were either not available on most European models, or would cost the earth as options on a luxury marque such as a BMW.

So off I went to the Honda dealership to look at the car and have a test drive. I couldn't see one in the showroom, but a salesman rushed over to me as I came in.

'I'm interested in the new Honda Prelude,' I said to him, 'can I have a look at one?'

'Very sorry but none in Hong Kong yet,' he responded. This was a bit of a shock to me.

'But the model was launched last year,' I said to him.

'Very true sir, but only available in Japan at first,' he replied. 'First shipment arrives in Hong Kong in two weeks,'

'I didn't realise that, but I am interested in one,' I said, realising I would have to rethink my plans to try for a discount. 'Can we look at what is needed for me to order one?'

'Of course, please come and sit down here,' he said, motioning me to a desk. He brought out a brochure and a colour chart for the paint work and interior, and ran through the many benefits of my buying the Prelude instead of another make.

'Ok, I'd like to order one please,' I finally stated. 'What colours are available for me from the first shipment you are getting?'

'Oh, so sorry,' was his reply. 'All first shipment already sold, let me check when next deliveries expected, perhaps six weeks' time.'

This was very frustrating. As with most people, having decided on a car, and being very excited about getting it, I didn't want to have to wait for ages.

I decided to try a test to see if the first cars really were all gone, and pulled out the company cheque book from my pocket and laid it on his desk.

'I'm sure you are correct that they are all sold,' I said very politely to him, 'but if there is any way you can get me one of the first cars, I can give you a company cheque for a large deposit here and now.'

'Very sorry, all sold,' he reiterated, 'but let me go and make some phone calls just to check.'

Of he went up some stairs to the first floor. I decided he was only doing this to give the impression that he had tried and nothing was going to come of it – I would just have to wait. He was gone a good five minutes, which I felt was stretching it out rather too much, but finally he came down the stairs again.

'I have spoken to most senior manager,' he stated. 'One of the cars was to have been for our showroom here, but he will let you have that one if you would like it. It is a metallic silver colour with a grey interior.'

Well, having expected a no this was great news, and while I didn't particularly care about the colour I would have chosen silver, so that was fantastic. Money talks in Hong Kong, I thought, and I had little doubt that the sight of that bright red HSBC Corporate cheque book sitting on his desk was too tempting to ignore.

He prepared all the paperwork and I signed and gave him the cheque. It was very handy at times such as this that only one authorised signatory was required.

A thought then struck me. 'Excuse me' I said to the salesman, 'but I am over six feet tall, I hope the front seats will have enough legroom for me to drive comfortably.'

'Oh, very good point,' he replied, 'please come over here,' and he guided me to a Renault Fuego. The dealership handled both Honda and Renault cars, hence this model being there. He opened the driver's door and pushed the seat back as far as it would go.

'Please sit and try out,' he said.

I couldn't see the point in this but went along with him.

'Is it comfortable, enough leg room?' he asked me after I was settled into the seat.

'Yes, it's fine,' I replied.

'Very good' was his response as he helped me back out of the Fuego. He then shook my hand and said he would call in about a week with an update on when the car should be ready.

I decided I would not take it any further as to how the legroom in a Renault could have any relevance to the legroom in a Honda – this was Hong Kong.

A few weeks later the opportunity arose to try another interesting food. During October to December there was a genuine gourmet delicacy available, 'Shanghai Hairy Crabs', and as I had never tried them Margaret, my secretary, had arranged a hairy crab party at her flat on the first Friday in December.

Also called Chinese mitten crabs, they are distinguishable by the fur on their claws which supposedly makes them resemble mittens, hence the name. They are native to Eastern China where they have been a delicacy for hundreds of years, with both the meat and the roe being considered very tasty. The crabs were so well thought of by Chinese gourmands that they were sent all over the world to cities with a large Chinese population, where they commanded extremely high prices. The roe is the most highly prized part, so they are only eaten during the last three months of the year when they are with roe. The female roe ripens at the start of this period so they are eaten first, followed by the males whose roe ripens later. The crabs are about the size of the palm of your hand and have an interesting lifecycle, living in freshwater until they are ready to breed when they travel to the coastal estuaries. The females overwinter in the sea in deeper water before returning to the estuaries to hatch their eggs, and the juvenile crabs then make their way back to freshwater and the cycle starts again.

The most prized crabs are those from Yangcheng Lake, which is near Shanghai and has an area of almost eight square miles. It is when the crabs are migrating from the lake to the nearby Yangtse River to breed that they are captured. Quite why these are supposed to be so much better than those from other lakes nearby I couldn't find out, but they command a much higher price and you had to be careful not to pay for 'fakes' masquerading as being from the famous lake. As the crabs from other lakes are exactly the same species, and indistinguishable from those in Yangcheng Lake, it seemed to me to be almost certain that many people would be ripped off. Margaret, however, said that as long as you bought them from a reputable shop they would be the real thing. I asked her if she could also get some 'fake' crabs so we could do a blind tasting, but she said she didn't know where to get non-Yangcheng crabs in Hong Kong, which I felt was a shame.

During the hairy crab season many up-market restaurants in Hong Kong had signs outside advertising that they were on the menu, and very pricey they were too, for what was, after all, just a crab. This was why we were having the party at Margaret's - apparently they were a sensible price if you bought and cooked them yourself and it was easy to do.

Arriving for the meal I went to look at the crabs, which were in the kitchen. There in a large wicker type basket were a goodly number of them, as there were eight of us for dinner. Being alive they were tightly tied up in some sort of dried grass or reed and the hair on the claws was clearly visible, although quite how this was supposed to make the claws look like mittens escaped me.

As was to be expected with such a delicacy they had to be cooked in a particular way, steamed sitting on top of sliced ginger and some sort of herbal leaf. These were to counter the fact that the Chinese consider crab to be a very 'cold' food, and the additions are supposed to reduce the effect of the coldness. They were served with a dipping sauce made with vinegar and shredded ginger.

Margaret had also supplied what she said was the traditional drink to go with the crabs. Called Huangjiu, which translates as yellow wine, this came in an interesting brown ceramic container, resembling a very large pear that had been upended with most of the stalk end cut off. There was a very pretty label on it which was all in Chinese, and a red ribbon around the stopper. When poured it was brown rather than yellow and was apparently made from fermented rice or other grains. It was just about drinkable, and on the basis of 'when in Rome' I stuck with it while eating the crab, but I was glad to move onto beer when we had finished.

The crabs themselves were delicious, but not for the squeamish. They arrived cooked, straight from the steamer, but otherwise untouched. You undid the grass binding, and then had to do all the messy preparation, that in the UK would have been done for you if you ordered a whole crab. This involved pulling off the underside of the crab, which was quite easy, then getting rid of the stomach and gills. The bright orange roe was then available. You eat this first and then went on to the normal crab meat. The roe was delicious and the texture reminded me of an almost hardboiled egg yolk. And the flesh when I ate that was very juicy and sweet, but given the small size of the crab there wasn't much of it.

It was certainly an experience, very enjoyable and so much better than trying the delicacy in the formal environment of a posh restaurant. I took the interesting Huangjiu wine container home as a memento of the evening, but unfortunately over the years it has been lost.

Two days later on the Sunday, I was helping at a Round Table day out for Vietnamese refugee children. After my introduction to the organisation at Easter, via my predecessor Clive, who had been a member, I had been a few times as a guest. I liked those involved and what they were doing and had therefore joined in May. The Round Table movement originated in the UK in 1927 as an organisation to bring together young businessman under 40, pool their knowledge and experience and contribute to local life. By the time I joined it was described to me as a group of guys who wanted to help out the less fortunate but have fun doing it. The intention was not just to throw money at an issue but to get together and provide manpower rather than cash; that way everyone could contribute equally, regardless of their financial situation. In fact I was told that there was a derogatory term, 'cheque book tables', for those where the members only provided money and did not get involved themselves in activities. Setting an upper age of 40 (later raised to 45 in the UK) was very specifically done to keep members young enough to be active, and to ensure new members were recruited to replace those retiring at 40, thus ensuring the organisation didn't stagnate with long-term members.

There were ten Round Tables in Hong Kong at that time, eight being English speaking and two Cantonese. I joined Hong Kong Round Table No. 1, which met at the Yacht Club, whose treasurer was one of the members. We used a function room which had wonderful views of the harbour and the room had its own bar and bar staff. The atmosphere at meetings was jovial and could be somewhat noisy as there was a lot of banter. If you were the shy retiring sort it wasn't for you, but interestingly, while I was a member, I saw a few people join who were fairly quiet, but within a few months they all gained confidence and could hold their own with anyone. Therefore together with excellent food the once every two week meetings were most enjoyable.

The Easter Fair, which had been my introduction to the movement, summed up the ideals; the members were organising and promoting the whole event and running the stalls, but the money raised coming from those who attended and what they spent.

Another charity fundraising activity they were involved with involved the famous Star Ferry. One member would get sponsored for each time he crossed the harbour on the ferry, going backwards and forwards as many times as possible in a day. This was much harder than it sounded as you could not stay on the ferry, but had to get off and run from the exit to the entry to get back on the same ferry, which involved a reasonable distance and stairs.

Another major fundraiser held once a year was a 'boxing smoker'. The format was that they would rent the ballroom of a top hotel and arrange for a boxing match between one of the local Chinese boxing clubs and boxers from the British army. In 1983 the venue was the Hilton Hotel in Central and the regiment was the Scots Guards who were stationed in Hong Kong at the time. It was a men-only 'black tie' event and the evening would start with a three-course dinner. There would be a few girls brought in to sell raffle tickets to boost the takings, and unofficial gambling would go on in respect of individual bouts, unofficial as gambling was illegal in Hong Kong except in very specific situations, such as at the racecourse. These events raised a large amount of money as they were well supported both by expatriate and local Chinese businessman.

The club also helped out every three or four weeks at Pinehill Village at Taipo in the New Territories. This was a home for disabled children about 15 miles from Kowloon. They had quite a lot of grassland there and we would cut this and do various maintenance jobs for them. Afterwards we had access to the swimming pool and basketball court and have a barbecue. One Sunday we were going out there with a stereo system that we were donating. I picked up a couple of other tablers and we set off. The weather was atrocious, pouring with rain and we had not gone very far when we hit a terrible traffic jam. There had been an accident in front of us and it took one hour and twenty minutes to do two miles. The whole time the rain was teeming down and we discussed aborting the trip, as given the weather, we would not be able to do anything. However the radio was saying 'weather fine, very hot, some showers'. We therefore carried on, thinking that this bad weather must be localised to Hong Kong and Kowloon as Taipo was the other side of a high range of hills. But no, after we had passed the hills and were getting closer the weather actually worsened.

As we had come so far, and had the stereo, we decided to drop this off and then go to a bar nearby run by a girl from Liverpool and aptly named 'The Liver Birds'. We had to carefully cross some flooded roads but finally made it to the home and, having dropped the stereo off, went to see if anyone else had been foolish enough to come. They hadn't and we were on our own. Off we went to the bar, which was a good five minutes' walk from the road down a pedestrian path, so we were soaked by the time we arrived there, only to find it was being knocked about and redecorated, as the girl had gone and a Cockney guy had taken it over and was doing it up. We had a beer each sitting on orange boxes and then drove home, ending up cooking the food we had brought for the barbecue on the stove!

On the Sunday we had chartered the *Huan*, a wooden sail training ship, to take out Vietnamese refugee children for the day. In keeping with a table event like this the members and their wives and children also came along, and the wives had organised the food and drink for the day.

Vietnamese refugees had been a major problem for Hong Kong since the mid 1970s. They had started arriving in 1975 after the Vietnamese war, initially due to worries about the impact of the communist government, and later that decade due to the 'ethnic cleansing' of those considered overseas Chinese rather than Vietnamese. By the early 1980s they were still arriving in very large numbers, although by now these were mostly economic refugees. In the early years most gained refugee status and were moved to other countries who accepted them.

However as so many refugees kept arriving these countries started to shut their borders. In response to this Hong Kong had to find a means to deter the refugees leaving Vietnam, and from mid-1982 they decided to create 'closed camps' to hold them in until they were either accepted elsewhere or, if not, forcibly repatriated back to Vietnam.

One such camp was called 'Kai Tak North' which was where our children came from. At its peak there were 15,000 people in the camp. They lived in family groups in buildings made of corrugated iron with rows of bunks that were often three high. Being children there was more flexibility and they were allowed out for supervised events such as ours.

The *Huan* had an interesting history. In the early 1970s three Europeans had commissioned its building, intending to use it to cruise the Mediterranean. However, before it was finished they ran out of money and sold it to a Hong Kong shipyard. Some eighteen months later, no further work having been done, an expatriate from the University identified its potential as a sail training ship for Hong Kong children. By 1978 the funds had been raised to buy her and complete the remaining work. She was about 90 feet long and built entirely of wood to a traditional Chinese three-masted junk design.

The crew had already collected the children by the time they arrived at Blake's Pier, by the city centre, to pick us up at 10.30. As none of us had the experience to sail her we used the engine to take us for a cruise for an hour or so and then anchored in a bay a short way from the shore. The *Huan*'s tender ferried those who wanted to go ashore to the beach. It was a lovely day although a bit challenging trying to communicate to the children, who spoke no English. It was clear however that they weren't bothered about trying to talk to a bunch of expats, and were perfectly happy just to play with their friends and enjoy the experience.

Less than two weeks after this I was heading back to the UK for Christmas and New Year via a couple of days in Singapore. So 1983 drew to a close very pleasantly catching up with family and friends, and having landed on the morning of the company's big Christmas bash at the Grosvenor Hotel in London, I was also able to attend it.

Chapter 9

Trials and tribulations - meeting Lita

A few days after arriving back in Hong Kong I went down with a very bad cold, in all likelihood picked up on the plane; being on a full flight from the UK in the middle of winter, who knows how many people had horrible bugs they were able to share with everyone via the ventilation system.

On Tuesday 11th January I was supposed to be going to a friend's birthday party. I felt pretty rough and almost didn't make it, but decided that as I had bought him a present I would deliver it, have a quick drink, and then go home for an early night.

David was a government surveyor who was a member of the Round Table. After a meeting we would usually head down to the bars in Wanchai, the nightlife area, for a nightcap and we had become quite friendly. At the party I had wished him many happy returns, given him his present and after a quick beer was about to depart when my eyes fell on an attractive Asian girl who had just arrived. She was about five feet two with long black hair all the way down to her waist, very pretty and dressed in the tightest black trousers with knee-length boots. She appeared to be on her own and was talking to David's fiancée Gloria and a couple of other girls. I hung around a bit longer than I had intended, keeping an eye on her and wondering if, in my present state, I should try to chat her up. Sense prevailed and I realised I looked awful with my streaming cold, so I decided not to. If I waited, I would also be able to find out more from David about her.

A couple of days later I called him. 'Hi David, how did the party go?' I said. 'I'm sorry I wasn't up to staying.'

'It went really well, didn't finish until four am' he replied, 'so a good job I had taken the next day off. How are you now, you looked terrible at the party?'

'On the mend at last,' I responded, then I moved onto the reason I had called. 'Look David, there was this really tasty Asian girl who arrived just before I left. Hair down to her bum and she seemed to be on her own.'

'That must have been Lita,' he replied.

'What's her situation, is she going out with anyone? I was really taken by her and I fancy asking her out'.

'She's a good friend of Gloria's and no, she doesn't have a boyfriend,' he replied, 'but I'm not letting you anywhere near her.'

'Why not?'

'Look, it's not you, but she's a really nice girl, and I don't want to see her hurt. She won't go to bed with you because she's not like that, so it wouldn't last long, and if you did somehow manage to get her into bed, she would be devastated when it finished and I'd blame myself for bringing you together.'

'Come on David, don't be like that, let me have her number. If she's that nice I'll be careful how I handle it. Why would I want to upset her if she's a friend of Gloria's?'

'Maybe' he replied, 'but you're still not getting her number no matter how much you badger me.'

As he was so adamant I left it at that. I wasn't going to give up, but clearly I would have to consider how else I could get to her.

I didn't have to wait long as about two weeks later I was at a Round Table meeting with David when he mentioned that he was in trouble with Gloria for coming between the two of us. He had told her about my phone call. It seemed that in her eyes I was not just a single expat looking for a fling but a very eligible bachelor, and if I was interested in

Lita she wanted to get us together. Apparently Gloria thought it best that we should go out as a foursome first, rather than my just calling her; and he said he would look for an opportunity to do this.

A couple of weeks later he called and said that the China Fleet Club had something on at the beginning of March. Gloria had invited Lita and she was able to make it, so if I was free that would be my chance. Luckily I was, so that was all fixed.

The evening went off well and I was even more attracted to her after it. She was from the Philippines like Gloria. Her parents had a farm but her father, who was also a carpenter, mostly worked as a foreman on larger building projects. She came from a big family as was common in the Philippines, with four sisters and three brothers. She was a nanny and had worked for families in the Philippines before coming to Hong Kong to look after three children for a wealthy Israeli family. She was friendly to me but rather reserved, with no indication that she might be interested in getting together. Towards the end of the evening Gloria whispered in my ear that I shouldn't do anything tonight, she would explain later.

We dropped her home first and as we drove away Gloria filled me in.

'Bernard, are you still interested in taking Lita out?' she asked.

'Absolutely,' I replied, 'she's very attractive and has a nice personality.'

'Well she likes you, but the trouble is she doesn't want a Western boyfriend. She thinks they are only after one thing, which of course most of them are. I sounded her out but if you call her she won't go out with you.'

'That's a pain, Gloria,' I replied. 'Of course I have no idea how the relationship might develop, but unless she gets to know me properly we'll never find out.'

'I think what you should do,' she said after some thought, 'is have a dinner party at your flat for the four of us. You're a good cook, and your apartment is really nice. That way she can get to know you better and she'll be impressed that you can put together a meal.'

'That's no problem, but will she come if she doesn't want to get too close to me?'

'Don't worry, I'll twist her arm if she's reluctant,' was Gloria's reply. 'Call me in the next couple of days and let me know some possible dates.'

So an evening was booked and they turned up for the dinner. They had picked Lita up and therefore arrived together. I was even more smitten when I opened the door. She looked lovely in a simple dress and was holding a cake she had baked for me as a thank you. As before, she was good company and we had a very nice evening. She seemed duly impressed by my efforts in the kitchen, and also that I had decorated and furnished the flat myself to such a high standard, without any interior designers being involved.

I had her phone number by now and after a couple of days I called her. Well, I didn't get anywhere. In the nicest possible way she rebuffed my attempts to get her to go out with me, basically saying she wasn't looking to get involved with anyone at the present time.

Well I didn't mind a challenge, and I was determined to see if I could get anywhere with her. But how? Unfortunately I could not make the next opportunity I would have had to see her and progress things. David and Gloria were getting married on the 24th March but I had to fly to London on business the night before so I would miss it. At least I reflected that I should have time on my side, as it didn't look like she would be going out with someone else anytime soon.

Arriving back from London and looking at my diary at what was coming up I saw I had a masonic ladies night I was going to on May 5th and this gave me an idea. It was a black tie do and, given it was a 'Ladies Night', I really should have one with me. So I called Lita up and laid it on that I needed a partner for the night, that she knew me quite well by now, there were no strings attached but it would mean a lot if she would accompany me. She clearly didn't want to say yes but I backed her into a corner and she did. Hooray! While there would be plenty of other people there, it was going to be much more of a 'date' than we'd had so far, so let's see what that leads to.

A couple of days later she called me. 'Bernard, I'm terribly sorry but I won't be able to come with you after all,' she said, 'I hope you still have time to find someone else.'

'Why, what's happened?' I asked her, thinking what a pain, just when I thought I'd cracked it.

'I just can't make it, I'm afraid,' was her less than helpful response.

'That's a real shame, I was so looking forward to it,' I said as a holding line while I rapidly thought what to do next. She was silent so I continued with a quickly thought out response. 'Well I'm not going to be able to find anyone else, you know I travel all the time and don't have another girl to ask, as I explained to you before.' I paused for a moment and went on 'so I won't be able to go then.'

'Yes you can,' she replied, 'just go on your own.'

'I can't do that,' I said. 'Just think what a sad person I'll look going to a ladies night on my own. Are you absolutely sure you can't make it?'

'I'm really sorry Bernard.' There was a pause and she went on, 'The trouble is I only have one evening dress, and I've just looked at it and it's not good enough for an event like this, and I can't afford to buy a new one.'

I breathed a mental sigh of relief. If that was the problem there was a good chance we could fix it.

'Oh, I'm glad that's all that's getting in the way,' I said. 'If that's the issue I'll be happy to buy you a new dress as a thank you for coming with me.'

Well it took a few more minutes to settle her concerns over this, but finally she agreed. I told her I knew someone who could get her a nice dress at a good price and arranged to meet her after work the next evening.

I did know someone who I thought should be able to help. Some of the members of the masonic lodge that was holding the event were from the Harilela family. They were very wealthy Indian businessmen with fingers in a number of pies, and one of these was that they had a number of tailors' shops in Hong Kong. I knew Mike (real name Mohan) the best, so I called him and asked the best way to get an evening dress at short notice. He told me to take Lita to any of his shops and get the manager to ring him. He would introduce me and that way I would get the best price and service.

So the next evening we turned up at one of the shops on Kowloon side. I had been expecting to just get a decent discount on a ready-to-wear dress, but it didn't work like that. This being Hong Kong the dresses were made to measure. The shop had catalogues from all the top designers, and from the photos you picked the one you wanted and they copied it.

It quickly became apparent that Lita was quite fussy about fashion. She spent what seemed to me to be ages going through all the books before settling on a simple black dress from one and a short white top from another. The manager took all her measurements and he arranged for her to come back in a couple of days for a fitting.

'Shall I give you the price now sir?' he said to me, nothing to do with cost having come into the discussions so far.

'No it's ok,' I said, 'I'll give you a call tomorrow'. I was not too bothered as given Mike's involvement I was happy the price could not be bettered.

'But I'd like to know how much it is,' chipped in Lita.

'Well as it's a present for you, I would rather you didn't know.'

But she wasn't having it and quietly but firmly insisted that she wanted to know how much her dress was. So the manager went to his desk and after some calculations came back with a price which absolutely stunned me. I didn't have much idea of what evening dresses cost but this was at least four times what I had been expecting, especially as Lita had chosen such a simple one.

She was the first to respond. 'That's very expensive' she said quite openly in front of the manager. 'Let me find something else for less money.'

'No it's fine,' I quickly replied, 'that's what I was expecting to pay so it's not a problem'. However, while that was what I said it wasn't what I thought.

She was going to say something else but I wrapped up the discussions by saying I would post a cheque to him and bundled her out of the shop.

We drove back under the tunnel to Hong Kong side. She clearly wasn't happy that the dress was so expensive and kept referring to this with me making light of it. But at the same time I was thinking it was going to be a very expensive evening if it didn't go anywhere.

I had been back in my flat for about twenty minutes when the phone rang, it was Lita. She said we had to talk, not on the phone, could I come to her apartment block and she would meet me in the car park. She was waiting when I arrived and got in the car.

'I can't possibly accept the dress,' she blurted out, 'it's far too much money. You'll just have to cancel the evening'.

Oh no, I thought, more grief. 'Look,' I said to her, 'I must admit I was very surprised at the cost, even though I told you I wasn't. I had no idea they were that expensive, but hopefully you'll wear it a number of times, and I really am very happy to buy it for you.'

'No' she replied. 'What are you expecting from me if you are willing to spend that much money?'

Over the next ten minutes I managed to calm her down and the evening was back on again. I drove away hoping that was that and matters would now progress with no more complications until the 5th.

Well, that was not to be. A few days before the ladies' night Margaret came into my office and said there was a Mr Dean in reception. He didn't have an appointment but was asking if he could see me for a few minutes. She gave me his card, which showed he was an EVP of Gulf Oil. As we did business only with banks I couldn't think what he might want, but then I noticed that the office address on his card was on the same floor as ours, and I recalled that Gulf had a small office for two or three of their most senior regional people, so I assumed it must be something about the building he wanted to discuss.

Margaret showed him into the office. We shook hands and I invited him to sit down.

'Many thanks for seeing me without an appointment,' he started off. 'The reason I've popped over is that Lita works for Mrs. Dean and myself'.

Unbelievable. Well it transpired that she had shown him my

business card the previous evening and he realised that our offices were not only in the same building but on the same floor. He then explained that Lita was like a daughter to them and they were hoping she would go back to the US when they returned, and they could get her US citizenship. We chatted on for a good few minutes. George was clearly a very nice guy but the underlying message was clear. He was letting me know that if I in anyway made Lita unhappy he would come after me!

After he had left I sat back in my chair and pondered the situation, rather bemused. All I had done was to see a girl at a party that I fancied and wanted to ask out. And this simple situation had taken me through all that had gone on this far. I wondered what the next chapter in this saga was going to be.

On the night I picked Lita up at her apartment, George opened the door and introduced me to his wife, Betty. They invited me in, as they wanted to take a photo of the two of us with Lita all dressed up, and I had to admit she looked stunning. After some pleasantries we left and on arriving at the venue I breathed a sigh of relief; we were finally here. The evening went off really well with a very good formal meal followed by dancing, which she turned out to be very good at. I could tell she was a bit nervous on arrival, but everyone on our table was very friendly and chatty and it was a very pleasant evening. By the time we left I was confident we had moved things along nicely. Unfortunately the Friday following the ladies night I had to travel to London for a planning meeting and would be away for two weeks. I had of course mentioned this to her during the evening, and when I dropped her home I said I would give her a call when I was back. Thankfully no rebuttal, so hopefully I had made progress.

I was aware that an upmarket new restaurant had just opened in Aberdeen called Casablanca, which was getting good reviews. When I called Lita on my return I explained that I wanted to try it and would love it if she could join me. She accepted. This was the end of May. I then took her out once more before just the two of us celebrated my 31st birthday at a very swanky restaurant called Cafe Amigo, which, despite the 'Cafe' part of the name, was just about as luxurious as you could get.

Our relationship developed very quickly from that point and was soon serious. We were very lucky that George and Betty really did treat her as a daughter, and she had almost complete freedom to see me, without the restrictions of only having Sunday off each week which applied to virtually everyone else in her situation.

There was a slightly difficult time for us at the end of July when my parents came to stay for two and a half weeks. It was their first time in Hong Kong and lovely having them there, but there was a definite sense of unease at my relationship with Lita. It didn't help that both my sisters' first marriages had failed and I was clearly the big hope for a successful one. While they treated her perfectly well when we were together, I knew that they would have reacted differently if she had been European and seen as someone I should look to marry.

At the end of 1984 we took a major step and travelled to the Philippines to meet her family. I was leaving on the 20th December to spend Christmas and the New Year in the UK and on getting back I was going to be very busy as the company's year-end was February. I therefore took just over a week's holiday from the 9th-18th November and, as always, there was no problem with George and Betty for Lita to go away.

The trip had three elements. Firstly we would meet up with her relatives in Manila, where a sister and brother were living, then we would head south on our own for a few days to Puerto Galera (Galleon Port), a very pretty group of islands where I had spent a week on my own at the end of August when I needed a break, and had loved it there. Then it was a full day's travel by bus to her parents' to meet everyone there. It was a great visit, fascinating being with her family, they were all so cheerful and friendly and fully adhered to the popular image of Filipinos as having a very hospitable culture.

1985 arrived and events took their course, and by the end of it Lita had moved in with me. This had caused much upset with George. When Lita had told him and Betty of her intentions I was asked to come for a talk with him. In keeping with how they felt about her this was very much her 'father' speaking to me. George stated how fond he and Betty were of me and seeing Lita so happy, but that he was old-fashioned and was completely against couples living together. If we married no one would be happier than him, but not this. We parted on good terms, but Lita said the last few days living there were very difficult. Betty had spoken to her though and said not to worry, he would get over it.

The situation with my parents also reared its head again at the end of 1985. By then Lita and I had been seeing each other for almost eighteen months and were living together, so we were clearly very serious as a couple. I was planning to go back to the UK again for Christmas and New Year but would take Lita this time. On a phone call to my parents I let them know this but my father, rather nervously, said he didn't think this was a good idea, that Christmas was a family time. Unfortunately they were still not accepting how close Lita and I were. I felt bad but had to say to him that I was going to be with Lita over the holiday and therefore they would either see both of us or neither of us. He relented, and to be fair, then said that if I felt like that of course she would be most welcome.

A few days later a letter arrived from him, about what I was putting them through. I felt terrible reading it, as we were a close family. It was very carefully worded and based on a realisation after the phone call that there was every possibility we would get married. He expressed their concerns that while Lita was a very nice person, and that we were obviously very happy together, had I considered the challenges of a mixed marriage, in particular for any children, and would she settle if we came back to the UK? It must have been extremely hard for him to sit down and write that letter.

What they hadn't appreciated was that I most likely had more concerns then they did. I was a traditionalist at heart, and one reason I was over thirty and unmarried was that I was being very choosy, too choosy I'm sure. I had every expectation of ending up living back in the UK, and therefore also doubts as to how happy she would be there, and of course the impact of other children on ours, knowing how nasty they could be to anyone who was in any way different.

Regardless of the situation, the trip went off very well. My parents and sisters could not have been more welcoming, and we visited a number of friends including David and Gloria, who were now living in the UK. Lita was fascinated to experience frozen puddles, snow and 'dead' trees and see London for the first time.

Following this visit to my parents, with the seriousness of our relationship absolutely clear to them, I was relieved that whatever their concerns, the situation was crystal clear.

Chapter 10

1984 – building the team

Arriving back in Hong Kong in early January from the UK, with the company's February year end not far away, brought with it the realisation that although it was the start of 1984 I had only been there for ten months. It was quite amazing to look back on just how much had happened in that time, both from a business as well as a personal perspective. My job in particular had been a very steep learning curve, specifically in how to handle so many activities in the time available, and when the pressure had been particularly high I had pondered on a well-known Chinese curse which translated as 'may you live in interesting times'!

As there was not much I could do at this late stage to influence the financial results of my first year, it would have been nice to have been able to sit back for a short while and take stock, but this was not to be. I had to 'hit the ground running' from the start of the new business year as I had another very challenging set of targets to achieve. My numbers were going to be rather disappointing, as sales and revenue were somewhat down on budget, but as I had managed the costs very carefully since September's 'Black Saturday' and 1997 crises my profit figure was going to be just over 90% of budget. Given that the sales and revenue numbers I had been given were almost double the previous year, and with the impact of my major market in Hong Kong putting almost all new spending on hold just over half way through the fiscal year, I felt this wasn't that bad.

There was a lot of pessimism in Hong Kong at the end of 1983 when we were working on budgets for 1984/85 and I had therefore gone in with a proposal to keep my numbers at the same level I was looking to achieve this year. The top management however were having none of this and seemed to take a stance akin to 'pessimism is for wimps'. They wanted significant global growth, and they saw the Asian market as being one to provide a large chunk of this, despite the Hong Kong situation. I had to up the numbers very substantially, but in recognition of my challenges I was told that there would be flexibility both in releasing key people to come to Asia and to pay for expatriate hires if the right people could not be found locally. From my knowledge of the countries I was responsible for, I doubted that the business was going to be there to achieve these budgets without Hong Kong coming good, but it was clear that such a view was falling on deaf ears. I therefore decided it was best to accept the situation with good grace, and determine if the promises in respect of my staffing had any substance.

On the sales front I had been struggling to get on board the senior local I wanted on my team. I had identified a few good candidates who were wanting to move from their current jobs, and seemed genuinely interested, but the reality was that top flight Chinese salespeople who could operate in a Western manner were as rare as hen's teeth. They ended up either moving to much larger companies than us or being given large pay increases to stop them leaving.

I had more success with finding a very good local Chinese junior salesman. Stephen joined us at the end of January and fitted in very well from the start. He was short of sales experience but willing and able to learn. The benefit of having a local on the sales team was shown with the first customer we were trying to get in Taiwan. With the lack of new business opportunities in Hong Kong, with almost everything on hold, I had ramped up activities in Taiwan, Korea, Japan, Thailand and the Philippines and had identified a large local Taiwanese bank prospect. Selling to them was very different to selling to Chinese businessmen in Hong Kong, most obviously in that everything we did with them involved what seemed to be hordes of people on their side, and most spoke little or no English. This was also the case when we came down to the contract negotiations, with every meeting having at least ten people present, representing every department involved. It was after the first couple of these meetings that Stephen came to me with a major concern.

'Bernard, we are going to have a problem with the bank on discounts,' he said.

'Well as we don't do discounts, if they want one it will be a problem,' I replied. I had already explained to Stephen that the company did not discount their software or maintenance fees, on the basis that if you did it for one prospective customer it would get out and you'd have to do it for everyone. There was some flexibility on how you structured project costs but licences and maintenance fees were sacrosanct.

'I know' he replied, ' but their culture is that if they do not get a discount then they have failed in the negotiations, so if we don't provide a discount it is very likely they will decide they no longer want our system, and will choose a competitor who will discount.'

'Seriously, they would walk away from their preferred product just because we would not give a discount?'

'I'm afraid so,' he confirmed, and went on to explain that one of the senior managers he had become friendly with had taken him aside to warn him about this, as the bank really wanted our system and were concerned, as they had heard that we did not discount.

'Well you're right, we have a big problem then' I responded. 'We wouldn't give a discount to the biggest global banks, so there's no way London will break their rule with a Taiwanese one they've never heard of.'

I felt we couldn't even involve my boss Charlie in this, as while he would clearly want the business and might help find a way around the problem, he was just as likely to tell me to stick to normal terms in which case, having involved him, I would have had no choice but to do so.

We mulled over what options we had and finally came up with a plan that had a good chance of working, provided nobody but the two of us knew about it. The company had a document called the 'Commercial Manual'. Every aspect of our pricing including licence fees, maintenance fees, daily billing rates, upgrade terms etc. for every country was included here. It was very strictly for company use only and was printed on very dark paper to make photocopying difficult. We decided we would reproduce the Hong Kong pricing page (which was also used for Taiwan) and uplift the prices by 15%. Stephen would have this in his briefcase. The contracts would show our normal prices, and when the bank started to discuss discounts Stephen would suggest I go out for ten minutes; saying he wanted to have a discussion in Chinese without slowing things down with translation, and therefore I could take a break. While I was out of the room he would then explain that he wanted to show them something in strictest confidence. He would pull out the uplifted price sheet and explain that as they were the first customer in Taiwan I had already given them a special reduced price as they could see, but it must not show as a discount on the contracts. He asked that they keep this confidential for obvious reasons.

When I came back the price topic was not referred to again and in the fullness of time the contracts were signed. While Stephen and I obviously had our concerns over this tactic, it kept everyone happy. It would never have worked without a local salesperson, and it also demonstrated how well thought of Stephen was by the bank.

Early in 1984 Charlie and I had decided that we had no option but to bring in the senior sales staff we needed from overseas. He had identified someone in Sydney (where we had an agent) who worked for IBM and was interested in a move to Hong Kong to take the sales manager's role, and there was an experienced salesman in London who was also interested in relocating to Hong Kong. Discussions with them went well and in March Jon arrived from London with his girlfriend Naomi, and a little while later Ross joined us, bringing with him his wife and young son from Sydney.

The final appointment in this respect was in Tokyo. We were

enjoying continuing success selling to Japanese head offices who were using the system in their overseas branches, but we were not managing to sell to the foreign banks in Tokyo, which should have been a good market for us. The major reason seemed to be that Toppan Moore were not actively selling to them, as in every case it meant dealing with non-Japanese senior managers in these branches, and they were not comfortable with this. Charlie had identified one of our US salesman who was single and interested in relocating to Tokyo and his appointment went ahead, although it would be some time before he was in place, and in the interim Jon took on the sales to these banks in Japan.

Before they arrived we had Chinese New Year. This was the biggest Chinese festival and lasted in total for fifteen days, although the key dates were New Year's Eve and New Year's Day. It was based on the lunar calendar, so the date varied significantly each year within a four-week period between 21st January and 20th February. This year it was the 2nd February and you had to allow for it as Hong Kong completely shut down on New Year's Day itself, and to a large extent on the days either side of it. Flights were booked up well in advance at this time, both by westerners taking holiday and Chinese flying into or out of Hong Kong to attend the most important event, the New Year's Eve family 'reunion dinner'.

At that time Hong Kong was resplendent in colourful decorations, with red and gold everywhere. Specially produced miniature tangerine trees and bushes with lots of small fruit on them were a key part of the decorations, as were 'lucky bamboo' plants grown in a spiral shape, although these were not in fact bamboo, but a similar plant. One of the other traditions, and one that I had to get involved in, was handing out 'Lai See' - lucky money. There were special red packets to put the money in and these were typically given to single people of any age by those who were married. They were however also given to people who worked for you, and therefore I needed to hand them out to the staff, my amah and Ah Kwok the boat boy.

Towards the end of January I took all the staff for a special New

Year dinner. The Hilton Hotel had a very good Chinese restaurant on its top floor called The Eagle's Nest with large round tables and great views across the harbour. We included wives and husbands and I also had a couple of company visitors in town, including Chris, the Finance Director of the Group we were a part of, so we were around 40 people. At the end of the meal one of those situations occurred which showed how different life was here as an expatriate businessman. I had planned to pay the bill on my credit card but when the maître d' gave it to me I asked if it was possible to send it to the office and I would pay by company cheque. He was fine with this, asked me to give him my business card and sign the bill and off he went. Chris was sitting next to me and asked if we had an account with the hotel. I said no and explained that I had never been to the restaurant or seen the maître d' before. He was understandably very surprised that they were prepared to trust the payment of such a large bill just on a business card I had handed over.

Jon, my English senior salesman, arrived on the 11th March, and was a breath of fresh air. He was not the easiest person to manage but he had bags of energy and a 'can do' attitude; and to have another person able to work full time on sales activity made a really big difference to how much ground we could cover. He and Stephen developed a very good relationship between them, which was a real plus.

Jon had brought his girlfriend Naomi with him. She worked as a graphic artist and had quickly found a job locally. In her first week she was working on an artwork when she had an interesting 'only in Hong Kong' experience. Arriving the morning after she had been applying a lot of paint, there was no trace at all of the white she had applied the previous day. All the other colours she had used were still there, but there wasn't the faintest trace of the white on the whole artwork. Being completely flummoxed by this and trying to work out what was going on she mentioned the situation to one of the other staff.

'Oh, sorry, Naomi,' this girl said to her, 'someone should have told you about that, the cockroaches come out at night and will eat any white paint they find. There's something in the white pigment they like. If you have anything with white paint you need to put it in a cupboard overnight.'

Nothing fazed Jon. A couple of months after he had arrived we had a situation with a bank in Macau who we were trying to get to buy our system. Macau, being a Portuguese territory, had a couple of branches of Portuguese banks. I had been working on a sale to one of them for some time, but it was proving difficult to win as they used a major competitor of ours in a number of other sites around the world. There were senior people in the Head Office in Lisbon telling Macau they had to use the same system, and our competitor was bending over backwards to stop us getting the business, as it would be embarrassing for them if we did.

I had managed to get the local staff, including the Portuguese General Manager, to decide they preferred our product, and liked working with us, and they had recommended to their Head Office that they take our system. The General Manager was in Lisbon to attend a board meeting, at which one of the topics was the system decision for Macau. Jon had taken over this sale and burst into my office on the day of the meeting in Lisbon. He had just been told that the GM was going to be railroaded at the meeting, and forced to take the incumbent system. Clearly, if this decision was taken at the board meeting it would be almost impossible to overturn. We decided that the only hope was to try and get hold of the GM in Lisbon and get him to ask for the topic to be deferred to a future meeting. If this could be done we would live to fight another day. But how to track him down?

Well, I had to hand it to Jon. He was straight on the phone to the Lisbon Head Office and somehow, after being passed to various different people, he managed to get through to a secretary who was sitting outside the room where the board meeting was taking place. We had hoped to get hold of the GM before he went into the meeting, but it had already started. Unbelievably Jon managed to get the secretary to agree to go into the meeting and get the GM to come out to take the phone call. He agreed to our suggestion and we heard later that he had successfully managed to get the decision deferred. And the outcome of all this – about three months later we did win the business!

One thing Jon was not good at was administration, whether it was completing his expense reports, filling in sales reporting documents or even paying his personal bills, as all this type of activity was an anathema to him. When his electricity and phone had been cut off for the second time for non-payment I decided to do something about it. As the expression went, you could lead a horse to water but you couldn't make it drink, so as other attempts to get Jon to keep on top of his admin had failed I asked him if he would be happy for Isabelle, the sales secretary, to take this over for him. He had no problems with this, anything to get it off his desk. Isabelle was a quiet, quite short lady, who despite giving the impression of being shy could be pretty feisty if needed. I asked her if she would mind doing all this personal activity for Jon and she was fine with it.

So every morning Jon would dump his post unopened on her desk, Isabelle would sort out any clearly personal mail and give that to him unopened but she handled everything else. Jon had given her a cheque book so any bills only needed his signature, and when he returned from a trip she would sit him down and go through what he had spent while it was fresh in his mind and fill out his expense reports. She would manage his 'to do' list and was very good at making him action the items that were due.

A couple of months later Ross arrived to head up the sales team. In addition to his management role, as we were a small team, he also was involved selling directly as I still was, although my primary focus in this respect was Japan and our agent there. Despite the additional sales resource it was still a tough environment to get the business needed to achieve my increased targets. Most of the countries in my territory except Hong Kong and Japan would not pay the prices we were charging, as ours was an expensive product, giving at best only a handful of prospects in each location. Hong Kong was still basically on hold as it would be early 1985 before the situation with China would become settled enough for businesses to start investing again, so the Japanese bank branches were the only hope. They were taking a long term view that Hong Kong would remain a good place to be, and we had some potential with them. With the sales team in place however, at least I had the resources to cover each location, hopefully leaving no stone unturned in terms of possible business.

With these appointments done I needed to turn my focus to the Operations area of the branch. Given the increased new business since I had arrived, and that this was becoming more geographically spread, together with the ever-increasing support workload for existing customers, the management of this area was causing issues. The technical side of the business in terms of the local programming and testing was very ably managed, as I have previously mentioned, by a Chinese lady called Winnie. Unfortunately I had not been so successful in finding suitable management in the area that looked after implementation of our system and ongoing customer support.

The head of implementation and the project/customer managers were very capable in terms of the detail work required, but unfortunately all of them were struggling in handling customers when difficult discussions were needed. The main areas for this were when a customer was not meeting its commitments under the project plan or was trying to expand the scope of the work outside what was agreed, and in protecting the company when we failed to deliver software on time or to an acceptable standard of quality. This also manifested itself in internal activities such as fighting their corner within the company when required.

Initially I felt I was dealing with individuals who lacked these abilities, but from discussions with a range of people including the recruitment companies it transpired it was a generic situation with local Chinese staff. The root cause was explained to me as being due to Chinese upbringing, which was aimed at making each person operate as part of the wider family unit, and not stand out as an individual. Unlike the typical Western model with parents bringing their children up to be able to stand on their own, leave the family and look after themselves, the historical background in China was based on family groups (including sibling families, grandparents, aunts and uncles and their families) living close together. To work this required a lack of confrontation and individualism, and a consensus approach being taken, with each person trying to establish the majority view and then going along with that. I had definitely experienced this in company meetings I had held in which, on asking for input from the floor, there was usually a deathly hush, no one wanting to stick their necks out with their personal view.

I decided that, unfortunately, we therefore needed another expatriate. Given the nature of this role however I didn't want to recruit externally, but to identify someone already in the company with good experience in operations management. They would then be able to support and train the local staff, as well as being fully aware of our development shortcomings out of London, and factor these in as needed. Rather surprisingly the person I came up with, who was very happy to move to Hong Kong with his family, had no fewer than four children to bring with them! David arrived in mid-August and was welcomed by his team, given his knowledge, and it was now up to him to handle these problem situations.

One other expatriate I had on the team at this time was one of our UK consultants, a single guy called Robert. I had put him in place to work with Toppan Moore, our Japanese agent in Tokyo, and support their staff in the implementation and support work they were doing for Japanese banks. For some of his time he was based in Hong Kong before going to live in Tokyo permanently.

Robert had some interesting traits. He was a nice guy, very calm and measured in his speech, and rarely ruffled. He certainly wasn't the most dynamic individual and had a habit of nodding off to sleep quite often, whether in a bar, a company meeting or in a restaurant after dinner. This somewhat 'laid back' personality however fed through into some interesting incidents. One of these was when he invited Lita and myself plus another couple for dinner at his flat a couple of weeks after he had arrived. I had managed to get him a leave flat and while it was not as palatial as the one I had had when I first arrived, it was very smart and came with the added benefit of not one but two maids, one of whom was a good cook. He therefore felt he should make use of this feature.

Halfway through the meal I needed to use the men's room. 'Robert' I asked him, 'could you tell me where the bathroom is please?'

'Use my en-suite' he replied. 'If you turn left and go to the end of the hall, my bedroom's there'.

I was just getting up when one of the maids in the dining room, who had overheard the exchange, spoke. 'Excuse me sir' she broke in, ' the guest bathroom is the door opposite if you'd prefer to use that.' As I walked around the table to go there, Robert exclaimed 'Oh, I wondered what was behind that door.' Amazingly, despite having lived in the flat for two weeks, he had never opened it!

A second Robert situation happened after he had left Hong Kong to relocate to Tokyo. He was in a normal furnished flat at that time and a few days after he had left we had a letter from the landlady claiming quite a large sum of money for a missing picture. I called him up in Tokyo.

'Robert, the landlady of your flat is claiming for a painting that she says is missing, do you know what she's on about?' I said to him.

'Oh that painting, yes I remember it,' he replied.

'Well was it there when you left, why is she saying it's missing?' I asked.

'Oh, I didn't like it, so I threw it out.'

'You threw it out?' I answered incredulously, 'but it was a rented flat, what made you do that, surely you realised she would charge for it?'

'Oh yes, it was rather stupid now I think about it, but I didn't like it.'

'So why didn't you do something such as put it under one of the beds, and put it back up when you left?'

He didn't say anything so I carried on. 'Well I'm sure she's now claiming much more than it's really worth, but that's your problem. The company isn't paying this, you will have to.'

'Yes, I suppose I will,' was all he said.

With these appointments in place, some excellent local recruits in more junior roles and with everyone now settled in the new offices, I felt quite proud of the transformation of the branch in what was only a little over a year since I had first arrived.

Taken at a management meeting in London – March 1983

View to Central from my flat in Elizabeth House

San Francisco Towers in Happy Valley

My living room in San Francisco Towers

At my desk – Hilton Hotel in background

Oxelotel II

Ah Kwok on Oxelotel II

Bottoms Up memorabilia

Lita with George and Betty

Our first night out together as a couple

Paradise Beach, Philippines (our hut on the right)

Puerto Galera, Philippines

One of the famous jeepneys

Lita's family at her parents in Pantar Sur

Lita's parents' farmhouse

Staff barbecue – Hong Kong style

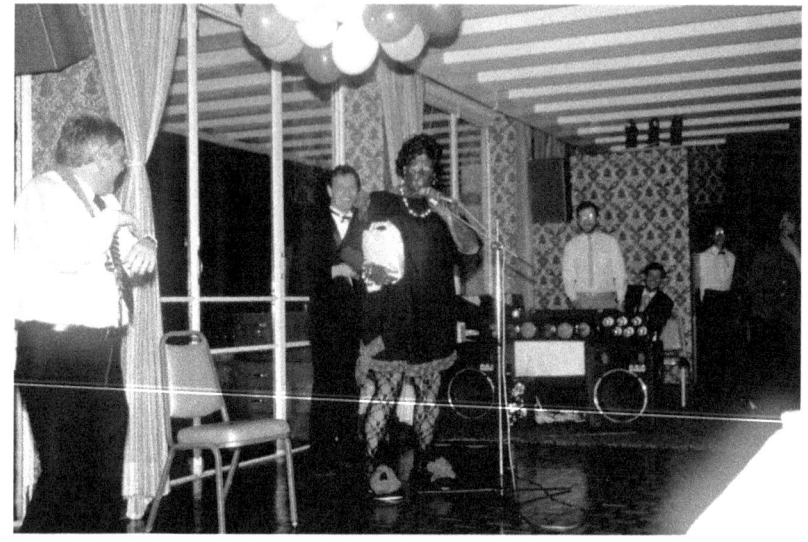

Dressed as Indira the Indian at a Round Table event

English roast meal at San Francisco Towers

With my parents and a Mini Moke in Macau

The broken-down taxi on the way to Batangas, Philippines

Paradise Beach, looking to the main house

With the staff of Paradise Beach

Lita arriving at Heathrow after her five-month wait for a visa

Chapter 11

Paradise Beach

A key event at this time was my parents' arrival on 23rd July for two and a half weeks. They had not been to Hong Kong before and of course found it fascinating, with trips on the Ox, visiting the office and having dim sum with the staff, in addition to normal sightseeing activities. Once they had left I had to put to bed the key staff additions, including getting David, the new Operations Manager, settled (he had arrived mid-August). It suddenly struck me on Friday 24th August that I did not have much on the next week, and what I did have was easily rescheduled. This was almost unheard of, so with Monday a public holiday I decided on the spur of the moment to go somewhere for the week. My boss, Charlie, had been in town for three days and was flying out that afternoon, so I squared it away with him and went looking for what to do.

Given the extremely short notice, and with it being only a four-day week, everything I fancied was booked up. I did however recall a friend giving me details of a holiday he had taken at a small beach resort in the Philippines, and decided to try for that. Apparently it was pretty basic, with nipa (reed) huts, and was run by a British guy. My friend had raved about it as idyllic, a perfect place to chill out and relax, which was just what I wanted, and as there were no telephones I would be uncontactable – a real bonus.

I was able to get a seat on a flight to Manila the next morning, and one back the following Sunday. My friend was away on holiday and I could not get hold of him, but I had all the information I needed to get there. Given the lack of a telephone I had no way to find out if the resort was full, but as it was in an area that was a popular holiday destination, I was pretty sure I would be able to find somewhere else if needed.

Enticingly named Paradise Beach Resort, it was on an island called Mindoro which was a short way off the south coast of the main island of Luzon, where Manila was. I had to get to a place called Puerto Galera on the north coast of the island, and then take transport from there to the resort. Puerto Galera (Galleon Port), named by the Spanish who arrived there in the mid 1550s, was a large and very scenic sheltered lagoon, considered to be one of the safest and most beautiful natural harbours in the world. Mindoro was a large mountainous island, the seventh biggest in the Philippines, its name coming from the one the Spaniards gave it, 'Mina de Oro', meaning mine of gold. They apparently came across some of the precious metal there when they first started exploring, although no major deposits have ever been found. While the area around Puerto Galera was a tourist destination, inland Mindoro was very remote and inaccessible and interestingly, living in the interior were the Mangyan, one of Asia's most backward tribes, who had experienced very little contact with the outside world.

There was a once-a-day ferry to Puerto Galera from Batangas, the nearest port on Luzon. As this ferry left at midday and the port was a two to three-hour bus ride south of Manila I had to stay overnight in the capital, as the earliest flight from Hong Kong arrived too late to be able to make the ferry.

I had decided to enjoy some luxury for my night in Manila, even though I was paying this time, and had booked into a five-star hotel, the Philippine Plaza. I had been told that this was the largest of a number of top-quality hotels completed in a rush in the mid 1970s, so that Manila could be hosts for a meeting of the World Bank and International Monetary Fund. This was the Marcos era, and they drove these projects through as they wanted the status of having such a prestigious meeting held in the Philippines. There was not enough business or tourist demand for this number of expensive hotel rooms at that time, and once the meetings were finished the hotels had very low occupancy. Ferdinand and Imelda Marcos were often in the news in Hong Kong for all the wrong reasons. Becoming President in the mid 1960s, Marcos initially had a positive impact on the country and economy, but unfortunately the couple succumbed to nepotism and cronyism and diverted much of the country's wealth to themselves and their family and friends. They also suppressed any opposition by jailing or forcing into exile key individuals, and just the year before we were there the main opposition leader, returning from exile, had been assassinated on his arrival at Manila Airport.

The hotel had been built on reclaimed land on Manila Bay, with great views over the bay from the rooms at the front; the sunsets were famous and it was close to the main business and tourist areas of the city.

The flight was fine and, thankfully, the airport, while busy, was not as frenetic as on the previous occasion when I had passed through it, and I was pretty quickly through and in a taxi. I had a front-facing room and true enough there were excellent views and the room itself was a very good size. I had thought about wandering around a few of the bars and clubs in the evening, but sense prevailed; I had to be up early and therefore decided that I would instead just have a nice meal in a nearby restaurant followed by a drink in the hotel bar.

I arrived at the BLTB bus terminal as dawn was breaking. I had been warned that the bus services in the Philippines were disorganised, not following a timetable, and that there was no reserved seating, so if you couldn't get on the bus that arrived you just had to wait for the next one and try to get on that. Given this, and that I had to be at the jetty by midday, I needed to ensure I had ample time, hence the early start.

Luckily the bus station was fairly quiet. I bought a ticket, found out which bus stop to use and, as none was there yet, went to the café for some breakfast. I saw someone getting an omelette sandwich, which looked fine, so I asked for that and a cup of coffee. When my sandwich arrived it had been liberally doused with banana ketchup, which I wouldn't have said yes to if asked, but on the basis of 'when in Rome...' I ate it as it was. It was delicious, and from that day I have put ketchup on omelettes and scrambled eggs. The banana ketchup looked and tasted the same as tomato ketchup. Not being a big grower of tomatoes, but having lots of bananas, the Filipinos had managed to concoct this version during World War II when there had been a tomato shortage.

There were no delays on the journey to Batangas, and I arrived in plenty of time at the jetty. The ferry was a very sorry excuse for a boat. It was made of wood, with most of the exterior paint gone and the timbers bleached by the sun. More worrying, given its tinder dry state, was that while we were making the crossing people were lighting portable stoves to cook on, but as nobody else seemed bothered by this I tried to put it out of my mind. Most of the seating was deckchairs with some upright wooden bench seats, and I managed to get a deckchair and relaxed in that for the two-hour trip, helped by a couple of San Miguel beers.

Arriving at Puerto Galera town I asked around and was told I needed to take a jeepney westwards along the coast road to get to the resort. Jeepneys were a uniquely Filipino form of transport, and originated with the US army jeeps that were abandoned after World War II. These were cut in half and lengthened to carry more passengers, a roof was added, and then each one was decorated to the tastes of the owner.

Perhaps the best description of them was one I came across in a book I had then titled *South East Asia On A Shoestring*: 'Take one ex-US army jeep, put two benches in the back with enough space for about twelve people, paint it every colour of the rainbow, add tassels, badges, horns, lights, aerials, about a dozen rear view mirrors, a tape deck, selection of Beatles' golden oldies, a chrome horse (or three) and anything else you can think of. Stuff twenty passengers on those benches for twelve, add four more in front and drive like a maniac'.

I found one going the route I wanted and sat inside. Jeepneys hung around until they were full, and often overfull, with people sitting on top and hanging off the back and sides. Once the driver felt there was no way anyone else could get on off we went. The distance was about five miles and after about thirty minutes of slow progress, dropping off and picking up people along the way, we arrived at the entrance to the Resort.

I was dropped off by a colourful sign which read 'Welcome To Paradise Beach Lodge, Bar & Restaurant, Cottages, Food & Drink'. Walking in I saw a large building in front of me and forming a V in front of it were four nipa huts on each side going towards the sea at an angle. I walked up to the big building and saw, sitting at a table on a large veranda doing paperwork, a man who I assumed to be the owner. This proved correct as on seeing me he stood up, came over to shake my hand, and introduced himself as Geffrye. Thankfully he did have empty cottages and he led me to one of the front two that faced the beach. On the way he showed me the bathroom, a small wooden building with a shower, basin and one toilet. He suggested I get settled and then join him for a drink on the veranda.

Surveying my home for the next week, I was perfectly happy. Yes it was basic, but there was a double bed, which was comfortable, and the room was very clean. On three sides it had large windows covered in gauze to keep out the bugs, a porch on the front and an electric light.

I went to join Geffrye and when he saw me he tidied up his papers and asked what I wanted to drink. I decided on a beer and he went into the building and I heard him ask someone for two San Miguels. He came back and sat down and I asked him how he came to be at Paradise.

'Well I'm sixty-two and British but I've spent most of my working life in Australia' he explained. 'I'm married but we have grown apart and I decided it was time to get away from it all. I heard about this place and arrived three years ago.'

'Is there much for you to do?' I asked him.

'Yes it's fine, if you don't want too much action. There are quite a few westerners who have retired here or are running bars, restaurants or resorts, so I meet up with them'.

At this point a girl came out of the house with our beers and he introduced her.

'This is Helen, she looks after all the day to day running of the resort,' he said. 'Anything you need, feel free to ask her.'

When she had gone back inside he went on, 'I have three other girls working here, one is local and the other two and Helen are from Manila. The Manila girls don't stay here that long as it's pretty boring for them, but I can always get replacements there. Lots of girls are looking for work and many have quite a good education and reasonable spoken English, which is important for me and the guests here as almost all of them are non-Filipinos.'

He went on to run through a few items to do with my stay. 'There will always be someone around to serve you,' he told me, 'just go in the kitchen or if there's no one there call up the stairs. There's a menu for food, but if there's anything else you would like, just let one of the girls know and they'll get it when they go into town, or there's another resort next door and they have a bigger selection if you want to eat there. Oh by the way, 'the water supply for the bathroom comes from a holding tank fed by a stream a long way up the hills behind us. You'll find that if you manage to be the first one to have a shower in the morning, the water will be warm, as the pipe will have been heated by the sun.'

Having had a second beer, I went exploring. The huts and the main building were set amongst coconut trees on a beautiful white sand beach, which was about half a mile long with a headland at each end. The main house was two storey, with the living accommodation for Geffrye and the girls on the first floor and the kitchen, restaurant and veranda on the ground floor. Looking along the beach to the right there was mostly virgin coast to the headland a few hundred yards away, and behind this in the distance you could see another bay with a sandy beach. This ended in a much higher headland and the island coast obviously turned right here, as there was no more land in view. To the left, as Geffrye had said, there was another resort next door and then a small river entered the sea, and after that were four wooden houses spaced quite widely apart, until the headland on that side was reached.

I wandered over to the resort next door. Talisay Beach Resort was more up market than Paradise, with better quality accommodation and a proper restaurant/bar area together with a separate beach bar. While I was very happy with the simple arrangements at Paradise, which was more akin to drinking and eating in a private house, it was a plus I hadn't expected to have somewhere like this only fifty yards away. I went out onto the road and walked along it for about half a mile. It was more a wide track than a road and there was nothing of note apart from the odd small wood and nipa house. I turned round and went back to my hut. I lay on the bed and had a nap to the sound of the lapping waves and rustling coconut palms coming through the open windows.

By the Wednesday I was nicely settled in and could appreciate everything that my friend had described: it was secluded, quiet, with beautiful beaches and coral for snorkelling, fantastic sunsets and warm, but with a light breeze all the time. But now the snag! He had been describing a visit in April. In August it was the wet season and the worst month to boot. It hadn't stopped raining since I had arrived and the ground was saturated. The sea was rough and dirty and you couldn't see a wonderful sunset as there was no sun. Geffrye had told me that I should get a couple of decent days, although August was rather hit or miss, especially as there was a typhoon nearby at the moment causing this particularly bad weather. Given the time of year it wasn't a big surprise that I was the only person staying, although this wasn't an issue as Geffrye often had friends around, and the beach resort next door had people staying who I could socialise with.

Other than the weather I was really enjoying myself, and it was certainly good value. My hut was £2 a night, beer 20p a bottle and an enormous plate of chicken curry and fried potatoes was £1. The local rum was excellent and particularly cheap, and at 50p for a half bottle not much more expensive than the coke to pour in it. The same could not be said of the local gin, which while as cheap as the rum, tasted as

I imagined lighter fuel would.

The terrible weather lasted until Thursday night and when I awoke on the Friday the sun was beaming down out of a blue sky, the sea was crystal clear, and the resort began to really live up to its name.

Helen had turned out to be a very bright and capable girl, well educated with excellent English and easy to talk to; not someone I would expect to find working in a small out of the way place like this. She came to see me before lunch on the Friday and said that I should take her and one of the other girls to the only disco in Mindoro, as a thank you for how well they had looked after me. I asked her how we would get there, as I had heard that the road was in a sorry state after all the rain, and she said no problem, we would take a boat.

This turned out to be one of the ubiquitous outrigger canoes. The boatman was interestingly named 'broken toe' and the journey there took an hour, during which we went past some delightful beaches and lagoons. We left at 9 pm and were back at 1 am with the cost for the boat being £8 plus two beers for broken toe.

The other girl was the local who helped Helen out at the resort. She was very attractive but like a wild animal, timid and nervous. Helen explained that she had never been outside the immediate area, let alone to a disco, and it would be an amazing experience for her. It was a very enjoyable evening and the boat trip back was magical, lots of phosphorescence, especially in the wake of the boat or if you put your hand in the water, and many glow worms flying around.

The next day I had to be up particularly early as the return ferry sailed at 7.30 am, and the continual wet weather had washed a large section of the road away, meaning the jeepney could not get to the resort. Geffrye had told me the night before that there was no guarantee the jeepneys would be running at all, but I should walk to the next village, where I would find out if they were; if not I would be able to get an outrigger canoe there to take me by sea. The walk to the village included fording a river but thankfully, on getting there, the jeepneys were running, and one was waiting for passengers when I arrived. On the journey to Puerto Galera I could see why Geffrye had been concerned as the road was in a terrible state in a number of places, especially where streams crossed it.

The boat ride back was fine as the sea was calm, but the journey to Manila was not pleasant as the bus was old, noisy and uncomfortable. I was staying at the Philippine Plaza again for one night, and unfortunately, the taxi that took me there from the bus station turned out to be one of the rip-off ones I had been told about before my first trip to Manila. I could see the meter going up at too fast a rate as we drove along and, arriving at the hotel, it showed seventy five pesos, whereas I knew from my identical journey the week before that the correct fare was about thirty. I adopted the recommended procedure in such cases and got out with my luggage before telling him I was only prepared to pay thirty pesos. He eventually came down to thirty-five, at which point I just gave him the thirty and walked into the hotel and he drove off.

Before going out that evening I totted up the cost of my week on Mindoro. The total for everything including the two bus and ferry rides, the accommodation, all my food and drink, the disco evening and a T-shirt was £60. In comparison, having stayed in a five-star hotel, my room cost for the two nights in Manila was over £100.

I was boring again that night and decided not to sample the delights of the venues catering to single male tourists and US serviceman in Ermita, the main red light area. If I had been with another guy it would have been fun, but on my own it didn't have the same attraction. I decided to go back to the Hobbit House restaurant where I had eaten in on my first visit to Manila, as the food had been good and the atmosphere busy and enjoyable. I did walk around for about half an hour first, taking in the ambience and being accosted regularly by taxis, girls and touts all offering some sort of exotic experience. I enjoyed the meal in the restaurant, and as I had done a week earlier, finished up with a drink and a cigar in the hotel bar.

Happily I did get back to Paradise Beach again that year, this time with Lita. We had been discussing what to do for Christmas and the New Year and felt that given how well we were getting on, it would be a good time for me to meet her family. However my parents were looking forward to having me back for the festivities, so we decided that to meet both objectives I would spend Christmas in the UK, but we would go to the Philippines just before I left for home. Given my work commitments, however, we ended up going earlier, leaving on Friday 9th November and flying back nine nights later on the Sunday, spending one night in Manila and three at Paradise Beach before going north to Lita's home.

It was great to be at Paradise Beach in fine weather, and in addition to relaxing we were able to explore the immediate area using the outrigger canoes. Unfortunately we only had two full days there due to our tight schedule, but a highlight was organising a lechon for dinner on the last night. A lechon is a whole barbecued pig and Lita had told me that it was traditional to have one for special occasions, and she thought the resort next door should be able to do one if we could get enough people to make it financially viable. We spoke to Talisay and they quoted to do the pig plus the vegetable, rice and potato side dishes. The price meant that we needed about ten to fifteen people to come in on it. This proved no problem when we asked the other guests at the two resorts, as everyone was very keen on the idea.

On the morning of the lechon dinner we walked around the bay to the headland on our left, having to wade the small river. On the way back we were level with Talisay Resort when the cook saw us and called us over, proudly pointing to what was obviously our pig, tethered to a stake and rooting around in the ground. Well I thought, at least we know it couldn't be fresher, but I wondered if it might put some of the people off eating the animal later if they saw it alive and oinking in front of them.

But worse was to come. About half an hour later we were relaxing back at our hut when a loud squealing started, and it was obvious the pig's time had come. The sound died down but didn't go away and after a couple of minutes I asked Lita what was going on. She answered that, unfortunately, the way they killed pigs in the countryside was to make a small incision in the artery in the neck so they could get all the blood, which meant that the poor animal took some time to die. I could have done without knowing this, but told myself that I had to allow for different values. This was rural Asia, not a squeaky clean supermarket in the Western world.

The pig was going to be slowly barbecuing all afternoon over a coconut husk fire, so later on we popped over for a drink and to see how it was cooking. A youngish couple who we had spoken to about the lechon (who were also staying at Paradise Beach) came and spoke to us and he introduced himself as Phil, an American who worked at the massive US Clark Air Force Base north of Manila and Janice, who was a Filipina. He told me he had wanted a holiday but none of his friends could make it, so he had decided to go on his own but find a bar girl to bring with him. He had picked Janice up in the red light area of Angeles City, the nearest town to the air base.

Lita chatted to Janice in Tagalog and told me later she was torn between fascination at talking to a genuine hooker and not feeling comfortable with her; especially as Janice did not have a great personality, and had confided to Lita how she was trying to extract as much money as possible from Phil. We left Talisay together and, walking back to our huts, Phil and I were in front and the girls someway behind.

We were chatting generally when he said to me, 'Hey Bernard, do you fancy doing a swap?'

'A swap of what?' I asked him.

'Well, the girls' he replied. 'Be nice to have a change, and while Janice isn't anywhere near as pretty as Lita, she's got a great body'.

'An interesting proposal' I responded, 'but as Lita's my girlfriend, and we're on our way to meet her family, I don't think she will go for it.'

He was genuinely shocked. 'I'm terribly sorry,' he exclaimed very apologetically, 'I hadn't realised that. I thought you had met her in Manila to bring here. I hope you realise I wouldn't have suggested it otherwise.'

'No, it's OK,' I said. 'Thinking back I didn't tell you anything about the two of us that would make you realise.'

Anyway when Lita and I were back in our hut I told her what he had said. She was incensed.

'What did you say, he asked you to do a swap?' she exploded at me. 'Do I look like a hooker?' She was seething. 'He thinks I'm the same sort of person as that ugly, uninteresting tart he picked up in Angeles.'

'Look, calm down, it was a genuine mistake' I managed to say before she had time to have another rant. That made matters worse.

'What do you mean, a mistake?' She was now annoyed at me. 'Are you saying I can be mistaken for someone like her?'

I decided it was best to keep quiet and let her fume until she had settled down.

Well the lechon was superb, thin crisp crackling and very tasty, tender meat. When everyone had finished we said the staff could have what was left, and invited the half-dozen young children who were hanging round outside the bar to help themselves. They were particularly excited, a fantastic treat for them, and it was great to see their faces as they tucked in. There were usually a few of the local children around. They were fascinated watching us tourists and every now and then someone would buy a bottle of coke for them to share.

It had been a short but fascinating break and the next morning we had the early start to get the ferry back to Batangas, and from there the bus to Manila.

Chapter 12

Mr Wong, new friends and a difficult colleague

Early July I had an interesting Hong Kong 'laissez faire' (a French expression often used in relation to Hong Kong to mean minimum government involvement) experience when I crashed my nice new car. Lita and I had been for dinner at Ross and Christine's (he was my new sales manager) on the south side of the island. On our way home, just after leaving them, we were on the winding, narrow two-lane road that was cut into the steep hills when suddenly, around a blind corner, came two cars at speed and parallel with each other, one trying to overtake the other. There was nowhere to go and I was facing a head-on accident. I instinctively pulled up onto the small footpath on my left, the seaward side of the road, and by a hair's breadth managed to get round the oncoming car. Unfortunately, on coming off the kerb to get back on the road I lost control, and after swerving a couple of times went up the kerb again, off the road, and straight into a tree. There was one hell of an impact and after I had regained my senses I checked Lita, who was ok apart from being hurt where the seat belt crossed her shoulder. It was a good job the tree had stopped us, as otherwise we would have gone down the steep hillside towards the sea.

The car was stable and not going anywhere and despite the extensive damage at the front the doors still opened. By the time we were out, standing by the car and getting our heads around what to do next, a few people had arrived from houses nearby. They said they had heard the impact and one mentioned that they had called an ambulance in case it was needed.

Sure enough a couple of minutes later sirens could be heard and the ambulance and a police car turned up.

One of the policeman, seeing we were basically all right, said to me, 'excuse me sir but if we or the ambulance get involved then the process will be very time consuming and bothersome, therefore if you are both all right and can get the car removed without our help that would be best for everyone.'

As I had not managed to get the licence number of either car as it had all happened so fast this was fine for me, especially as while I did not think I was over the alcohol limit, I could not be sure, as I had been drinking.

'That would be great,' I said, 'but the car is not capable of being driven and while my girlfriend is basically all right her shoulder hurts and she may be rather shocked.'

The two policeman then spoke together in Cantonese and then went off to the ambulance and spoke to the medics. After a short time they came back.

'My brother in law has a garage,' one of the policeman said. 'I'll get him to come and get the car and you can arrange with him where to take it. If you give me your keys and contact details I will give them to him. I have also agreed that the ambulance people will have a look at your girlfriend unofficially and if they don't need to take her in the ambulance that will be that.'

I thanked him very much and while Lita was being looked at I gave the policeman my details. By then she had returned and said they had given her the all clear, except for bruising to her shoulder and the side of her head where it had hit the inside of the car at some point. The policeman then gave me a lift back to the apartment. I can't imagine that was the experience I would have had in similar circumstances in England.

The next morning I arranged for the car to be taken back to my parking spot at the flat and contacted the insurance company to get it repaired. Disappointingly it took well over two months before the car was repaired; apparently as the model was so new, and the damage so extensive, that they did not have some of the spare parts in Hong Kong, so they had to be shipped from Japan.

In September I played my first round of golf in Hong Kong. I owned a set of clubs but was not very good at the game and had never even had a lesson. However I could get around a golf course well enough to enjoy a game, and therefore, when I received an invitation from the Hong Kong Management Association to a Golf Day at Fanling, I accepted.

It was not easy to play golf in Hong Kong as there were virtually no courses. The Royal Hong Kong Golf Club (RHKGC) created the first eighteen-hole course in 1889 at Happy Valley on Hong Kong Island. However space restrictions led to it being relocated to Fanling in the New Territories near the Chinese border in 1911, over twenty miles from the centre of Hong Kong. Fanling had been expanded over time to three eighteen-hole courses, and a nine-hole course, also belonging to the club, had existed at Deepwater Bay on Hong Kong Island since 1898. It had only been last year that a second eighteen-hole course had become available with the completion of one at Discovery Bay on Lantau Island (requiring a ferry ride to reach it). I had read that a third was just starting construction at a place called Clearwater Bay in the New Territories.

It was just about impossible for a normal person to become a member of the RHKGC due to the lack of memberships and the cost if any were made available, but it was possible to play by buying an expensive day ticket. I had been hoping to get the chance to have a game there one day and it was good to have the opportunity to do this as part of an organised event.

One problem though with playing in September was that it was the hottest and most humid time of the year, made even worse on the day we played by a complete absence of any breeze. I was boiling and as I was prone to sweating anyway when I was hot, particularly from my face, I was dripping the whole way round. However as these conditions were normal in the summer months Fanling provided a special benefit I had not seen anywhere else: there were two bars actually on the course, one at the 9th hole and the other at the 14th. As well as a very welcome cold drink the bars also had jars of salt tablets on the tables to replenish what you lost from the sweating.

It was an excellent day and apart from the heat and humidity most enjoyable. I knew quite a number of the other players and was introduced to some good contacts, and I played quite well given my lack of ability and didn't disgrace myself. The event finished with a very good dinner and a prize giving, with enough prizes to allow everyone to win at least one, mine being a nice bottle of Scotch and an umbrella.

A couple of days after the golf match I acquired 'Mr Wong', a very attractive zebra finch with a bright red beak. He was presented to me by Naomi, the girlfriend of our English salesman, Jon who, having introduced a cat into their flat realised it wasn't such a good idea to have both. She said that a couple of times she had caught the cat creeping up slowly to Mr Wong, clearly with evil intentions.

I had never had a bird before but was very pleased by him. He did not have a very attractive song, more of a tweet, tweet, but it was pleasant to hear him as it was not too loud. Naomi had also given me the cage he was in, which was a very attractive circular one in Chinese style made of what looked like reddish-brown reed. True enough, as Naomi had told me, if you put Mr Wong under the shower to give him a wash he would fall over and play dead for some reason - very cute.

At the end of September there were two arrivals in Hong Kong who would become very good friends of mine. Bob was coming out from London to take up a new role of Regional Sales Manager for the balance of the company's financial year - until the end of February. I had not really known him in the London office, where he had been in sales management, as our paths hadn't crossed much, but earlier in the year, when I was back for a management meeting, we started talking and found we got on well. On the second day of the meeting he told me that he lived quite close to the hotel and did I fancy skipping the hotel dinner and going back to his house for a meal and staying the night there. He said his wife was a very good cook and the food would be much better than at the hotel, as would the wine.

Sandie turned out to be a lovely lady, very good company and, as Bob had said an excellent cook. And he turned out to be a bit of a wine buff, with an excellent cellar. I had a most enjoyable evening and the three of us hit it off very well.

Bob's arrival heralded the finalisation of a change of role for me next year. I had heard in recent weeks that the Group MD in London had been trying to get Charlie to release me to come back to the UK. The global business was growing rapidly, and the company was very short of senior managers with my mix of operational and sales experience, so he felt I would be better utilised if I had a head office-based role. I had even written recently in a letter to my parents that the likelihood was I would be back in March 2005. My preference however was to stay in Hong Kong, not only because I enjoyed the life and the people I worked with, but also as I wanted to have a little longer for Lita and myself to determine our future, without being pressured by a deadline.

The plan now was for Bob to take over the Hong Kong branch from me on March 1st (the start of the company's year) and I would move into a new regional marketing role, still being based in Hong Kong, although the regional office was in Singapore. This was a great move for me. While I enjoyed the role of running the branch it was going to be wonderful to relinquish the day-to-day responsibilities for sales, admin, staff and customer issues and move into this more strategic role. In addition, while my travel would most likely increase, the trips would be to a more diverse set of locations with a very different agenda.

It transpired that Charlie had managed to get London to agree for me to stay in Asia as I would be supporting all the business units in the region (including our Australian agents), thus spreading my skills. He also felt that with Bob only having a sales background it would be valuable to have me in Hong Kong to assist him in dealing with the technical and operational issues that would arise, as well as any support required in respect of Toppan Moore our Japanese agent.

On the last Friday in September, Lita and I had an interesting evening. The Australian Society, of which we knew a few members, including Ross, my sales manager, invited us along for an evening at the Frog and Toad pub on Lantau Island. This was a converted private house in a small place called Tai Long Wan. There were no roads to the village and just about everyone arrived by boat, although there were walking tracks to it from other parts of the island. If you didn't have your own boat transport then you would normally get a ferry to Cheung Chau Island, and use a kaito (small local ferry) to take you there. It had only recently opened and was run by a Joe Lee (who was Hong Kong Chinese). It was closed on weekdays unless you contacted him, and if there was a large enough group he would open up.

It could get quite busy at weekends, mostly with westerners, but it was at its most frenetic in October when Joe would arrange a mud wrestling competition which would see hundreds of people converge on it. I never witnessed this as I couldn't get up any enthusiasm to watch people getting themselves completely covered in liquid dirt.

Lita came with me and we had a very pleasant evening away from the hustle and bustle of Hong Kong, although unfortunately she was badly attacked by mosquitos. I had never known her to be bitten so badly and felt very sorry for her. It made it worse that she had worn a dress, so they were able to get at her legs, and she was further frustrated as I didn't suffer a single bite. I had found on arriving in Asia that I was very fortunate in this regard; for whatever reason mosquitos never bit me, even if I was sleeping only in shorts in a bedroom with loads of them.

About a month after Bob and Sandie arrived they invited me round for dinner. They had recently moved into a temporary flat while they were looking for a long term place. Bob told me the apartment came with an elderly Chinese amah with the wonderful name of 'Ah Yuk'. She was happy to cook and Bob had been enthusing about her ability with steak, and said I had to come over and try one.

On arrival I was introduced to the venerable lady, who was certainly pretty aged and very wrinkly, but with a lovely almost toothless smile.

When she was ready to cook Sandie took me into the kitchen to show me the special technique Ah Yuk used. This centred on an enormous, very heavy, very battered saucepan which she would ensure was at a high temperature before the steaks went in.

When my steak arrived it was clear why her abilities were highly regarded. It was crisp and brown on the outside and juicy inside, cooked exactly as requested. She beamed with pleasure when I congratulated her on her cooking and later in the evening I put myself even more in her good books when I gave her the nice box of chocolates I had brought along. Sandie said they would be far better presented to her than eaten by us.

During the evening Sandie had brought up the subject of the Red Lips and Bottoms Up bars which she had heard of from Bob but never been to herself. I told her I had an interesting 'tourist' evening I had taken people on previously that included the two bars and an interesting Indian restaurant, so why didn't we do that? I said I would get Lita along as well and we made a date for the following week.

On the agreed evening we met up on Hong Kong side at the Star Ferry and took this across the harbour. It was only a short walk to the start of the evening, the basement bar of the Sheraton hotel in Kowloon. This was called 'Someplace Else', and as would be expected being in the Sheraton it was upmarket and very pleasant. The cocktails were very good there and with my sweet tooth I was partial to a drink with an umbrella in it; so Sandie and I had a couple, Bob stuck to beer and Lita to water. After this we headed off for dinner, which was at a block of flats called Chungking Mansions. This was a large building on Nathan Road, which was quite close by. It was over twenty years old and although originally built as residential flats had become so run down that virtually no normal families lived there anymore. Instead the apartments had been taken over for a wide range of other uses such as unlicensed restaurants, cheap guesthouses, illegal tape copying and fake watch manufacturers, as well as a number of one or two-girl brothels, obviously at the bottom end of the market.

The common areas were decrepit and filthy and on entering Sandie queried if it was a joke bringing us to somewhere like this.

'It's no joke, Sandie' said Lita with disdain, 'this is where we are eating.'

Despite the state of the place the lifts were working (important as the block was seventeen storeys high) and we went up. The Nanuk Mess was housed in one of the two bedroom apartments and was run by an Indian family. Entering through the front door the very small, dark and dingy kitchen was on your left with a couple of cooks beavering away. Next you passed the bathroom with its original pink suite, now in a terrible state with the bath more white than pink from wear. Well, what you could see of the bath that is, as this is where all the dirty plates glasses and crockery were dumped, the washing up clearly being done at the end of the evening, or if they ran out of clean stuff.

Then we arrived at what had been the living room and the two bedrooms, now kitted out with tables and chairs. We found a table for four and sat down.

Lita hated the place as she considered it uncomfortable and unhygienic in the extreme. However I had been there a few times before and knew a number of people who frequented it, and had never heard of any stomach troubles. I could fully understand why those of a more sensitive or fussy nature could be put off, but the food was really good and both it and the beer were dirt cheap.

I explained all this to Bob and Sandie. Having heard this he was quite happy but she was clearly apprehensive. I ordered some beer which came in very large bottles and a can of coke for Lita. On the table were a couple of stacks of clear melamine type beakers, which were badly scratched and opaque from long use.

'I'm sorry Sandie' said Lita, 'but I'm not going to eat very much if anything here and I won't drink out of these, I'll drink from the can. But Bernard's right, he's always been fine when he's been here so I suppose it is ok so don't let me put you off.'

'Well, in for a penny in for a pound' said Sandie, holding a beaker out to me for filling up, 'but if I am ill after this, Bernard, you will have to go out of your way to make it up to me.'

The beer was ice cold and the food was excellent as always, some of the best I had ever had, and in a completely different league to what I was used to in the UK. When the bill came, even though they had been expecting it to be cheap, Bob and Sandie were still amazed at the low price, with the beer not costing much more than at a supermarket.

Red Lips was the next stop. It was still early when we arrived and very quiet, and apart from a couple of older guys we were the only ones there. The girls were suitably impressed by the 1970s decor and ambience but shocked at the age and decrepit state of the 'girls', despite being prepared for it.

'Surely no guy would ever make out with one of those, would they?' queried Sandie.

'Apparently it does happen,' I answered her, 'although I agree that with the attractive girls available at other bars I am amazed as well.'

'I suppose you could come in here very drunk and just not realise,' she went on.

'Can you imagine waking up to one of these ladies in the morning,' I said, 'having a terrible hangover and then the shock of seeing what is lying next to you?'

'Stop it, Bernard!' she exclaimed. 'I don't want to think about it.'

We only stayed for one drink. Apart from the fact that it was not a particularly pleasant place to drink in, we did feel rather out of place, being two couples who were clearly only there as tourists.

Bottoms Up of course was completely different. It was an enjoyable place to spend a bit of time, even with your girlfriend or wife. Yes, the girl in front of you was topless, but if that did not offend you then the bar was fine. Sandie ordered the Typhoon, both to try one and as she wanted one of the glasses as a memento of her time in Hong Kong. Unfortunately Pat Sephton, the manager, wasn't there that night as they had hoped to meet her, being so well known. It was pretty quiet as well, being early in the evening, but this did allow Bob and Sandie to chat with the bar girl about life working in such a famous watering hole. As it was still quite early we had a nightcap back at the Sheraton before going home.

It was about this time that we had a photo shoot in my office. My secretary Margaret's boyfriend Nigel was a journalist and at that time he was looking after a magazine called *The Executive*. For the October 1984 edition the theme was executive stress, and Nigel wanted the picture on the front of the magazine to be of a very stressed-out manager sitting at a desk which was a shambles. He had asked me if he could use my office and if I could be the manager. Much as I would have liked having a picture of myself on the front page as a reminder of my time in Hong Kong, I decided that the topic was not a good one for my image. I told Nigel I was happy for him to use my office but he needed someone else to be the manager.

Nigel and the photographer, together with a friend of his as the model, arrived, and as they were setting up I realised that it also was not likely to go down well with some people in the company if the company's name was visible and linked to a negative topic. Perhaps I was being overly sensitive, but having witnessed how some of the senior people could react to insignificant matters I felt it better to be on the safe side. So I moved away or covered up anything with our name or logo that might be visible before we went ahead. Nigel showed me the proofs a couple of days later and I perused them carefully to make sure I hadn't missed anything. I gave Nigel the go ahead, but when the magazine came out, with the picture blown up to A4 size I spotted a logo I had missed on a page in a file that was open on the desk. However I decided that it was so small it wasn't an issue and that in fact it was quite a good thing to have a tiny indication that the office was mine.

As September finished I leafed through my diary and it was clear the last three months of the year would rush by. October was going to be busy as I had to be in Singapore for a week, and had various members of the company's senior management in town for different reasons, including a fairly big staff event at the end of the month with some of them doing presentations. At the start of November I had to be in Taiwan, followed only a couple of days later by my holiday in the Philippines with Lita. Two days after returning I had to travel to

London for ten days for a variety of meetings and then it was December and after another trip to Taiwan I was back on a plane to London on the 20th for Christmas and New Year.

The first visit in October was one I could well have done without, so I was not looking forward to it. Derek, the Global Operations Director, was coming for three days, including a staff session when he wanted to give a morale-boosting presentation, as he put it. Derek was a rough diamond, arrogant and extremely unpleasant. While, of course, the company had a few people I was not fond of he was the only one I actively disliked. He had arrived a few months earlier from Xerox where, I was told, he had been responsible for a team selling photocopiers. I had seen him at work at company meetings, and on previous visits to Asia, and also had some unpleasant calls from him when he was unable to get my boss, Charlie. From what I understood he had obviously enjoyed some sales success at Xerox by beating up his sales team, on the basis that the more hours they put in the more sales would be achieved. This might well have worked for photocopiers, but our product was very expensive in comparison and also included quite a complex implementation project, with a range of software customisations. Being nasty to our sales people and management, including threats of the sack, did not translate into a bigger sales pipeline or the quicker closing of deals we were working on. This frustrated him, and he became even more difficult.

Normally when I was dealing with him Charlie was there as well, and Derek tended to work through him, which was fine for me. Unfortunately this time he was on his own, but thankfully he was only in Hong Kong for two days, with his staff event on the second evening. He said he wanted to go through in detail with me the situation on the numbers for both sales and revenue but didn't want to eat into my working day; he therefore suggested I meet him at 8 pm in his hotel room, so we could order some room service and work there uninterrupted. I called Charlie to get his input on how I should handle the session and he told me to play it as it was. He wasn't certain about it, but felt Derek thought he was massaging my figures and status analyses, hence him wanting a one-on-one with me.

I arrived at Derek's hotel room door with some trepidation and knocked. After some introductory pleasantries he gave me the room service menu, and asked what I wanted to drink. After he'd ordered we started work, and apart from a break for the food we carried on continuously until gone 1 am, during which time he managed to work his way through almost four bottles of wine, while I stayed very sober.

The evening turned out be a revelation. He could have been a completely different person from the one I had known to date. As we went through my original budget and current forecast and the opportunities and risks he was supportive, constructive and easy going, and he came up with some good suggestions and insights. If I suggested something he disagreed with, rather than implying I was an idiot, his historic norm, he would calmly explain why he felt differently, and, most times, he was correct.

I went home very relieved. The evening had been enjoyable and beneficial and had gone so well I felt I still had my job. It was clear from this example that he did have a lot to offer, but unfortunately this side of his character was not one I ever saw again. He continued in his normal style all the other times I came across him afterwards.

Chapter 13

The real Philippines

The time rushed by, and suddenly it was the 9th November and Lita and I were on our way to the Philippines for me to meet her family.

At Manila airport, Arca, Lita's brother in law, was waiting for us and took us on the 30-minute drive to his house. There I was introduced to Lita's sister Nora and her children, Neil and Cathy, fourteen and thirteen respectively. When we sat down I told Lita not to bother about me, but to talk in her own language with them, as they had a lot to catch up on, but as they all spoke excellent English they only rarely switched into Tagalog. We left at 6.30 pm as we had a restaurant booking for 7 pm, and piled into the car to go there. Lita had decided in Hong Kong that as her brother Tony and his wife and five children were joining us, it would be better to go out for dinner rather than Nora organising something at her home.

The restaurant was called Josephine's and was situated on Roxas Boulevard, a long street that ran along the waterfront which I had walked along previously as it was close to both the Manila Hotel and the Philippine Plaza Hotel, where I had stayed. It could handle large groups and provided live music and entertainment, including a magic show. Tony, his wife Cion and their children were already at the table. I was introduced to them. They had two sons and three daughters, all under twelve. The girls were very cute in gorgeous dresses, one white, one pink and one yellow.

The food was pretty good, and with so many people we were able to order a large selection, so I could try a number of local dishes I had not tasted yet. The Philippines was not renowned for its food, which did not make use of strong spices or chillis, and some of the dishes had Spanish origins from the time when the Philippines was a Spanish colony (which ended in 1898 after over three hundred years). There were however a number of interesting dishes, with those that were more palatable to Western palates including adobo, a rich stew of pork and/or chicken with soy sauce and vinegar, crispy pata, pork knuckle deep fried until the skin was really crispy, sinigang, pork or fish in a sour, watery soup and lumpia, like a large Chinese spring roll, either steamed so the outside wrapper is soft, or fried when they are called lumpia Shanghai. A meal would include rice, often noodles (called pancit), and a fish condiment called Bagoong, made by fermenting small fish. Dishes that were not so palatable had ingredients such as pork blood, intestines and a very bitter knobbly courgette type vegetable.

It was a lovely evening. The magician got me up on stage to help with a 'stick swords in the woman' act, and I had a good opportunity to get to know the adults, as they all spoke excellent English. After the meal Tony and his family headed home as they lived in a different part of Manila, and it was apparently a slow journey given the traffic, which would still be heavy even at that time of night. We went back to Nora and Arca's house for a drink and then he drove us to the hotel, not too late as we had an early start to go to Paradise Beach the next day.

After an excellent three-night break at Puerto Galera we had a full day's journey from there to get to Lita's parents. From the BLTB bus terminal where we arrived at in Manila, we had to take a taxi about six miles to the Philippine Rabbit bus station to get a bus to Balaoan in La Union Province, the nearest town to their farm. This bus company had no schedules (or none that anyone seemed to know about) and it was a case of waiting around again. The journey was going to take seven to eight hours, as the town was about 190 miles from Manila, and because of the distance Lita said we should take an air-conditioned bus. Apparently these were interspersed randomly amongst the normal buses, so it was a case of waiting for one to arrive. After a couple of the basic types had turned up, an air-con model arrived and we were on our way.

The journey was 'interesting'. Initially we crawled through Manila, with its terrible traffic, but after leaving the outskirts we came to a stretch of dual carriageway. This was a promising development, but Lita told me there wasn't much of it, and sure enough fairly soon we were onto a normal road. I had learnt from the buses going to Batangas that it was best for one's peace of mind not to look out of the front windows, and there was even more reason not to on the trip north. Much of the road had dwellings either side with a lot of people walking on the verges, slow mopeds weaving in and out, tricycles, jeepneys, buffaloes pulling carts and ancient trucks, all getting in the way or stopped on the side of the road. There were a lot of other long-distance buses and these were driven as fast as possible, with each one intent on passing anything in their way at the first possible opportunity. It was particularly scary that when overtaking bigger vehicles, the buses did so on the presumption that anything coming the other way that was smaller than them would pull into the side of the road to let them through. All very well if the roadside was empty, but most times it wasn't. I couldn't imagine what the accident rate was compared to the UK.

We stopped three times on the journey, with the middle stop longer to allow for a sit-down meal. The look of the food at these cafés did not encourage me to partake, so we stuck to what we had brought with us. At the bigger towns we went through vendors would jump on the bus at the start and jump off again the other side of town. They did quite a good trade selling a variety of items including Chicharon, a type of pork scratching which was given to you in a plastic bag into which was poured some vinegar. They also sold a food called balut which was strictly for the very adventurous. This was a hard-boiled duck egg, which sounds fine until you find out that the embryo has been allowed to develop enough for the chick inside to be partly formed before it's cooked! Apparently the bones were quite soft but the beak could be too hard to eat, so you had to spit this out. The thought of eating it was quite revolting. I did try to do it three times when in the Philippines, but I never managed to go through with it.

Soft drinks were also available from these vendors. They came in glass bottles which they would open and pour into a plastic bag with a straw in it, so they could retain the bottles.

Just before getting to our destination the bus went through the regional capital of San Fernando, which Lita told me was the main town nearest to them. She said that the town was well known by international yacht racers due to the 'San Fernando Race'. This took place every two years, starting from Hong Kong and finishing here, a distance of 480 miles.

Eighteen miles north of the town we finally arrived at Balaoan where Lita's sister Edith, together with some of the children, was waiting for us. With no way of phoning we had not been able to tell the family when we would arrive, and she had been there for a couple of hours. Edith said she was pretty sure we would take an air-con bus, and as this was the first one for some time she guessed we would be on it.

The family home was in a hamlet called Pantar Sur which was about a mile away, and we had to take a tricycle to get there. These tricycles were the backbone of public transport in the countryside. You could get three smallish people inside, another one sitting behind the driver and at least one on the back. You would also see them almost completely hidden with goods piled in and on them until it was physically impossible to add more. How the little motorbike engines coped with the load I couldn't imagine.

Edith went across the road to the market place where the tricycles congregated to find a couple of them whose drivers she knew well, and we were soon off. We went north along the main road for a few minutes and just after crossing a river turned right onto a dirt track. We spent most of the journey going along tracks between farmland or beside irrigation channels, passing the occasional house, before arriving at a stretch of concrete road through Lita's village where she pointed out some relatives' houses and the local school.

Just after the village and close to a river we came to her parents' house. This was set back from the road with a sizeable yard in the front, and a large welcoming group came out to greet us as we pulled up. In addition to her parents there were her brother Jaime, who now managed the farm, and her sisters Auring and Hilling with some of their families. Having done the introductions, we all went into the house for drinks and dinner.

We had finished the meal and were drinking coffee when Lita turned to me. 'It's about the right time for us to go outside and say hello to everyone,' she said.

'Pardon?' I responded, perplexed.

'Oh I haven't told you yet, have I' she replied, 'if you go outside you'll find lots of people from the village and surrounding area. It's an event if someone like me is home so they turn out to be part of the welcome. In fact there will be more than normal as you are here. Word would have spread that my 'Americano' boyfriend is with me and they will all want to see you. Just walk around and say hello to them, and then we can come back inside. We'll all go out and join them a bit later.'

And sure enough when I went outside the yard was packed with people, adults and children. They had brought chairs and were comfortably settled and clearly enjoying the chance to get together. I wandered around, shaking hands and saying hello. Just as I had got round most of them Lita's mother came out with an enormous pot of spaghetti, and with the help of Edith and Auring she handed out plates of food to everyone.

'It's our tradition to give food to visitors so mother knew we would need a large amount and made the spaghetti earlier,' Lita explained.

After all those outside had finished eating we joined them. That was a late night, at least for Lita and her family. The visitors started to drift off home from about 10 pm, and when most had left we went back into the house. I was very tired by midnight, given the long journey and early start, and went to bed, but they all carried on well into the early hours.

I woke the next morning at about 6 am to the sound of cockerels crowing, the smell of wood smoke and the tinkling of a bell at the front of the house. It was a lovely temperature at that time but it was rising quite quickly, and by 9 am I would find it was very hot, continuing so for the rest of the day. Washing was rather basic, although everything was very clean. The bathroom was a large room downstairs with a water pump in it. There was no shower, bath or fixed washbasin. Instead there were a couple of large buckets and you filled these from the pump, and then with what looked like a plastic saucepan you would pour water over yourself to emulate a shower, or fill a large round basin to wash in. Toilet facilities were provided by an outside WC in a small building about twenty yards from the back of the house, and this was flushed with water from an enormous ceramic pot, which was kept topped up from the pump.

After I had washed and dressed I went down to the kitchen and Lita handed me a cup of coffee and some pandisal. These were small bread rolls, soft and still warm from the oven, and they had been the reason for the tinkling bell. The pandisal man cycled around with the rolls in a large Styrofoam box to keep them warm, and announced his arrival with the bell. These little rolls were eaten with sandwich spread, but this was different from the UK version, being made with thick sweetish mayonnaise containing less chopped pickle than the version I was used to. This was the 'first course', followed a short while later by breakfast proper, with a choice of garlic or plain rice, tinapa (a smoked fish), tuyo (dried salted fish), longanisa (sausages), fried eggs and tusino (strips of sweet pork). Everyone ate at a large table in the kitchen.

After breakfast Lita took me out to show me around the house and garden. At the rear was a wet kitchen and an outdoor cooking area, and further back a small pigsty with a pig in it and a couple of other cages. The chickens were wandering around freely and there was a large water buffalo harnessed to a stake. She explained that her mother was quite fussy with anything that was going to be eaten so the pig, chickens and ducks for instance would be kept here for a reasonable time before they were killed. That way her mother could control what they ate and ensure it was clean.

Walking a fair way back from the house we came to some fields which extended far into the distance. There was a row of massive electricity pylons overhead and Lita took me to a large concrete pad set into the ground under the pylons and by a field. She said that this had been their old house, much bigger than the current one, and being on the edge of the fields it had picked up the breezes. They had been forced to move when Ferdinand Marcos, the dictator president, had decided to run electricity to his home area, which was north of there, and the route of the pylons was, as I could see, right over their house. She explained that it was bad enough that they had received virtually no compensation, but because of the minimum distance the new house had to be from the pylons, they had been forced to build near the road. On one corner of the concrete she showed me her initials and those of her brothers and sisters, written when it had still been wet. She was clearly very upset at the loss of the house, talking about all the great times the family had enjoyed there, and how nice it was having the views across to the hills in the distance. We walked back and went into the kitchen, where Lita made coffee.

I had been hobbling around since just before we had boarded the bus to come north, as I had sprained my ankle at the bus terminal. I had stupidly not been looking where I was walking, not a sensible thing to do in the Philippines given the general state of the roads and pavements. It was quite a bad sprain and during the journey the ankle had ballooned, and I struggled to walk. By that morning the bruising had spread up my leg to the knee in vivid colours including dark blue, yellow and brown. and looked very impressive.

I had put my leg up on a stool while drinking the coffee when Lita's brother Tony came in. He had travelled up overnight to be with us while we were there.

He looked at me and said 'Your ankle looks very painful, would you like me to massage it?'

'Thanks for the offer, but it's painful enough as it is, so perhaps not,' I said. I actually wanted to say what a stupid suggestion it was, but felt I shouldn't be rude, having only recently met him.

'No, maybe he should,' piped up Lita. 'It's a good idea and it could make it a lot better.'

'No, I don't think it's a good idea at all,' I replied rather testily. 'Let's just leave my ankle alone, shall we.'

'You don't understand,' she responded. 'Tony has been taught how to massage and is very good at it, you should give it a go if he thinks it will improve it. What do you think Tony?'

He came over to have a closer look. 'I can make it much, much better and get rid of most of the swelling,' he said, 'but I have to warn you it will be very, very painful for the first few minutes after I start'.

I was very undecided. I did not of course want to experience the level of pain he was indicating, but the ankle was hurting quite a lot and if this could be reduced significantly it would be good.

'It's up to you,' Lita chimed in again, 'but he was trained to massage as one of the children had a joint problem, and the doctors said massage would be very beneficial. He really does know what he's doing'.

So I agreed. Tony sat me in a rocking chair on the veranda and asked if I was ready, and reiterated how painful it would be initially. I had second thoughts. but was now committed.

Boy was he right! It was excruciatingly painful, really terrible and I was in agony as he massaged up and down around the ankle. But amazingly, after three or four minutes the pain started to lessen and then I could see the swelling start to reduce. He carried on for about twenty minutes and when he had finished I couldn't believe it. All signs of swelling had gone completely, and when I stood up and walked around I had no pain whatsoever.

'You see, it really did work, didn't it?' Lita said to me.

I had incurred bad sprains before, so bad in one case I had taken myself to hospital, but had never been advised to consider massage.

While I was having the treatment Lita's sister Hilling had arrived. She wanted us to come and see her house and farm and have lunch. It was decided that as my ankle was now ok we would walk there, as it was only about twenty minutes away, and they could show me the farm and what was going on, this being rice harvesting time. Edith and Nora (who had arrived from Manila) with some of the children joined us and we set off. It was fairly slow going as we were walking across fields were the rice had been harvested, and only the stubble remained. All around into the distance were people harvesting rice. They stopped work when they saw me and stood looking. Lita explained that very few westerners ever came to this area and they were therefore fascinated by me, especially given that I was large and fair-haired. At one point I went over to a group of eight people working threshing rice and had their photos taken with me.

Hilling and her husband Tino proudly showed off their house, which was a good size, and after lunch they walked us around the neighbourhood. One of the cash crops they grew was tobacco and they showed me a very tall building with mud walls, open at the top but with a thatched roof. This was a pugon, the place where the tobacco was cured. The leaves would be threaded onto thin bamboo sticks and an enormous number of these would be stacked in multiple levels in the pugon. A fire was then lit at the base and the smoke would permeate upwards, curing the leaves, which were then sold to buyers from Manila. Hilling had a supply of the cured leaf for their own use and, having seen that I smoked, said I should try a proper cigarette rather than the namby pamby tailor made ones I had. She proceeded to roll what was basically a cigar. It looked pretty rough and when lit it lived up to its looks. The smoke was acrid and sharp and I coughed after a few puffs, at which everyone fell about laughing, so I lost a lot of credibility regarding my ability to smoke.

On arriving back at Lita's parents' place everyone was gathered outside at the back of the house, and the reason for my seeing a pig there earlier became clear. We were going to have another lechon, and there it was, just starting to turn brown on the spit. This was a special event to celebrate our visit, and everyone was clearly enjoying it hugely, with all the guys drinking some form of alcohol together with plates of nibbles. I had already found out that when drinking alcohol in the Philippines it was de rigueur to have a variety of small things to eat, called polutan. These could be almost anything from simple items such as peanuts and prawn crackers to dishes of chopped up pigs' ears, marinated intestines and chicken feet.

The following day, having asked if I could try some coconut, a party of us waded across the river, as on the opposite side the family had land where coconut palms grew. With us was Poldo, who was going to climb the trees to get them. He had come to Lita's family as a very young boy. He lived close by and his parents were so poor they were struggling to feed all the children properly, so Lita's parents had offered to include him in their meals in return for which he would do odd jobs. This had grown over time until he had become a close and indispensable part of the family, and he now did much of the work around the farm helping Lita's brother Jaime. When Poldo had a serious girlfriend and was going to get married, Lita's parents gave him a piece of their land so he could build a house for himself.

Poldo was amazing; he scaled the trees without any aid whatsoever. I had seen TV programmes of people climbing coconut trees with just a leather loop around them and the tree, but he used nothing. He went up about four trees until we had enough. Some of the fresh green coconuts were opened there; we drank the refreshing milk and everyone except me ate the soft flesh, an old brown one having been opened for me. This young flesh was very different from the thick flesh of a mature one, which was all I had seen in the UK. We returned to the house with our spoils and Poldo opened another of the brown coconuts for me. Gathered around us were a number of the local children, who, as usual, found me an interesting sight. When I put the first piece of thick white coconut flesh in my mouth their eyes widened in surprise, and then they burst out laughing. The reason was that these mature coconuts were not eaten in the Philippines but only fed to animals, the locals only eating the thin, tender flesh of the nuts when green. The children couldn't believe that I was eating what to them was pig food!

Our stay ended all too quickly and a jeepney had been booked to take us to town, given the number of people who wanted to come and see us off. Unfortunately we would not have time to see anyone in Manila as we were arriving very late, staying again at the Manila Hotel with a morning flight back to Hong Kong.

Chapter 14

My new role, Australia and around the world in a month

After arriving back in Hong Kong on the 18th November, the remaining time until Christmas just raced by. Three days later on the 21st I had to fly to London for a number of key meetings, mostly to do with the next financial year, including getting up to speed on a major presentation. This covered the company's five-year product plans and was to be given globally during March and April, to staff, customers, the press and the market in general. In my new role I was tasked with doing the presentations across Asia, Australia and New Zealand.

After arriving back from London on the 2nd December I had a trip to Taiwan, then the company's Christmas party on the 15th, before I flew back to London on the 20th for my holiday.

The Christmas party turned out to be specially interesting for me. We had decided to do it properly this year and had booked one of the five-star hotels. It would start with drinks and mah jong, then a formal dinner before finishing the evening in the hotel's disco. Everything was going smoothly until the end of the meal, when I was told by a couple of the senior local managers that, as I was the boss, I should have an individual toast with each of the staff as this would bring good luck. I hadn't banked on this but recalled being told that at Chinese weddings the groom was required to do many individual toasts but allowed to delegate much of the toasting to his best man, so it was he would suffer the effects rather than the groom.

The drink to be used apparently was very expensive XO cognac, and as there were almost thirty people I had to have a drink with I realised I would be in trouble at the end of it, not least as I had already had a few drinks plus a fair bit of wine with the meal. I decided that I would handle this by shooting off to the men's room when it had finished to get the alcohol out of my system! We just about finished two bottles of XO by the time I had 'yum singed' (meaning cheers) with everyone, so I had drunk the best part of a whole bottle in 15 minutes. This was in alcohol poisoning territory and a couple of worried wives came up to me with the same concerns.

I was waylaid here and there on my way to the toilets and never made it. Instead I ended up at the disco, where I had three or four more XOs over the next ninety minutes or so. I was obviously well gone but not ridiculously so, and surprisingly didn't embarrass myself.

Very stupidly, at the end of the evening, I then drove home! As this was our corporate hotel they had given me one of the three parking places at the front of the hotel, and I had driven there with the intention of getting the car the next day. One effect of all the alcohol was that any ability to act sensibly had disappeared, and despite Lita's voluble remonstrations off I went. I couldn't remember the journey at all the next day, but she said that surprisingly I drove well, except that I didn't exceed 20 mph the whole way. Luckily it was only about a ten-minute journey back to the apartment.

I may have been generally all right that night, but did I then suffer. Lita said I staggered into the bedroom and collapsed on the bed fully clothed with my feet on the pillow and my head at the foot end, and she couldn't get me to move, so I stayed that way most of the night. The next day I couldn't stand up and felt absolutely atrocious. I spent it either lying on the bed or the sofa feeling very sorry for myself. The second day I was only marginally better; I had the most appalling headache and all my joints ached as if I had flu. The third day (being

Monday) I did make it to the office, but just felt like putting my head on my arms on the desk rather than doing any work. Never before or since have I been anything like as bad as that from alcohol.

Christmas in the UK went very well and when it was only a couple of days to New Year I realised that there was nothing very interesting I'd been invited to on the 31st. However I knew that Charlie was having a do at his place in Singapore and decided this would be much more fun than what was on offer in the UK. I managed to get my flight changed to arrive in Singapore on New Year's Eve at about 7 pm. I couldn't get Charlie or his wife Christine on the phone to tell them I was coming, but I felt sure the evening was on and I could sleep on their sofa if they had guests and no one else there had a bed for me, so off I went.

The flight was wonderful. I was on Singapore Airlines, always excellent, but this time it was something special. There was hardly anyone in Business Class and I had a seat on the upper deck of the plane. With only a couple of other passengers up there the service was great, made particularly special as it was the last flight for one of the stewardesses before she was getting married. The crew were therefore having a party for her in the upstairs cabin, and they would pop up in ones and twos for a short time to join in and wish her well. She had the captain's hat on and had a wonderful time, as did we; they brought up Dom Perignon champagne from First Class for us and made wonderful cocktails to complement the poncy champagne.

I arrived at Christine and Charlie's at about 8 pm and as the door opened and everyone saw me there were loud shouts and laughter. Charlie had told me before I left for London that I was welcome to join them, but he felt that as he hadn't heard from me I wasn't going to be there. There was a 50/50 split between everyone as to if I wouldn't make it or would just turn up unannounced, as I had, and some bets had been made. It was a wonderful evening and as we opened each bottle of champagne we had bets as to being able to get the cork in the pool, about ten yards and two storeys away. After Auld Lang Syne Charlie put Land Of Hope and Glory and other Last Night of The Proms type music on full blast, and with all the noise we must have really disturbed the neighbours (who were also their landlords), who were Singaporean, and having a refined dinner party on their balcony.

It was gone 4 am before we went to bed and New Year's Day dawned very slowly. At 12.30 I was told to hurry up, as breakfast was at 1 pm! This consisted of very spicy Bloody Marys, strong coffee and bacon and tomato sandwiches. We met up with various people over the next couple of days as we continued celebrating the New Year and had a wonderful time, and my visit to Singapore was rounded off perfectly when on the flight to Hong Kong I was upgraded to First Class.

I arrived back on Thursday 3rd January and the following week we had a staff meeting to make public the new roles for Bob and myself. As the change would not technically take place until 1st March we continued as usual as we wrapped up the year. However, with Chinese New Year starting on 20th Feb and lasting effectively five days until Monday 25th, we used the first two weeks in February to have meetings with customers and other key contacts to explain the changes and my new role. We had decided that Monday 4th March would be the first physical day of the change, with Bob and myself swapping offices and a company party to celebrate the end of the year.

After I had sorted out where everything went in my new office, I sat back and pondered the future. I was now truly free of the day-to-day detail and responsibility of running the branch, a refreshing thought. I had an excellent working relationship with the managers in Asia and Australia, and almost all of them had become as much friends as colleagues. I had almost complete control over what I would be doing, subject to Charlie concurring with me as to what I had planned. I also had a separate set of cost budgets just for myself, and had won agreement to a generous travel and entertainment figure, so that was not a constraining factor. All in all I decided I was really looking forward to the next year.

I then ran through what I should be doing in the short and medium term and realised I had two immediate priorities. The first was to organise a very belated flat-warming party. This was something I had been intending to have from about a month after I moved in, but it had become one of those activities that was always to be done next month. I told myself that there was no excuse now my schedule was so much under my control so I settled on Saturday 16th March, about two months shy of two years from when I had moved in! The invitations went out, and while initially I was going to organise the drinks and food myself, I soon decided to get my club, the FCC, to do it. This would obviously be much more expensive but would leave me free to enjoy the party myself and spend more time with everyone. It turned out to be a wise move, as a week before the party IBM called me and said they were organising an Open Day in their offices for that Saturday, and could I do a presentation and be there to mix with attendees.

Margaret, who was still my secretary and also looked after Bob, was great - she went to my apartment early to arrange matters and help the FCC people setup. It was a very pleasant evening and the apartment was packed. The FCC had provided a barman and two waiters and they were rushed off their feet. When everyone had left and I was presented with the bill to sign it was quite a large one, but I decided that was fine as it reflected the success of the party.

The second priority was to organise a visit to Australia. Sydney and Melbourne were important cities for us, not only because of the bank branches in those locations, but as we needed to be in contact with the head offices there, as a number used our software elsewhere in the world. We had a small branch in Sydney but the Group also had a relationship with a local software house called JBA. This company had software in different areas to us including hotel systems, and also acted as our agent. Australia was Charlie's responsibility and I had therefore not been involved there before, but my new role required me to work directly with them. It was going to be a busy visit, as in addition to introducing myself to JBA people I needed to meet customers, IBM and other key people, and also had to give the big presentation mentioned previously (which we had called a Statement Of Direction) a number of times.

I had never been to Australia, so this was going to be an exciting trip. I decided I should use the opportunity of the long flight to see

Alice Springs and Ayres Rock in the very centre of the country. I would therefore leave Hong Kong on a Monday night and fly to Melbourne and have Tuesday to Thursday as holiday, arriving in Sydney on the Friday. After the weekend I would commence the business part of the trip.

I arrived in Melbourne on 25th March and the next day took a plane to Alice Springs, where I spent the night, before heading off the next morning on a pre-booked tour with a Trailways bus for the five-hour journey to Ayres Rock. I spent one night at Ayres Rock as the trip included seeing it during the day and at sunset, when it was known for the colour change that occurred, as well as seeing other sights including the Olgas, a weirdly shaped rock formation.

It was at the Ayres Rock hotel where I first experienced the flies that Australia is known for. I had tried to go and sit outside, but you couldn't. The flies immediately converged on your head and were very intrusive, getting into your mouth, your nose, your ears and your eyes. When I gave up and went in someone told me that it was the moisture the flies were after as there was almost none outside. I couldn't work out where all these flies came from as the hotel (which was very new) was in the middle of nowhere, and there was just miles and miles of bone-dry arid semi-desert all around. There were no large animals in evidence which could have given them excrement to breed in, but the flies were there, and in their thousands by the look of it.

I flew back to Alice Springs to save time and had another night there before getting a flight to Sydney on the Friday. I found Alice Springs much bigger and more refined than I had been expecting. It originally came into being in 1872 as the site of a repeater station for the telegraph line that went from Port Augusta in South Australia right across the centre to Darwin in the North, where it went into the sea. From there it ultimately reached Europe. I had hired a car and therefore managed to see the sights in the area, including the repeater station, the small old airport where the Flying Doctor service was based and Château Hornsby. I had no idea there was a vineyard in such a dry and desolate spot until I saw a sign to it. As a memento I bought a bottle, which eventually made its way back to the UK.

The Kentucky Fried Chicken outlet in the centre of town also provided a memorable if quite sad experience. I was sitting inside having some lunch when the door opened and in walked an enormous, quite old Aboriginal woman, in an absolutely filthy white dress. My table was by the door and she stopped right by me. Phew, she certainly whiffed, and I was willing her to carry on towards the counter and away from me. She did this and then proceeded to try and get something to eat for free. The staff refused and politely suggested she should leave the restaurant. She turned around and spoke to us all, difficult to make out as she seemed to only have a handful of teeth, but I think she was asking who would give her some money. Everyone kept their heads down including me. On getting no response, she bent down and pulled the white dress over her head – she had nothing on underneath! At this point one of the girls behind the counter bravely came out with a box of food and started to guide her to the door. Initially she followed, but then she stopped right by my table and seeing the empty chairs made as if to sit down! It was a very unsettling moment but the young girl, thankfully still holding the food, took her arm and gently propelled her to the door. I turned around to watch her go. She now had the food box and started to eat a chicken leg as she was walking along the road. She was struggling to hold both the box and her dress while eating with the other hand and obviously decided the easiest thing to do was ditch the dress, which she dropped on the ground before calmly continuing on her way.

On arriving in Sydney I was met at the airport by our local manager, Jenny, who was English, and her Australian husband John. I had met them first in 1980 when Jenny and I had both worked in our New York office for a few months. We had become good friends there and I was very much looking forward to catching up with them. They had suggested I stay with them rather than a hotel, which I was very happy to do. They lived in Mosman, which was a suburb of Sydney, on a promontory very close to the central business district. It was the location of Sydney Zoo and the road down to the water, which passed the zoo, ended at a pier where you could get a ferry into Circular Quay, the water transport hub of the city, so they were very well located.

As I had not been to Sydney before they said that my first proper sight of the harbour should be from the water; in their 37-foot sailing boat, so, the next day being Saturday, after breakfast we went to where it was moored.

The weather was perfect, and as we sailed round into the city part of the harbour there was the iconic Opera House and the Harbour Bridge in full view. As it was a Saturday the harbour was teaming with ferries, tour boats, water taxis and pleasure craft in general, particularly sailing boats, many of which were clearly taking part in races. We sailed right up to the Opera House before turning back and were on the mooring again by 1 pm. For lunch John and Jenny took me to The Oaks. This was a well-known pub that had been around since the late 1800s and was in the suburb of Neutral Bay, about ten minutes north of the Harbour Bridge. It had a very large outdoor area in which stood the enormous oak tree from which it derived its name. The speciality here was food rather than alcohol, particularly the beef. Inside the pub was a salad bar and a meat counter with a selection of steak, chops, chicken and fish. You helped yourself to bread and salads, selected your choice of meat and then took it outside and cooked it yourself on large barbecues. There was someone there who would cook it for you, but it made it a much more interesting occasion to do it yourself.

On the Sunday we went for lunch to a very well-known restaurant, Doyles, which had started in 1885. This served predominantly fish and stood on the beach at Watson's Bay, which, if you were at a table outside, had a stunning view up to the Sydney business district, the Harbour Bridge and the Opera House. Watson's Bay was directly across the harbour from Mosman and quite a long drive from there so we took the boat across, moored and went to shore in the tender. Many Sydney restaurants were BYO (Bring Your Own) and didn't charge corkage and this was the case at Doyles; Jenny and I joined the queue for a table and John went off to the nearest bottle shop. The food was very good and when we had made it back to Mosman they took me for a drive around Sydney, stopping at the famous Bondi beach.

I was in Australia for two weeks, giving me plenty of time to see the main sites, although I was very busy with meetings and presentations, including two trips to Melbourne. There was a fair bit of rivalry between Sydney and Melbourne. On arrival at Melbourne people would say to me 'I expect you're glad to have left Sydney,' and in Sydney when I was back there the reverse occurred.

Despite the amount of work I had to do I had managed to plan the trip around Easter and had the four-day holiday in Sydney. On the Saturday I managed to meet up with good friends from the time I was based in Belgium in 1980. Barbara had stayed with me when coming through Hong Kong just after I arrived but I had not seen Philip since 1980, and I had not met Barbara's husband Judd. Philip was English but had grown up in Brussels as his parents lived there; he had worked for me and it was through him I had met Barbara. Coincidentally they had both ended up living in Sydney, where Barbara had met Judd, who was English.

On the Wednesday after Easter I had managed the timing to be able to attend a Phil Collins concert and it was quite special when he kicked off saying 'Hello Sydney', and there I was.

On the Saturday Jenny and I flew to Singapore together to attend a regional meeting before I finally landed back in Hong Kong on the 18th April, three and a half weeks after I had left.

While I had been in Australia the sale of the Oxelotel had gone through, and there waiting for me in the office was a cheque for my share. I decided that given the enjoyment I had had from the junk this money shouldn't just disappear into my bank account but be put to a more interesting use. After some thought I decided to spend most of it on a video camera and a portable recorder. In 1985 video recorders had been around for some time, but realistically priced video cameras had only recently become available. Mind you realistically priced did not mean inexpensive, quite the opposite. After some research I chose a Hitachi recorder and a separate Hitachi camera. The recorder was the same size as a normal video recorder but half of it could be unplugged from the base to allow mobile recording, and it also had editing capabilities such as being able to dub a soundtrack without losing the original recording. The alternative was an all-in-one camcorder, but these were large and had to be rested on your shoulder. The basic price was high enough but on going to buy it I found that it did not include the extras such as rechargeable batteries, the battery charger to use when away from home and a carry case, and these bumped the price up a fair bit.

Of course having this new toy was one thing, but having the time to play with it was another. I was still travelling somewhere most weeks and this meant packing a lot of activity into the time I was in Hong Kong, so my initial plan of putting together a tape of Hong Kong life, both for family in the UK and as a reminder for me in the future, did not progress very quickly.

In June I had another extended trip when I was away for a month. I had fancied doing a 'round the world trip' for some time but needed justification, and in my new role this was possible. These trips were based on airline tickets that gave you heavily discounted travel as long as you continued around the world in the same direction, ending up back where you left; you paid one price and could have as many stops as you wanted. They were available with different airline combinations so you had to balance the route you wanted to take with what airline combination was available to do it. I found I could do what I wanted using Cathay Pacific and Pan Am, and a ticket using these two airlines was available. I was only going to do four stops and knew my dates, but you could make bookings as you were travelling, so you had total flexibility on dates as long as seats were available. In the 1980s this was rarely a problem as the days of airline alliances had not arrived and planes usually had spare seats, often a lot of them. The round the world ticket itself was still a paper ticket 'book style', but they would insert pages with blank flight details, and then as you booked a leg the airline staff would write the details in.

I left on the 5th June for London, where I had to attend a three-day planning meeting and spend a few days in the London office. I took a couple of days' holiday while in the UK and was there for three weekends, giving me a decent amount of time to catch up with friends and family. On Monday 24th June I flew to New York, where we had a large office; I had been based there for a couple of stints and therefore knew quite a few people. On Friday 28th I flew to San Francisco, where a banker friend who had worked for one of our customers lived. The plan had been to stay with him and his wife. However, a few days before Keith had called me up. 'Bernard, I need to ask you if you've had chicken pox,' he asked.

'I don't know,' I replied, 'I've had a disease with spots when I was a child, but which one I have no idea.'

'Well the trouble is our son has just been diagnosed with it and apparently, if you get it for the first time as an adult it can be quite nasty. It's then called shingles and it can cause things like sterility. If you haven't had it, I expect it would be best if you didn't stay here and we'll get you a hotel, but it's up to you.'

'Best thing is I'll call my mother,' I said, 'I'm sure she'll remember, as she was a nurse. I'll call you back after I've spoken to her.'

Well it turned out it wasn't chicken pox that had caused my spots but measles, so a hotel it was going to be for me. They looked after me really well and it turned out that, without realising it, I had picked a great weekend to be in San Francisco. On the Sunday was the Gay Freedom Day Parade, the largest in the world. It was a fantastic experience to be there as the Parade was amazing and I captured all the best bits on the video camera – of course I had taken my new toy with me. On the Monday I went to Alcatraz Island, and while waiting in the queue to board the ferry to it who did I see coming off the arriving boat but one of the couples who had been partners in the Oxelotel. I was aware that they were on their way back to Europe, as the husband had been posted to Paris, but not that they were stopping off in San Francisco. We arranged to meet for dinner the next evening and the following morning I left for Tokyo.

This flight was the most boring one I had ever taken, and being in Business Class didn't make it any better. It was 11 hours nonstop. I couldn't get to sleep and as we crossed the dateline, it meant that while I left at midday we didn't arrive until 3 pm the following day. This was 2 am my time, a horrible time difference. I managed to get two hours' sleep before waking feeling terrible; I was meeting our two Tokyo-based English staff for dinner but would have much preferred to stay in bed for longer.

It was only a quick stop in Tokyo with a half day in the office and I was back in Hong Kong on Friday evening, the 5th of July. The flight there was on Pan Am and you could see that the airline was not doing well. All of their planes were ancient, but this one almost defied description. It was very tired inside with stained seats, threadbare carpet, all the plastic yellowed and the entertainment system didn't work- it must have been one of the oldest in the fleet. The service on board also indicated why they had problems. For instance they served lunch after we had taken off, and having given me the meal tray the stewardess enquired 'What would you like to drink, sir?'

'What wine do you have?' I asked.

'I'll go and bring the selection to you sir.'

This sounded promising, but a couple of minutes later she was back holding a small screw top bottle in each hand. Very formally she presented them to me. 'This is the white' she said, holding one out to me, 'and this is the red,' she said, holding out the other. Why did she bother with this charade instead of just asking if I wanted red or white?

Chapter 15

'Cousin Ken', dodgy PCs and visiting China

One of the results of my job involving so much travel, customer entertaining and other reclaimable costs was that I never knew just how much money I really had in the bank unless I did a reconciliation. At any one time I had a number of financial factors in play all of which combined to hide the true position, whether good or bad. These consisted of expense forms I had completed and submitted, some having been paid and others not, expenses I had incurred but were not yet on an expense form (mostly scribbled into my diary), credit card statements that had arrived and were or were not paid off yet, and items on credit cards where a statement had not yet arrived. Complicating matters further was that the company would give me a cash advance to help my cash flow, which also had to be taken into account.

Given the scale of the round-the-world expenses I had just incurred, I decided now was a good time to get all my expenses up to date and do a reconciliation. Normally when I did one of these it disappointingly showed me having much less money of my own than I had estimated, but on this occasion the result was a reasonable positive situation, and I also still had the balance of the Ox sale proceeds, which were in my savings account.

I had been thinking about dipping my toe into the stock market for quite a while and this time I did something about it. I opened up an account with a stockbroker using the spare cash to buy shares in a couple of companies, having canvassed a few contacts as to any recommendations. Over the next months these managed to neither make nor lose me any money, as when one was up the other was down the same amount and vice versa, and I did not add to my holdings as I never had any spare cash again. In early September however I did get a real benefit from this investment decision, as my stockbroker called me and asked if I fancied a cheap weekend in Sabah on Borneo Island. Apparently a new Hong Kong-based airline called Dragonair had just been started and was flying there with empty seats; he told me that if I called the airline's MD he would get me a deal to go there for less than the hotel on its own would have cost.

So I called him ('hi Steve, you've never heard of me but...') and sure enough I ended up with a booking for four of us, including a friend of mine and Jon, one of our salesmen, and his girlfriend. It was possible that there was extra availability as we were flying on Friday 13th! We boarded flight DE001 at 5 pm and despite the ominous date we had a good journey and enjoyed a wonderful time at Kota Kinabalu. The Tanjung Aru Beach Hotel had only recently been completed and was rated five stars, and it was very nice. The whole weekend including flights, hotel, transfers, a day trip to a coral island, breakfast and some free drinks cost £70 each, which even in 1985 was a bargain.

The Wednesday following this I had another opportunity to provide my 'Kowloon evening tourist tour', as previously described. The twenty-year-old cousin of Sandie, my colleague Bob's wife, was over for a holiday from Perth in Scotland. She asked if we could show Ken the sights as I had done for her and Bob previously, as it would be a great experience for him. So a party of seven of us started off as usual at Someplace Else, the up-market bar at the Sheraton hotel, and followed this up with another excellent and very cheap curry at the extremely down market Chungking Mansions. Then it was off to Red Lips before finishing the evening as usual at Bottoms Up.

At Red Lips, despite being a mixed group, a couple of the old ladies joined us. One of them managed to sit next to Ken and was trying to see if she could get anywhere with him. Ken was quite a character, despite his relative youth, and was up for a bit of fun so he showed some interest, despite her age and looks. After some minutes she had started stroking Ken's arm and neck and asking if he liked massages. Sandie turned to me and I could see she wasn't happy.

'Bernard, I think it's time to leave,' she said. 'I don't like the idea of that old hag touching Ken and what she might be saying to him.'

'Fair enough, Sandie' I said, 'but it's only a bit of fun and as you can see Ken is happy joining in.'

'Well I'm not happy with it. Can you pay the bill and we'll go.'

'No problem' I replied and went to the bar to settle up.

At the bar I decided that the situation could be the basis for a little wind-up at Sandie's expense. She was a good sport, so I thought, why not?

As well as paying the bill I asked the mama-san (the female manager) how much it would cost to take the girl who was with Ken out of the bar for one hour. I explained that there would be no hanky-panky, we just wanted her to stay with us at the next bar we were going to and then she would return. On this basis the price was quite low, so I agreed. The mama-san went over and had a quiet word with Ken's 'girl' while I returned and told everyone we were going.

Ken's companion stood up and walked off into the back room of the bar, much to Sandie's obvious relief, and I took the opportunity of the disruption while everyone was getting up to have a quiet word with Ken and Bob to set things up.

My brief to them was that the girl was going to join us for a short while but we would make Sandie think that Ken wanted her to join him for the evening. At a suitable time at Bottoms Up I would arrange for her to leave.

It couldn't have worked out better. We were all just about to move off from outside the door of Red Lips when she appeared again, and, really helping the situation I was trying to create, she had with her what looked like a small overnight bag.

'What is she doing here?' Sandie asked me with a look of concern on her face.

'Ken told me he quite liked being with her, so I've paid the bar fine so she can come with us.'

'You've what!' Sandie exclaimed, pulling me aside to be out of earshot of Ken. 'How could you even think of doing that, Bernard? She's gross!'

At this point Bob joined in. 'Calm down Sandie, it'll be fun for Ken and we're all together, so what's the problem?'

'What do you mean, what's the problem?' she said to him with feeling. 'I don't want that horrible old hag anywhere near my cousin, and I can't believe he has any interest in being with her.'

By now we were walking to Bottoms Up and Ken had made matters worse for Sandie by holding the girl's hand. We entered Bottoms Up and sat around one of the circular bars. Ken was doing a marvellous job of staying very close to the girl and whispering in her ear.

'Bernard, I want you to get rid of that thing,' Sandie said to me. 'How could you do this? Ken's only twenty and I told his mother I'd look after him.'

Lita now also started having a go at me, as I had not let her into what we were up to.

'What do you think you are doing?' she said to me. 'Sandie's quite right, it's horrible to see, get rid of her.'

'I don't know why you're both getting so difficult,' Bob said. 'He's a young lad, be understanding.'

Sandie was obviously just about to have a go at him for this comment, but changed her mind and didn't say anything. Instead she sat sullenly, glaring at me from time to time.

Shortly afterwards Sandie and Lita went to the toilet and I decided the joke had run its course and we should finish it. With Sandie being in the ladies, however, the opportunity existed to end on a high. I told Ken to go outside with the girl and let her go back to Red Lips, and after a few minutes to come back into the bar.

Well, the look on Sandie's face when she arrived back and saw they were both missing was a picture.

'Where is Ken?' she asked me, with a look of alarm on her face.

'They've gone off somewhere,' I said to her. 'He said he'd be back in under an hour and I told him if we had left we would be at Someplace Else, it's fine.'

'It's completely not fine Bernard!' she shot back at me with some force. 'She's absolutely horrible. I wouldn't agree to it if she was really good looking, let alone that haggard old tart.'

As she paused to draw breath, Lita laid into me again. 'I can't think what you are up to. It's totally unacceptable!'

'How could you do this to me, Bernard?' Sandie said. 'I'll never forgive you.'

At this point I realised enough was enough and was just about to put her out of her misery when I saw her look up. A change came over her face and she started to smile. I turned around and there was Ken in the doorway with a broad grin on his face.

'Bernard, I'll kill you, I was taken in so completely,' said Sandie. 'I should have realised you and Bob wouldn't have agreed to this, I'm really annoyed with myself for being so gullible.'

It was lucky she was such a good sport, as I had never envisioned the joke would work out so effectively and Sandie would be so convinced it was genuine.

That October I decided to spend some more money on technology, even though I was still getting to grips with video photography and editing. I went and bought a PC. One of the main reasons was that I was regularly asked by people about PCs, as they assumed that because I was in IT I could give them some advice. However I knew nothing about them - the systems I had always worked with filled small rooms, and there was effectively no crossover at all between how they worked and the tiny desktop home computers. I felt that it would be beneficial for me to gain an understanding, both to fill in this gap in my IT awareness and to be aware of the capabilities of PCs as they might apply to our customers, and our own use in the office. And the best way was clearly to get one of my own.

Prior to 1977 home computers were for hobbyists as they had to be built from kit parts and provided very little real benefit to a user. However in that year three ready assembled home computers became available, the Commodore PET, Apple II and Tandy TRS-80. These were able to provide some real world applications, as evidenced by an Associated Press article that year which described the TRS-80 computer as being able to 'do a payroll for up to 15 people in a small business, teach children mathematics, store your favourite recipes or keep track of an investment portfolio. It can also play cards.'

From then on the capabilities of new models grew rapidly, the market took off, and their use expanded outside of the home and into businesses of all sizes. So much so that in 1980 (the year before the IBM PC was launched in August 1981) over fifty new PC systems came on the market targeted at business users. The problem with this was that there was no standardisation, with each manufacturer doing their own thing. This was less of a problem for the home user but a significant one for the business community.

The IBM PC however changed this. Technically it was nothing special, but in making it available, IBM, being the IT behemoth it was, created a standard. Their reputation in corporate computing meant that the IBM PC architecture took a very substantial market share of business applications in a short time, and it wasn't long before, apart from Apple and specialist companies, a PC manufacturer or software supplier had to be 'IBM compatible' to survive.

The IBM machine however was priced for business use, as was the software for it from the likes of Microsoft and Lotus, and completely unaffordable for home use. Even the early legitimate 'clone' PC's were still priced at a very high level, and though they were cheaper than IBM these did nothing to address the software price. Unfortunately I needed to get to grips with an IBM PC and its business software to really benefit. Outside Asia the cost would have completely ruled it out, but in Hong Kong there was another option. The Golden

Shopping Arcade in Kowloon was the place to go for anything to do with computers, especially fake IBM PCs and illegally copied software. It was well known outside Hong Kong, and many of their sales were to overseas visitors who took their purchases back in their suitcases. There were about 80 small shops selling anything IT related. The IBM PC was easy to copy, as the genuine article only had a couple of electronic chips on the circuit board and some associated software that IBM could call their own, with everything else being standard components available to anyone; in fact you could get a custom built fake that was much better configured than the IBM offering. For the software the trick was to be able to circumvent the copy protection that was built in. The boffins at the centre very quickly found a way to break each new type of protection, and you could even buy software or a piece of hardware to enable you to do your own copying.

Being in IT myself I shouldn't really have condoned the situation by buying such hardware and software. However as the price of the legitimate products was aimed at big companies, with no likelihood of a home user being able to pay such prices, I felt I was not losing them any money.

One of the staff at work who was up on such things came with me and I ended up with the PC, a genuine Epson printer and a range of software (business and games) together with the manuals, which had also been copied and printed. Until relatively recently the cost of the printer would have been a major issue, but at the start of the 1980s more sensibly priced dot matrix printers had come on the market and by 1985 there were a number available. I was also able to have a hard disk, a truly expensive option if from IBM, but a much more sensible, though still costly item in Kowloon. Most PCs at this time came with one or two 'floppy' disk drives to read the programme and the data disk. These could slow the computer down quite a lot if what you were doing required reading and writing to the floppies, as this took time. The hard disk was similar to a floppy but solid, like a CD, and fully enclosed. This allowed it to run at a vastly greater speed, which meant that reading and writing information was done quickly.

I carted all this home and then struggled to get it all set up and working, which was not easy. Luckily the manager of a sister company of ours and his wife had recently bought a PC and were therefore up to speed. I invited them round for a nice dinner on the basis that they would help me get it working, which they did. There was much to learn, but I found it fascinating, and the odd spare evening would rush by as I tried to get to grips with this new toy.

A couple of months later I did the right thing and bought a legal IBM clone made by Epson. Prices for these had started to come down and while it was a fair bit more than my fake I had realised my PC was here to stay, and with a move back to the UK I would be better off with something that was genuine and could be repaired. I had also been able to get it at the wholesale price from a company we dealt with who marketed Epson computers, as they felt that if someone like myself had one it would create more visibility and promote the viability of such an IBM-compatible machine. I had a ready buyer for my PC as Margaret, my secretary, on hearing I was thinking of buying a new one, told me she would like it, as she wanted to earn extra money from doing word processing out of office hours.

If you lived in Hong Kong there was, of course, the opportunity to go into China. Having a proper holiday in China was a major event, but it was easy and interesting to do a day trip there. By 1985 there were a number of ways to get to China from Hong Kong (the most used being the train journey via the Lowu border crossing in the New Territories), but for a day trip the best option was to go via Macau.

Prior to the creation of the People's Republic of China in 1949 there was no border between Hong Kong and the mainland and travel was therefore simple. However from that time China effectively became a closed country, certainly in terms of tourism, with Mao Tse-Tung considering leisure travel to be bourgeois. By the time of Mao's death in 1976, however, it had become clear to the government that they needed to open up the country to be able to improve economic conditions and gain foreign exchange. In early 1979 under Deng

Xiaoping, by then the most powerful politician, major reforms were initiated, including allowing tourists to visit.

I had done the day trip via Macau more than once, the first time with a British member of our staff and his wife, and then a couple of times when my parents and friends were visiting. You had to do it as part of an official tour, as you entered on a group visa. Meeting up at the Macau ferry terminal a hydrofoil took you on the 45-minute journey to Macau, where you boarded a bus and had a tour around Macau itself before going through the border gate. After some form filling and the fairly perfunctory involvement of customs officers, you were able to change money to yuan at a Bank of China office before re-boarding your bus.

Surprisingly, you did not get a passport stamp as standard but were directed to a window where they could be obtained. It might be better to miss out on the stamp if you had plans to visit Taiwan, an island about 100 miles from the Chinese mainland. Having been the losers in the Chinese Civil War, in 1949 the Chinese Nationalist Party (The Kuomintang), the previous government, decamped to Taiwan and proclaimed themselves the Republic of China (ROC), as opposed to the People's Republic of China (PRC), as the communist winners under Mao Tse-Tung called themselves. About two million people went with them (Taiwan only had a population of six million before they all arrived) and they also brought with them a horde of national treasures and much of China's gold and foreign exchange reserves. The ROC had a stated aim of getting back control of mainland China in time, so there was a lot of friction between the two. Apparently if you turned up at either country with the other's stamp in your passport they might well refuse to admit you, with China being much more sensitive than Taiwan. Regular travellers to both countries would have two passports therefore and were even advised that to be safe they should cut out any tags from clothes bought in Taiwan when going into China in case they were confiscated.

Leaving the border, the views as we drove along were very agricultural: duck farms, rice paddies, dust roads over small bridges (some of which we used) and canals with small boats. There was virtually no motorised traffic apart from the odd lorry with soldiers and rare two-wheeled tractors, just an open engine sitting on an axle which was hitched up to a cart. Everyone walked or used pedal cycles to get around, and there were no motorbikes or mopeds.

The first stop was at the Chung Shan Hot Springs Resort. This was the first Chinese/foreign joint venture for the tourism market and was funded by Hong Kong and Macau entrepreneurs. It was seen as such an important project that Deng Xiao Ping himself attended the grand opening on 28th December 1980. We had lunch here with the only option being Chinese food, and while it was perfectly acceptable it was not great, being similar to basic Chinese food served in UK takeaways. This was not really surprising, as the Communist system, in place since 1949, did not allow for restaurants so chefs were non-existent and the availability of food was such that even home cooking was extremely basic. I was told by the staff in the office that, unlike the mainland, Taiwan was excellent for Chinese food, as many of the good chefs in China had gone there after the Communists had won the civil war. They had realised that there would be no use for their talents under the Communist system!

There were three other stops, the first one at a village called Cuiheng where you visited the home of Dr Sun Yat Sen, a revolutionary and one of the founding fathers of the Republic of China, then a small farming village and finally the town of Zhongshan about twenty five miles from Macau. This was a very interesting stop and you were allowed thirty minutes to wander around. The first thing that struck you was the bikes. They were absolutely everywhere, with no other form of transport at all. As you walked around many people would look at you, and at one stage when we were in a shop I turned around and there were a number of people standing looking at us through the window. I took a photo of them. We said to our guide that we were surprised by this interest in us, given that the border had been open some time. He explained that many of the people would only come to town two or three times a year and it was quite possible that for a number of them we were the first westerners they would have seen, added to which we had a girl with blonde hair, which was especially interesting to them.

At the end of 1985 Lita and I spent Christmas and New Year in the UK, the first time she had been there. We were there almost three weeks, which gave me plenty of time to show her London, visit friends and have time with my parents. As described previously they were clearly concerned that all the indications were that we would get married, how this would work in terms of Lita settling into the UK, and how our children would fare being from a mixed marriage. I was a bit nervous as to how this might manifest itself with us staying with them, but it was absolutely fine and they treated her so well you wouldn't have thought there were any issues, quite the opposite in fact.

While I took her around the major sights in London we spent most of the time with family and friends. Of course we did a lot of what people normally do in the UK, and on returning to Hong Kong, when Lita was asked how she liked her time there, she would reply that it was fine, but she hadn't expected to spend so much time in pubs and Indian restaurants!

The subject of my return to the UK raised its head again while I was there when I popped into the office one day. I only had a few informal meetings but one of them was with the MD, and during this he mentioned that if I wanted to come back to London he could offer me a couple of very interesting roles. Clearly he thought basing me in the UK was a better use for me than leaving me out in Asia.

Chapter 16

Business travel, and Lita requests a hangover

Early in 1986 I was asked to take on responsibility for sales activity in Tokyo. Charlie had put a full-time salesman from the US there, but he had left, and given the enormous cost of an expatriate in Tokyo for the relatively limited business opportunities, it made more sense for me to look after it. I was happy with this as Tokyo was an interesting place both to visit and to do business in, and I knew it and our Japanese agents pretty well. In addition, the marketing role I had, which had looked so attractive at first, turned out to be rather bland. The company culture was by this time very heavily short term sales oriented, and given this sales focus there wasn't any real appetite to take a more holistic view to position us for longer term success. Being such a long way from the UK head office, it was difficult for me to influence thinking on the subject. The chance to be able to bring some real revenue in again was therefore appealing.

Looking at how the next twelve months might pan out, I had to factor into my planning that it was now pretty clear I would be back in the UK by, at the latest, the start of the next financial year in March 1987. My friendly chat with the MD in London at Christmas had progressed by February, and quite a lot of pressure was now being applied to release me to do a bigger role in the UK. I made it clear that I was not ready to go back yet, but I would be happy to do so in ten to twelve months. Up until the end of March I felt there was a significantly worse than 50/50 chance of my staying in Asia for more than a couple of months. By then, however, discussion on the subject had abated, due principally it appeared to a view that if they forced me back now there was a significant chance of my resigning to stay in Hong Kong.

In parallel therefore with my business trips around the region I also looked at any opportunity to add on a tourist element, something that, with a couple of small exceptions, I had not done to date, given how busy I had been. In this respect it was helpful that the company took a relaxed approach to travel arrangements. I was entitled to business class flights and five-star hotels, and as long as they paid a fair price for these, and my business commitments weren't compromised, I could be flexible as to how I spent this money. I therefore asked our travel agent to keep an eye out for any special deals that I might be able to use.

Early February was Chinese New Year with a four-day break and shortly after it was Valentine's Day, so I had asked Lita if there was a restaurant she would like me to book for dinner. 'I don't want to go to a restaurant,' she said, 'You can cook me a meal at home, because I want to get drunk.'

This was a particular surprise as, in common with most Asian women, she didn't drink alcohol, but for no other reason than she didn't like the taste.

She went on, 'I've never been drunk in my life and I want to feel what it's like, and to experience a hangover'.

'Getting drunk is one thing' I said to her, 'but you certainly don't want to have a hangover, you've seen how awful I feel when I have one, why would you want to experience that?'

'Well, I think it's time I found out what it's like.'

'Fair enough. What do you want to get drunk on?'

'Champagne' she stated immediately, obviously having given it some thought.

So Valentine's evening comes along and I've prepared a nice dinner for us and there's champagne chilling in the fridge. I served the starter, opened a bottle, and poured it out for both of us.

'Happy Valentine's Day darling,' I said, raising my glass for a toast.

'Yes, and to you too,' she responded, taking a small sip of her drink. She grimaced. 'It's not very nice is it?'

'You know you don't like champagne,' I replied, 'but it's actually a very good one and delicious'.

She managed a very slightly larger sip than before and again flinched. The level of champagne in her glass when she put it down was almost the same as when I'd poured it.

We ate our starter without her drinking any more.

'You'd better get that first glass down you while I'm getting the main course,' I said to her. 'You'd better have a few more to drink if you do intend to get drunk.'

When I came back in she'd managed about half the glass.

'Come on,' I said, 'you need to start drinking in earnest, knock the rest of that glass back and I'll pour you another.' Very reluctantly, she did so.

We were five minutes into eating the main course when she said to me, 'I'm drunk, darling'.

'No you're not,' I answered her, 'even with your non-tolerance of alcohol, you won't get drunk on one glass.'

By the end of the meal she had struggled through about half of the second glass but that was it. She didn't want any more, and although she took the glass with her when we left the table, she didn't have another drop that evening.

The next morning when the alarm went off, she immediately sat up in bed and then shook me awake. 'So this is what a hangover feels like,' she said.

'No it doesn't, you don't have one,' I said. 'The tiny amount you drank won't do anything.'

'I definitely feel different,' she said.

'Do you have a terrible headache, feel like you have flu, have a sore stomach and you're dehydrated?'

'No,' she said.

'Well you haven't got a hangover then. Why don't you go and make some tea?'

The first opportunity to apply my new model of combined holiday and business trip came in March. I had to be in Singapore on business and on booking the flights our agent told me that I could add Cairo to the routing for no additional money. Apparently Singapore Airlines had just started their Singapore to Cairo service and during March, if you flew into Singapore with them, you could do a return Singapore-Cairo-Singapore flight for just one US dollar. Given that the flight time was around thirteen hours, this was a fantastic deal. I therefore booked a week's holiday and organised a couple of days in Cairo and a Nile cruise.

The trip turned out to be an experience and a half. It started on arrival at Cairo Airport, which was not well looked after or well run. After queuing up at immigration I arrived at customs. This was a shambles. They were checking everyone and the customs officers were dressed in ordinary clothes, so you couldn't tell the difference between them and other airport workers or passengers. I had brought my video camera, and this caused a lot of aggravation. As personal video cameras were very new, customs assumed you were a professional photographer on business and wanted to charge an extortionate fee to bring the equipment in. Finally they relented, but they filled almost a page of my passport with the details of the camera and recorder, as I had to still have them when I flew out, not being allowed to sell them in Egypt.

By the time we left the airport it was the middle of the rush hour and with no mass transit system, the traffic was appalling. It seemed that every car was dented and scratched from the constant jockeying for position, with motorbikes weaving in and out and pedestrians everywhere. By now I had been travelling for over twenty hours and was feeling decidedly jaded by the time we arrived at my hotel, the

Cleopatra, at 9.15 am. It was in Tahir Square, the main one in Cairo. The benefits of this hotel stopped at that. It was an absolute tip although rated as a four star, dingy and decrepit with only one lift working, and that had to be seen to be believed. My room was on the 12th floor and when I was ready to go out, given the state of the lift, I decided to walk down to check the fire escape route. At the 9th floor you couldn't go any further as there was a family living there and they had closed up access either via the staircase or the door on that floor! Peering over the handrails this seemed to be the state of the rest of the staircase going down.

I set off to find Thomas Cook's Cairo office, where I had to arrange to meet my guide and pick up a book of vouchers. I managed to get there without getting lost (though having to fend off droves of local touts) only to find a large sign saying they had moved! Luckily when I read the sign in more detail and looked at the map they had only gone around the corner. I organised everything there, including getting them to reconfirm my flights (a problem in Egypt as the phone lines were very bad) and change my hotel for my return, having told them what I thought of the Cleopatra. I then went back to the hotel, where my guide would meet me to take me to the Pyramids. I found the hotel bar and ordered a beer, which gratifyingly turned out to be a very large, very cold bottle of Stella that tasted excellent. On asking if they had any cigarettes they sent someone out to get me some. On arrival they had the same name as the hotel, so there I was smoking a Cleopatra in the Cleopatra.

The guide showed up and the first stop was the Egyptian Museum, also on Tahir Square, where the star exhibits were the finds from Tutankhamen's Tomb. We then set off by car to the Pyramids, with the final stretch being an unimpressive dual carriageway, dead straight and with the central reservation full of hedges cut in pyramid shapes, very naff. On the way there and down the straight road there were signs of the security police riots a couple of weeks before. This had been the result of hundreds of the most junior conscripts hearing a rumour that their conscription was going to be increased from three to four years.

The violence was very serious with a large number of tourist buildings being set on fire, including hotels. The government sent the army in with tanks to restore order, and these and the troops were still all over the tourist areas.

At one point I had the video camera out to record the burnt-out buildings and the tanks when a number of the troops started shouting and waving at us, obviously unhappy with the camera, and wanting us to stop. The guide just drove through them, shouting out that I was a cinema reporter. Thankfully they let us go, but it was a worrying moment, and I kept the camera out of sight after that when soldiers were in evidence.

Having finished seeing the Pyramids and the Sphinx, and undertaken the obligatory camel ride, which my guide videoed for me, I was dropped off at the hotel and told to be ready at 4.30 am the next morning to be picked up for the flight to Luxor, where I was joining a Nile cruise boat. It was now after 5 pm and I had been awake for over 32 hours. I was completely whacked and, faced with getting up at 3.45 a.m. decided I needed a sleep, even though I was very hungry.

In the lift was a notice from a tour manager to his group from three days before recommending a restaurant around the corner, so I decided to eat there. I set the alarm for 7.30 pm, threw off my clothes and collapsed into bed. I fell into a deep sleep and awoke much refreshed - at 1.30 am! It transpired that I had set the alarm correctly but in the process I had switched the time from pm to am, so I was twelve hours out. I couldn't get back to sleep, so with nothing else to do I read until it was time to get ready.

I arrived at the cruise boat, the MS *Giza*, at about 8.30 am and was told the cabins would not be available until midday. I was not inclined to go out and explore as I just wanted to relax, and therefore decided to stay on the boat. I was absolutely famished and realised I had not eaten for about 27 hours, since the uninspiring breakfast on the plane from Singapore. The crew told me I could join the departing passengers for breakfast as long as I paid two Egyptian pounds (about £1 British). It was of the cold continental variety and I had grapefruit, eggs and cheese, together with bread rolls. I also sampled a cold meat sausage that was thinly sliced like salami and looked like salami, but I avoided it thereafter as it tasted as if it was 90% sawdust.

Feeling much improved, I bought some postcards from the shop and repaired to the lounge to write them out, assisted by a Stella beer. At 10.15 a.m. they announced that the cabins were ready, a nice surprise, and mine was very pleasant: spotlessly clean with a large picture window, a sofa bed, a second pull-down bed and a nice little bathroom, the shower of which amazingly had as much pressure as any shower I had ever used.

At lunchtime the new arrivals gathered in the dining room and I was directed to a table which had the majority of the English speaking contingent assigned to it. There were eight adults in addition to myself, three couples in their 50s and a young Australian husband and wife with a gorgeous twelve-month-old daughter who couldn't have behaved better for the whole five days we were on the cruise. In one of those coincidences that happen when you travel, one of the group knew Lita's boss George well, as he also worked at Gulf Oil. The rest of the passengers mostly consisted of two enormous tour groups, one French and the other Italian, and thankfully these groups had their own guides and itineraries. It transpired that I had fallen on my feet here as not only did our small group get on famously together, but our guide was really excellent.

That afternoon we went to visit the temples in Luxor, and I was in my cabin after we returned when there was a knock at the door. It was Peter, the Gulf Oil man, and his wife, and they asked if I wanted to meet them for drinks before dinner. They told me that they had found out that the boat was semi-dry as the owner was a Muslim. I was aware of this but not bothered as I was happy with beer and wine, which they did serve. They were rather indignant though and had bribed a crew member to go and buy them some spirits. When I met them in the bar they had a British Airways flight bag under the table in which were bottles of vodka, scotch and Armagnac. I didn't have the heart to say I preferred a beer, given all the trouble they had been to, so I had a vodka tonic, which Peter poured out surreptitiously under the table. At dinner I made the mistake of getting a bottle of Egyptian Omar Khayyam wine, which was as rough as rough could be and only drinkable if you didn't give your taste buds a chance to recover by eating any food; after that I drank beer with dinner instead of Château Detergent. After the meal I had an Armagnac from Peter's bag and then excused myself. It had been a very, very long day.

The Nile cruise was really good, with very interesting sightseeing on land mixed with the ever-changing vista of the river bank when we were underway to our next location; fisherman, women walking to get water with jars on their heads, goatherds, small houses and villages, absolutely fascinating. One frustration however continued to be the video camera. As with customs when I entered the country, every site we went to assumed I was a professional and demanded an extortionate fee to take the camera in which I refused to pay (at the Egyptian Museum in Cairo they had wanted the equivalent of £50 sterling). I was forced to leave my expensive equipment with the man who took the entrance fee, but he could have been anyone as they were always so disreputably dressed.

The cruise finished at Aswan, where I was staying a couple of nights in a hotel to allow me to fly to Abu Simbel to see the sites there. I had been booked into a boring hotel, but having gone with our group for a drink at the Old Cataract Hotel while still staying on the boat I managed to get myself moved there. This hotel had been built in 1899 and was so named because of the cataracts it looked over, areas of shallow water with rocks and boulders making navigation very difficult. It was an old world hotel, un-modernised with lots of character and a stunning location with a fabulous outside terrace overlooking the Nile. Agatha Christie had based part of her book *Death On The Nile* there and it had lovely, un-manicured gardens. Unfortunately I did not get to see Abu Simbel, because on arriving at the airport for the short flight there we were told it was cancelled due to sandstorms. This was quite a common occurrence, but it was a shame to have travelled so far and not manage the final stage.

So it was back to Cairo for a night before heading home. Thomas Cook had, as promised, moved me to a different hotel, the El Nil. Saying that it was better than the Cleopatra only shows how bad the Cleopatra was. The El Nil had the weirdest layout, particularly my room. My door opened onto an 18 foot by 4 foot corridor that had a light on permanently and two other doors, one to the bedroom and one to the bathroom, the latter being the biggest, oddest-shaped room I'd ever seen. It had no window and was dingy in the extreme, despite the suite being light blue and the half tiled walls also light blue. This was in part due to the floor, which was made up of bands of black and white tiles. The white tiles were filthy, either due to ingrained dirt or possibly mould. In fact the whole bathroom was dirty and very downmarket but, very incongruously, it had a bidet.

Before going out to dinner I started reading a book on the Mediterranean by Eric Newby. I noticed that one of the chapters was on the Pyramids and turned to that first. Imagine my surprise when the opening words of the chapter were 'As no one at the El Nil Hotel, one of the less expensive caravanserais...' another travel coincidence. Next morning I left for the airport where, thankfully, a Thomas Cook man helped me get through all the stages at the airport for my flight back. This was a real benefit as it was a long-winded affair to fill in all the forms and deal with the various officials, compounded by my video kit. The customs man made me take out both the recorder and camera to show him the serial numbers in case I had swapped them for identical models while in Egypt.

It had been a wonderful visit but it was a tiring country to experience given the constant hassle from the locals, touting for everything under the sun, so you never had any peace when walking around. In addition the effort of having to bargain for ages for anything you wanted to buy to get even a half sensible price, meant I bought fewer things back than I wanted to. It was a relief to get to Singapore and normality.

However Egypt, had one final present for me. I had been feeling unwell on the flight, and my stomach was getting worse and worse in the taxi to the hotel. Luckily I made it before the Egyptian equivalent of Delhi Belly properly hit me. Thankfully I only had a day in Singapore before flying back to Hong Kong and I survived until I was back at my apartment by using various 'dry you up' medicines, but twenty four hours after getting back to Hong Kong I was no better so I went to see the doctor. When he interrogated me and found out I had eaten some salad for dinner the night before I left Cairo, his response was in that case he had no sympathy for me, I should have known better. He arranged for some tests and gave me some general tablets to take while waiting for the results.

These were going to take three days, and by the end of the second day I was no better despite the tablets. Margaret suggested I try some Chinese medicine. She said she swore by this for tummy problems so I thought, why not? Po Chai pills came in clear plastic phials with a large number of what looked like tiny aniseed balls in each. One dose was a whole phial of these. As with a number of Chinese medicines they claimed to fix just about anything including headaches, which was believable, to repairing broken bones, which wasn't. Well they did the trick and within twelve hours I was so much better.

When I went back to the doctor (who was English) to get the test results he asked me how I was. I told him that his tablets hadn't done anything so I had tried Po Chai pills.

To my surprise he said, 'Po Chai pills, wonderful aren't they? I give them to my family if they're poorly, they work really well. Unfortunately I can't prescribe them as we don't know what's in them. Anyway, your tests haven't come back with anything, so I suggest you keep taking the Po Chai pills if they are working for you.'

I organised three other business/holiday trips that year. The first week in May I combined a trip to Tokyo with a holiday in Japan. I took Lita with me and we flew on a Sunday, spending two weeks there. As the Monday after we arrived was a Japanese holiday we spent that sightseeing in Tokyo, I worked the Tuesday to Friday and we then spent the weekend in Tokyo, including going to Mount Fuji. On the second week I worked the Monday and Tuesday and then Wednesday to Sunday was holiday, flying home Sunday night.

I had an interesting experience in Tokyo when I took Lita for dinner to one of my favourite restaurants, which also happened to be the most expensive restaurant I normally used. This was called Inakaya and was a Robotoyaki restaurant, which meant that you sat at large square U shaped counters around the chef, with all the raw food laid out in front of him. The counters sat about four people on each side, therefore twelve in all. You didn't book places but would join other diners already seated. When you had selected what to eat from what was on display in front of you, the chef cooked it on a brazier and then passed the plate to you using a long wooden paddle, as it was too far for him to hand it to you directly. I have no idea why this type of restaurant was so much more costly than other very good ones, but it was; the meal that night for the two of us, with no expensive alcohol, just beer for me and tea for Lita was 30,000 Yen, which was around £130, a large amount of money in 1986.

That night, in addition to the excellent experience of eating there I had two additional memorable events. When we arrived we were taken to our seats and I very quickly realised that the diner to Lita's right was Bill Gates, of Microsoft fame, together with two of his executives. At that time he and Microsoft had not achieved the enormous visibility with the general public that they later experienced, but to someone like myself, who worked in IT, he was already a big name. It was quite common at Inakaya to talk to the people either side of you, and so it was with Bill. Clearly most of the conversation was between him and his two colleagues, but it was interesting to discuss a number of topics with them.

The second interesting part of the evening was that at Inakaya warm sake came in the ceramic flagons that are common in Japanese restaurants worldwide. But if you had cold sake, which I liked, it was served in a square wooden box. This was the most unsuitable drinking vessel imaginable. The wooden box was placed on a small dish and the waiter would fill it up until the box overflowed into the dish. Well that night, as Lita and Bill Gates were there, I decided I would like to take my box home as a memento. When I was ready to pay the bill I asked the waiter, in English of course, if he could include the cost of the box so I could take it away with me. He couldn't comprehend what I was talking about. I tried again, very slowly but he was still at a complete loss. He called a colleague over but he fared no better at understanding what it was I was asking for. Finally the manager arrived, and initially I still had no success, but suddenly comprehension dawned on him.

'Ah you are asking how much to pay to take the saki box home with you,' he said.

'Yes please' I replied, very glad that I had finally been understood, as I had been wondering what to do next.

'Oh no, of course no charge, you are welcome to have it as our gift to you,' he said. He took it away and presented it back to me a short while later, beautifully wrapped up in a lovely gift package, something the Japanese were so good at.

It dawned on me after we had left that it was not my English that had been confusing them, they just had never been asked to take the wooden box away, and therefore were looking for some other meaning to what I was saying. I have the box in front of me as I write. It is three inches square and two inches high with finger joints at each corner, and some Japanese characters burned into it.

On the Wednesday of the second week we went to Tokyo Disneyland with our local manager (from the UK) and his wife, and that evening we took the bullet train to Kyoto, where we stayed for four nights. This was the old capital of Japan, and had a number of very attractive temples, shrines and gardens, and there was plenty to do. We flew back to Hong Kong from Osaka (which is only about 25 miles from Kyoto), the trip had been most enjoyable and I was glad to have finally seen somewhere else but Tokyo; in ten trips there up to that time I had only had two half-days off.

In June I managed a super deal. I had to go to Tokyo again and the agent came up with a package trip from Hong Kong to Tokyo, then to Hawaii and back to Hong Kong. Including the flights, hotels and transfers this actually cost less than the normal ticket and hotels I used to go to Tokyo only. The hotel in Tokyo was unsurprisingly rather basic and a long way out and I had to use the subway, and I was flying economy rather than business. But getting to see Honolulu and Oahu and staying on Waikiki beach was tremendous, although I hadn't realised exactly where Hawaii is until then – slap bang in the middle of the Pacific Ocean. Mind you, because of the low price of the package the flight back from Honolulu was via Tokyo with a three-hour connection, which meant it took eighteen hours.

One interesting aspect of the Tokyo to Honolulu flight was that you crossed the dateline. This was wonderful going there, as I left Tokyo at 9 pm on Friday night and arrived in Hawaii after an eight-hour flight at 8 am the same day, Friday morning. Unfortunately, as I was not continuing eastward I suffered the reverse on the way back. I left Hawaii at 10 am on June 16th and seven hours later when I landed at Tokyo it was 2.15 pm the next day, 17th June.

In September I took Lita to Australia and Singapore for four weeks, spending three days in Singapore and the rest in Australia. Of the 24 days in Australia I had ten days working, including three in Melbourne, and was pretty busy. There were two weekends in Sydney to show Lita the sights and ten days proper holiday, driving and flying up to Cairns to see the Great Barrier Reef via the wine-growing area of Hunter Valley and the Gold Coast. Despite the amount of holiday I took on this trip, the bills the company covered for flights and hotels for twelve working days across the two locations paid a very large part of the cost, given that we had travelled economy and stayed with our local managers in Singapore and Sydney.

Chapter 17

Winding down, a Mini Moke and a big decision

The second half of 1986 saw me as busy travelling as usual, and despite my spending four weeks in September in Australia and my parents being in Hong Kong for a month from the middle of October I still made a dozen overseas trips before heading off to Manila on the 19th December for Christmas and New Year.

One reason for this was Japan, where my sales activity was reaping results. In July I closed a significant piece of business which came in at double the value I had been expecting and a good two to three months earlier than I thought it would. It was also a complete surprise to the company, but a very pleasant one, as I had not shown it on sales forecasts. I had the luxury of operating this way given the special nature of Japan (with a local agent and a historic low level of domestic business), coupled with my main role being a regional marketing one. No formal sales budget, commission plan or the like were in place for Japan, and I was not subject to a normal sales review process. I did do monthly reports of sales activity and prospects, but never included everything I was aware of to allow me to better manage the forecast, dropping prospects out and including them as it suited me.

I celebrated with the client by buying the two people I had worked most closely with a slap-up lunch costing £360, a lot of money in

1986, but then again it was Tokyo. Our poor waiter had a disastrous experience though - I had ordered a very expensive bottle of wine and as he uncorked it the bottle slipped through his fingers and smashed on the floor. All four of us were stunned into silence looking at the broken bottle, with its expensive contents completely wasted.

But the really big one was a massive deal with one of the UK high street banks for their Tokyo Branch, and this was the highest value single location piece of business the company had ever won at that time. Despite the size I had also been able to keep quiet just how active this one was, until it was basically a done deal. A key reason for this was that the General Manager of the bank in Japan wanted it kept hush hush to make sure he would get the system he wanted. He felt that if his head office computer people were involved too early they might push for an alternative that didn't suit him before he was in a position to justify his team's choice, and he could be forced down that route. Keeping things under wraps would not have worked at our end if we had a normal sales person on the account but, given my seniority, coupled with my operational experience planning and running projects, I could handle virtually all the high level project scoping and planning myself.

When 'Project Japan', as the local GM had titled it, went public, no one in either company outside Asia was prepared for it, although it was known that the bank were going to be looking into what they needed longer term in Tokyo. With such a senior sponsor driving it, and all the key elements determined, all that was really left to get the contract signed were the legal terms and some detailed documents to be put in place. I was not greatly involved thereafter as from the point where the local General Manager had involved his head office the majority of the activities were between them and our UK-based people. This suited me fine as by this time I was moving into the final phase before I returned to London.

We arrived back from our month-long trip to Australia and Singapore on the 8th October, only five days before my parents arrived for their second visit. It was going to be lovely having them back in Hong Kong, but as we waited for them at the airport there was some nervousness in the air. While Lita and I were already living together when we had spent the previous Christmas in London, we had been in separate bedrooms at my parents', but now they would be staying with us. To make matters worse, while I would be in Hong Kong for their first day, the next morning I had to leave first thing to fly to Singapore for a Regional Meeting, and would be away three nights. Lita was understandably concerned about being on her own with them. Luckily their flight arrived at 9 am and it was a public holiday, the Chung Yeung Festival, when families would go to their ancestral graves or have a picnic, preferably in a high place, which is supposed to bring luck. I therefore had the whole day and evening with them, everything was fine and Mum and Dad seemed perfectly at ease, despite their only son cohabiting out of wedlock under the same roof.

I left at 8.45 am the next day and it wasn't until later that night that I was able to telephone. Lita said everything was going fine, my parents were very friendly, she was very relieved and the biggest problem had been with the carrots at dinner.

'The carrots?' I queried.

'Yes' she replied, 'I remembered you said your parents liked their food well-cooked so I boiled them for longer than usual'.

'But not enough, obviously,' I responded.

'Well the other vegetables were all right but your Dad said the carrots were rather underdone for him, and could I give them a bit longer,' she explained. 'They still weren't cooked enough the second and third time he tried them, so I then cooked them till they were really mushy, when thankfully he said they were now ok.'

They stayed for a month, which flew by very quickly, and my father had his 66th birthday while they were with us. Bob and Sandie's parents were also in Hong Kong at the same time and the two couples hit it off and became good friends. They looked after themselves during the day and in the evenings we made use of the wide variety of good restaurants, sometimes with Bob and Sandie and their parents or other friends, and Margaret also arranged a hairy crab party at her flat so they could experience that delicacy. Very surprisingly, my father enjoyed them. He was very much a 'meat and potatoes' person were food was concerned and the crabs were difficult to eat, messy and required eating the roe, which I had not thought he would be keen on.

We did have one special experience while they were with us in that we spent a Thursday to Saturday in Macau. While I had been to Macau many times on business, and had stayed there a couple of times with friends who lived there, I had only seen the centre of the city. For this trip I had booked us into an old fashioned Portuguese Inn (a Pousada) on the farthest island, Coloane. This had been built as a private house in the 1930s and converted into a hotel in the 1970s. It was unattractive externally as they had built a number of sea-facing rooms on the front in a now very dated 1970s style, and it was rather basic but quiet and laid back. One reason for its quietness was that it was a quite a way from the main part of Macau. You had to cross a long bridge to get from the mainland to Taipa Island, and then at the southern end of Taipa you took a causeway to Coloane Island.

Staying there however gave me a good reason to do something I had wanted to do in Macau for some time - hire a Mini Moke. This was very like a scaled-down Jeep, and it had initially been targeted for sale to the military, but its low ground clearance and small wheels had made it a failure in this market. It took most of its parts from the Mini (hence the name) with Moke being an archaic name for a donkey. Having given up on the military market, British Motor Corporation (BMC) produced a civilian version in 1964. This achieved cult status in the 60s, and when I was growing up I remember seeing them on TV and in magazines, many brightly decked out, for example in Union Jack colours, and driven by the likes of the model Twiggy. In 1968 they stopped being built in the UK but continued in Australia, where they were made from 1966 to 1981. From 1980 until the early 1990s they were made in Portugal, a key reason they were present in Macau, with a number available to hire. Here they were also used as the official transport for the police.

We took a jetfoil, this being the fastest way to get there, and left Hong Kong at 3.30 pm. The rental company was a short walk from the ferry terminal, and as I had not told my parents or Lita about the Moke they were very surprised when they realised that was what we were hiring. Our Moke turned out to be very fetching, with plum-red sides and a bright yellow bonnet and spare wheel cover. The roof (which was fabric) was in deckchair stripes of blue, white, red and yellow.

The weather stayed dry while we were there, a particular benefit if you are driving around in a vehicle like a Moke. Macau did not have much to offer in terms of tourist sights, but the general ambience of the town was worth experiencing, food was very good, particularly as was to be expected, Portuguese dishes, and the casino was fascinating, constantly throbbing with Chinese gamblers.

We did the major places to visit such as the fort (Fortaleza do Monte) and the old Jesuit St Paul's Church. This latter, the most visible landmark of Macau, only consists of the front of the building, built in the early 1600s. The rest was destroyed in a typhoon in 1835. This facade was imposing, sitting on a small hill with 68 steps leading up to it. One of the nicest old buildings was the Bela Vista Hotel, pretty run down but in an elevated position with (as the name implies) good views out to sea, partly spoiled by 1986 with landfill development. This had been built in the 1870s as a private house but fairly quickly converted to a hotel, it had gone through various uses over the years reverting back to being a hotel in 1948.

We stopped for lunch one day at the Pousada de Sao Tiago, a small hotel in a converted fort that dated from the early 1600s which had a lovely terrace. It was near the sea, at the southern end of the town, and had a memorable entrance, as you had to walk up a stone staircase in a stone tunnel with a small stream of water running by the side of the steps. We had a lovely cold bottle of Portuguese Vinho Verde sitting on the terrace. The Moke gave us the chance to explore the islands of Taipa and Coloane but there was not much to see other than small temples, and on Coloane we found a pretty yellow church with a memorial to the last pirate attack in 1910 in front of it. The sea views were distinctly uninspiring, the water being very shallow and muddy, and the islands themselves were plain, with unattractive beaches; it was clear that it was the town where Macau's attractions lay. It was a lovely break and I was glad it was just the four of us together. Then much too quickly it seemed, we were on the jetfoil back to Hong Kong.

A few days before my parents arrived our rosewood dining suite had been delivered, this being the biggest of my going-home purchases. This was quite a common buy for expatriates as rosewood furniture was built from solid timber and was very much more expensive in the UK. Rosewood is a tropical hardwood, so named as the timber had a distinctive rose smell. It had an interesting grain with the natural colour of the rosewood used in Hong Kong being a golden brown. We had originally intended just to get a table and eight chairs, but after a few visits to different makers we decided to splash out and include a drinks cabinet, a sideboard, a large cutlery chest and a nest of tables. Despite the extra cost this would ensure that we would have all matching furniture, as we had decided it would be hard to buy furniture in the UK that would complement the table and chairs. It could be stained a different colour to the natural brown and after some thought we went for a dark walnut finish.

It was pointed out to us that as solid wood was used this would expand and contract depending on the humidity, with a large difference between damp Hong Kong and the relative dryness of the UK. This was handled by the use of what were termed 'floating panels'. The large panels in the furniture were built to fit into grooves instead of being glued in place, which allowed them to move without warping or splitting the panel. The finish was a high gloss polish and every salesman we spoke to made a point of holding a lighter to the polished surface to show how strong the lacquer was, as it was not affected by the flame. However we soon found out that the surface, while resistant to heat, was not so to simple ordinary water, which left a milky mark!

The cost of this luxury purchase was just over HK$22,000, about £2,000, but we felt it would last a lifetime and was therefore worth it. Our biggest concern however was not the cost but that it would fit into the dining room of our future house. It certainly would not fit into my current house, which was a modern three-bedroom semi.

Three other types of items were also worth buying before I returned – ceramics, silver plate and brass. There were a number of ceramic manufacturers offering a range of goods at very low prices and we started buying items we wanted to store ready to be shipped back. These included two large Chinese-style elephants about two feet high designed as ornaments and with a flat top for a plant, an umbrella stand, various vases and plant pots both for inside and out and a number of smaller items. We also decided that it would be a good chance to get Christmas presents – there was a range of very attractive lamps on sale based on porcelain bases and we bought a mixture of these. When we were writing out our Christmas cards later in the year to those in the UK who were getting a gift, we included a photograph of the lamp they would receive, but noted that they would have to wait for the arrival of our goods in the UK next year before getting their hands on it.

To add to the ceramic goods we also bought a 92-piece Chinese dinner service from China Products, the main Chinese Government outlet store. One reason for getting this was that friends who were also going back to the UK told us they planned to have Chinese themed dinner parties when they returned. Given that most of the effort in a Chinese dish was preparation, with the cooking being very quick, they planned to get each couple to bring one or two prepared dishes which they would then go to the kitchen to cook one after the other. That way the work would be spread out and no one need be absent for more than a few minutes to end up with eight to ten dishes. This sounded a great idea and we wanted to do the same.

For the brass and silver-plated items you went to the factory and were taken into their showrooms, which had a massive range of items on display. We didn't need much of the brass but did go to town on the silverware; the prices were so low it was hard not to buy everything that took your fancy' especially as the showroom was run by an amazing Italian girl called Luciana who was very persuasive. A wine cooler with its own three-foot stand stood out and as we browsed we selected butter dishes, cruet sets, chopstick rests, coasters for glasses, large ornamental plates to use for a dinner party on which the normal plates would rest, bread baskets, even toothpick holders. All were silver-plated and a number had some gold plate finishing them off, such as the butter dishes where the handle on top was a gold plated acorn.

In early December I bought myself one other expensive item - a Swiss Baume et Mercier watch in steel and gold. I had been thinking about buying it for some time but couldn't make my mind up. This was partly due to it being a costly item, partly as my top of the range Seiko digital had loads of functions whereas this was just the time and date, and partly as I wondered why I was thinking about getting it at all. True I had been very attracted to the design for some months as it was often in adverts, but it was only a watch and quite a lot of money.

I have mentioned previously how important designer items were to Hong Kong Chinese, no matter how junior they were. If they could possibly afford something with status they would save and save until they had the money to buy it. I had been completely the opposite when I arrived in 1983, as someone brought up in a North London suburb. I was not bothered at all by the logo on my belt or tie, that my wallet was not from someone like Louis Vuitton, that my glasses didn't have a prestigious name such as Dunhill on them and that my pen was not a Mont Blanc. But being enmeshed in the Hong Kong psyche for this long had changed me. I knew the names of designers and top quality manufacturers, I was aware of the cost of such premium articles, I recognised logos, and I admired these brands. Yes, I really liked the look of this watch, but I realised that I was also attracted as much, if not more, by the brand - Baume et Mercier. My mind was made up. I decided that I would buy the watch both as a personal memento from Hong Kong and to remind me of the power of marketing, without which I would never have considered its purchase.

During November I had been actively considering a very important subject – should I stay in Hong Kong? It would mean leaving the company, but I was quite happy with that. I had enjoyed some wonderful times since joining, but growth had, not unexpectedly, changed its nature and unfortunately not for the better, particularly in London. Another factor in favour of leaving was that the days of it being a good thing to be at one employer for a long time had gone. For someone in my position it was actually more of a negative, implying you were what was termed institutionalised (not brave enough to move), as well as not having the breadth of knowledge that would be gained from working at multiple companies. I also enjoyed life in Hong Kong very much and could understand why so many expatriates didn't leave until they had retired, so a job move while remaining in Hong Kong was attractive. It was also clear that Lita and I were going to be married and for her, staying in Hong Kong meant she kept all her friends and didn't have to go through establishing a new life a long way from her family.

Getting a new job was not going to be a problem. Not only did I have lots of contacts but the job market was very active, and I was regularly being contacted by recruiters and head hunters and was even on the advisory groups of a couple of the latter. It would mean hardly seeing my family and UK friends going forward, but that was manageable.

However I did have to factor in what marrying Lita would mean. I did see myself going back to the UK in the medium term, and therefore how she would settle needed to be considered, and as we both wanted children their education when they were older was an issue, as neither of us wanted them to be sent away to board.

Towards the end of November a situation arose that forced me to make my decision. The owner of the most successful of my direct competitors called and asked me to have lunch. John had been a friend from soon after I arrived, as given the small size of Hong Kong, individuals in similar roles tended to meet up, despite the competitive situation. He was a New Zealander and a nice guy, and in addition he had also joined the Round Table, so we met socially a reasonable amount. John knew I was planning to go back to the UK and over lunch asked me if I would consider joining his company. They had been growing strongly all the time I had known him and were much bigger than us, as in addition to having the agency for the product that was competitive they had become a major partner with IBM, selling their mid-range computers, and therefore had a number of other products on their books that ran on this hardware. So all I had to do was accept his offer, hand in my resignation and a new phase of my life would start.

It was clear that the only thing that would stop me was the situation with Lita. After some very hard thinking, and with a great deal of disappointment, I finally decided I needed to return to the UK. I could look to get a new job once I was there, but the key was to see how happy Lita would be in the UK. Perhaps I was being overly sensitive, but I felt the best thing in terms of our future was for her to go back with me as my fiancée, for us to get married in the UK and settle down and start a family (we were in our mid-thirties, so we couldn't wait too long on this front). If she was happy that would be fine, but if not I had a backup plan to move to Sydney. We both had friends in Sydney, I knew a number of business people there, the lifestyle was excellent and the weather was infinitely better than the UK. I would be happy having older children in Australia, which was not the case with Hong Kong. I had to establish sooner rather than later which country we were going to make our home.

With this decision I realised that there was something very important that I hadn't actually done yet – I had to properly ask Lita to marry me! Thankfully, but I expect unsurprisingly, she said yes and we were officially engaged.

Chapter 18

Fun & Games - Christmas and New Year in the Philippines

For my last Christmas before going back to the UK, we were going to the Philippines. Bob and Sandie, who had become very good friends, had been fascinated by our stories and pictures of Paradise Beach and wanted to go there. I had explained to them how basic the nipa huts where, given that their holidays to date had been in much more salubrious accommodation, but they were fully up for it. Lita and I had decided we would holiday in Asia, as there was no point going elsewhere given our relocation to Europe, and we were very happy to go to Puerto Galera with them. We would stay in Manila for a couple of nights, then at Paradise Beach until just after the New Year, with Lita staying on to spend time with her family. She would have wanted to do this anyway, but as I had to go to Florida on the 10th January there was no point being in the flat on her own when, as she was already in the Philippines, she could be with her family until I arrived back in Hong Kong.

We left for Manila on Saturday 20th December and were staying again at the Manila Hotel, meeting up with Bob and Sandie there, as they had gone a day earlier. The flight to Manila had gone smoothly and thankfully the queues were short at immigration and our luggage arrived quite quickly, but on walking through the doors of the arrivals building our relatively relaxed journey came to an abrupt end. In front of us was a heaving mass of people in every direction. They were jam packed and, having filled to capacity the hangar-like area in front of arrivals, the crowd continued outside each entrance. It was an absolute zoo, much worse than the previous times I had been there, and they were bad enough.

Lita's brother Mario was meeting us at the airport but she couldn't see him anywhere, and I couldn't help as I had never met him. She said he was very reliable and would definitely be there, but where? As Lita is only a little over five foot tall she couldn't see easily, and after a few minutes of looking intently she told me to stay with the luggage and she would walk around and try and spot him. She was gone a fair time but returned disappointed and frustrated. She was certain he was in the crowd, but they could not find each other.

I couldn't see any reason for there being so many people, as inside the airport it hadn't seemed to be that busy, but Lita said whole families would often turn out to meet someone, particularly at Christmas, which would swell numbers substantially. Wherever you looked people were trying to make themselves visible. Some had brought boxes to stand on, others were waving brightly coloured materials and some of the more organised even had banners and placards they were holding above their heads. But these created their own problem by hiding those behind them, who were pushing their way through to try and get in front of the obstructions.

After waiting around for another ten minutes with no joy I went back inside and arranged a car with the Manila Hotel desk. On the way we bribed the driver with 50 pesos to take us via Lita's sister to drop off presents and let them know what was happening. They were very surprised to see us on our own and said that Lita's brother and two nieces had left for the airport at 10 am to be sure not to miss us, and it was now 3.30 pm! We were spending that first evening with Bob and Sandie and then meeting up with the family the next day, so we didn't stay long before the car took us to the hotel.

That first evening we went to Josephine's, the big restaurant we had been to before, as we felt it would be a good introduction for Bob and Sandie. Mario (Lita's youngest brother) came with us. She had not seen him for about five years as his job had taken him out of the country, but he was now back in Manila. Even with five of us I greatly over-ordered including suckling pig, a marinated roasted chicken, grilled whole fish, spring rolls and noodles. It was all excellent and restored Sandie's faith in Filipino food. She told us that for lunch that day in the hotel's coffee shop, wanting to try something local, she had ordered Kare Kare; she had first asked the waitress what it was and been told it was pork and vegetables in sauce, which sounded fine. On its arrival she was rather put off by the look of the dish but decided to start with one of the big white noodles. On putting it into her mouth she realised it was not noodle but boiled intestine! Prodding through the dish she recognised a piece of tripe and decided that all the other meat seemed to be other types of offal. She was quite an adventurous eater, but this was a step too far.

The next day Mario met us at the hotel in the morning to take us to a local market, as Sandie wanted to buy a solid wood-carved water buffalo; she had been told this was something worth bringing back from the Philippines. With Mario was Gerry, a cousin of Lita's from her home village who was at college in Manila. We went by jeepney to a totally local artefacts market, with not another tourist in sight. Sandie ended up buying two buffaloes (called caribou in the Philippines) which by the end of the holiday she had named Rum and Calamansi, to remind her of one of her favourite drinks. Calamansi were tiny sour tangerines, the juice of which, mixed with water, went very well with the local rum.

That evening we were meeting up with all Lita's family who were living in Manila. We had booked Pistang Pilipino, a large restaurant serving Filipino food, with a stage on which a variety of acts appeared throughout the evening. These were all of a high quality and very professional, including an outstanding magician. The whole group of us numbered seventeen including some quite young nephews and nieces who were torn between eating what, to them, was a very special meal, watching the acts on stage which enthralled them and looking at Bob, Sandie and me, which they seemed to find as interesting as the other two diversions. It was an excellent evening, as all the adults in the family spoke very good English and were good company, and Bob and Sandie told us later how lucky they felt to have this opportunity to be with a local family. We didn't stay out too late as we had an early start the next morning for the journey to Paradise Beach.

We left the hotel at 8 am to go to the bus station about 30 minutes away. It would take about two and a half hours for the bus ride to the port, where we would get the ferry to Mindoro Island, on which was Puerto Galera. Arriving at the bus station we were met with a scene of utter chaos. With so many people travelling just before Christmas, the weak organisation, which at the best of times only just coped, had failed completely. There were lines of people all over the station, virtually no buses arriving, no timetable for bus arrivals and no guarantee that joining a line would get you a bus as, unlike the orderly British queuing mentality, people were just pushing in all along the lines. I also established that we had no chance to get an air-conditioned bus as these had a booking system and were all fully booked.

There were however any number of unofficial touts, who told us that for the equivalent of £1 each they would get us seats on a non-air-con one. It transpired from a bus that had just arrived that this was achieved by these entrepreneurs climbing in through the back windows of the bus while it was disgorging its passengers. They would then lay claim to the seat until you could get on board. Surprisingly, even for the Philippines, no one from the bus company was preventing this. We decided that this route was too fraught, especially as we had to get to the port before 12.30 pm, when the one ferry of the day left. Luckily I had half expected something like this, and the previous day I had looked into a fall-back option, to use one of the hotel taxis to take us for US$50. While it would have been an easier option to go for this in the first place, I wanted to try and get the bus, as I felt it would be a real experience for Bob and Sandie. With the bus not a viable option we went back to the hotel, and were soon on our way in a nice modern taxi feeling much relieved.

We had just left Manila behind us and were on the expressway to Batangas province when the taxi started to make an ominous noise, and after less than a minute the driver pulled over to the side of the road. The clutch had completely failed. We all got out and I wondered what we were going to do now, miles from anywhere, encumbered with all our luggage and the driver standing there scratching his head. Almost immediately, a couple of empty jeepneys pulled over and asked if they could help. Our driver negotiated with one of them to take us to Batangas, which didn't seem to be a problem, and while I was rather concerned about this the taxi driver said not to worry, we would be safe and he had the number of the jeepney. As the Manila Hotel taxi drivers are almost part of the staff, and only drive hotel guests, his assurances were valid. We agreed to give the taxi driver 200 Pesos (£8) for his troubles, as we felt sorry for him stuck miles from anywhere, and the jeepney wanted 400 Pesos (£15) so it ended up being a cheaper trip.

The journey to Batangas town went without any more problems, although the weather worsened and it started to rain. With time getting tight we were held up by a big traffic jam on the way to the port, but we made the jetty by midday, giving us half an hour to spare.

As we passed the port gates someone we took to be an official asked us where we were going. On telling them the Puerto Galera ferry they said 'too late, ferry already gone, you can see it in the distance'. And sure enough you could make out a white boat steaming away from land, obviously having just left the jetty. Sandie asked when the next ferry would be. 'No more today' our mentor said, 'but I can arrange special trip for you'.

At this I decided that I could smell a rat, even though it had been two years since I was last here and the ferry schedule might well have changed. I told the jeepney driver to go to the end of the pier, where I could see a boat. By now a couple of porters had joined us. 'Ferry gone' they both confirmed, looking sorrowful, and they and the official jumped onto the jeepney as it moved off. I almost believed them as there was no action around the boat on the jetty, and if this was the ferry which was leaving in half an hour, I would have expected to see people milling around.

The jeepney was not allowed to drive the last forty yards, so I walked up. Thankfully the boat had 'Puerto Galera' boldly painted on its side, and when I checked with one of the crew he confirmed it was the official ferry leaving at 12.30. I waived to the jeepney and gave the thumbs-up. As I was on my way back to it the heavens opened, the deluge just lasting the time it took for me to get to the vehicle, long enough for me to get drenched to the skin.

The 'official' and the porters had scarpered by the time I was back, and Lita said that after I had given the thumbs up Bob had turned on the erstwhile helpers with a face that boded them no good, and one of the porters had said in Filipino 'quick, he looks nasty, let's get out of here'.

It was not the best start to a holiday. This was the same basic boat that Lita and I had been on before, made worse this time as due to the inclement weather they had put up rough plywood covers on the sides, so you couldn't look out. Bob and I commandeered deckchairs and settled down, while the girls sat on a bench seat. We turned down the offers of egg and hamburger sandwiches from the hawkers, but Bob and I paid an inflated price of 40p each for a San Miguel beer. The ferry left at 12.50 pm and two hours later we were on the jetty at Puerto Galera.

The last leg of our journey to the resort was a five-mile jeepney ride. Normally this was not an issue, you waited for a jeepney to fill up with passengers and then off you went. Unfortunately today was not normal - it was obviously going to be difficult the whole way for us! When we arrived at the place where the jeepneys congregated none were there, but about 40 people were waiting - obviously there were problems. After fifteen minutes one arrived and whoosh, it was full up even before we had picked our bags up. It then started to rain and rain. On leaving Hong Kong I had seen in the paper that a typhoon was threatening the Philippines, and while it appeared highly unlikely that this one would actually hit us, the wide bands of rain and wind around the typhoon affect large areas. This was undoubtedly the cause of all the rain we were experiencing, as the weather should have been idyllic at this time of year.

If we felt uncomfortable while we waited, we felt rather sorry for a party of five in front of us who had told us they were staying at the resort next to ours. Obviously not aware that the places we were staying in were rather basic, they were very well dressed with matching sets of clearly quite expensive suitcases – they looked very incongruous and out of place in this setting.

I was pondering what we should do. Having been here before I knew that the road to the resort was poor, particularly the last section, which required two rivers to be forded, and with all this rain they might well be impassable. In addition we needed at least two more jeepneys before we would be able to get on one, and it might be getting dark by then, not ideal in these conditions. There was an option to take an outrigger canoe, but we would get soaked, and there was the question as to how rough the sea would be. In the end we decided to go for the boat as it was the quickest and surest option. We found one and he agreed to take us for 300 Pesos, twice the normal fare. We were joined by a young lad in the queue who worked at our resort.

The canoe ride was fast, but as expected in the conditions, very wet. One more potential complication materialised during the trip, which had me wondering if the day had any more surprises in store for us. In talking to the young lad it transpired that Geffrye, the owner, who I knew from previous visits and had booked with, had left the week before and the place was now being run by someone called Martin. I hoped we would not arrive to find we did not have a reservation and the place was full up, to really finish off the day. With Christmas the busiest time we might well have problems finding somewhere else.

As we arrived at the bay the two resorts were on, the boatman said that because of the bad weather he would have to drop us the other side of a small river from them, and we would need to wade this. As we were coming in we saw the party of five, who had also decided to go by sea, making their way across the river - we felt so sorry for them in their good clothes, carrying their expensive suitcases on their shoulders, but thankfully none of them tripped up. We jumped off into knee-deep water, offloaded our luggage and trudged the hundred and fifty yards to the resort. We must have looked a sight when we arrived, as we were soaked through and pretty worn out.

Thankfully they knew about our booking, although as we were a day early (we had decided not to hang around in Manila) the two huts needed to be made ready. Sandie and Lita went off to dry themselves in the communal toilets while Bob and I ordered a bottle of rum and some coke, and started to warm up. While the girls were changing one of the rooms became available and Bob and I put on dry clothes, and very soon we were feeling much better, helped along by the rum.

When Martin arrived he turned out to be British and very likeable. He worked on seismic oil exploration in China and did two months on and two months off, using Puerto Galera as his base for the off months. He said he wasn't running Paradise as a commercial venture, but when Geffrye was looking for someone to lease it he had decided to take it on, more on the basis of allowing him to live rent free rather than as a way of making money.

So everything was coming good, although we did have one final interesting experience before going to bed. Martin had just taken on a young Filipina girl called Judith to run the kitchen. She was very nice but very nervous about having to cook us a full dinner, as she wasn't yet used to the kitchen. Martin had been recommending to his other guests that they should eat at the next door resort until she was up to speed. After our stressful day we didn't fancy this, and just wanted to chill out were we were. Lita went to talk to her and arranged a dinner for us that she could cook at her leisure. It was then about 6 pm and we told her there was no hurry, we were happy relaxing on the balcony, and any time between 8 pm and 9 pm would be fine.

At 8.30 pm we sat down to a fine-looking dinner and were congratulating Judith and pooh pooing her nervousness. The noodles were delicious, the vegetables lovely and the fried rice spot on, but when we tried the pork stew it had a very strange taste. We couldn't work out what it was, but it wasn't pleasant so we called Martin over to try it, and after one spoonful he said 'yuck' and went to the kitchen. He was soon back and announced that the strange flavour was kerosene! The bad weather had resulted in a blackout and Judith had hung a pressure lamp over the stove to cook by, but it had been overfilled and unknown to her the excess had dripped into the pot. We told her not to worry, there were plenty of the other dishes so we would be fine, but this incident devastated her new-found confidence.

It's worth noting that power failures were not called blackouts in the Philippines – they were 'brownouts', but I could never find out why the word brown was used. Another strange use of a colour was for pornographic films, which were referred to as 'green' movies. Again I never found out why when almost everywhere else in the world that was English speaking these were called blue movies.

We spent twelve days at the resort, very relaxing, but the weather could have been better. There were apparently not one but two typhoons nearby, and while the weather wasn't too bad, and we had a number of lovely sunny days, it was in general unseasonably windy and showery. We became very sociable with the resident expatriates who lived at Talipanan Beach. They were a mixed bag with Martin, a couple of young Australian oil workers sitting out a recession, an English writer who had spent twenty years in Japan and was working on his next book (but only from 9 am to midday), the father of one of the oil workers who was having a boat built in the Philippines, and Curly, the manager of the resort next door, who seemed to be taking a couple of years off to live on a beach. The two Australians had just finished building a fabulous house in the middle of a coconut plantation for themselves. As foreigners they were not allowed to own land, but had done a deal with the village headman, so his name was on the official documents. We were invited to the house-warming party and the whole village turned out as they were very popular. A pig and two goats had been spit roasted and they had a Banca (one of the outrigger canoes) transported to the house to fill with ice to keep the drinks cool.

These two lads were on a mission over the whole holiday period.

There was a young boy in the village who had a cleft palate and they had decided to raise the money to get it operated on. They found a very pretty girl with a great body in Batangas, squeezed her into a very tight fitting pair of micro shorts and top and took her around all the island resorts selling kisses with her. They were well on track to raise the money needed for the good cause and this novel way of getting money from people made them even more popular with the local people.

Christmas Day happened to be Sandie's birthday, and we had brought with us a bottle of real champagne to celebrate. At lunchtime we went to the beach bar at Paradise with Martin, opened the bubbly and toasted Sandie's health. That evening a special meal of a whole spit-roasted pig had been arranged at the restaurant and afterwards we had Christmas pudding! My parents had brought a small one with them when they had last come to Hong Kong, as they knew I would not be back for the festivities. None of the normal accompaniments were available though, so we ate it with evaporated milk.

New Year's Eve was surprisingly restrained and everyone on the beach congregated around the beach bar of the next-door resort. One of the Christmas and New Year specialties in the Philippines was illegal firecrackers. They were very powerful and the largest, called Thunders, really let off a bang. All week these had been going off, but they really came into use on New Year's Eve. There was a big bonfire on the beach and every five minutes one would go off, and you would be showered with cinders as it had been thrown in the fire. Unfortunately at 11.40 pm it started to drizzle and this gradually became heavier. We carried on for another hour before, sopping wet, everyone decided to call it a night.

While we spent most of the holiday relaxing at the resort, we took a day out to hire a Banca to show Bob and Sandie the whole area, having lunch at a resort near Puerto Galera and doing some snorkelling. We also had a couple of trips on the jeepney into the town, and on one of these I had a most unpleasant experience. By the time it arrived at Puerto Galera the jeepney was absolutely packed, completely jammed full inside, with four people hanging off the back and two on the roof together with two goats. We were just pulling up when I realised I was being drenched - I was rather flummoxed initially as to where the liquid was coming from, but then realised it was goat urine! I couldn't move an inch as we were so tightly packed in, and just had to sit there and endure it until the goat was finished.

One saga which reached its finale a couple of days before we left concerned the restaurant at Talisay, the resort next door. This resort, although quite small, had been well set up by the two Australians who owned it. They were away on an extended holiday but this did not affect the popularity of their beach bar (built under a tree) or the restaurant, both of which were the best examples of their type for miles, and people would come there by boat and jeepney from neighbouring beaches. Unfortunately it soon became clear that without their involvement the kitchen could not cope. The cook, Ally, was perfectly able to produce good food but had virtually no organisational skills. The first evening we ate there it took an hour for our meal to arrive, the second an hour and a half. We realised that if we were going to eat there in future it would be best for Lita to pop over before service started to give the order to Ally, and book a time for it to be served.

This proved a wise move as the next time we ate there our food arrived as arranged at 8 pm. The people next to us, who ordered at 8 pm, didn't get their meal until 11.45! A couple of days later we pre-ordered again, which saved us the long delays the other diners experienced, but by now you could see tensions rising between Ally, the other staff and customers. It also became apparent that she was incapable of managing stock, and she kept running out of the most basic items such as bread and flour. We did wonder what Curly's role was as he didn't seem capable of sorting this out.

Then one of the owner's wives arrived back, but this didn't help. She was obviously more used to talking then doing, and spent a day and a half telling the cook, Curly and the other staff what they were doing wrong, rather than taking steps to put things right.

Then came the fatal night when we went there without having pre-ordered. Bob and Sandie went for omelette and chips (to make it easy),

I asked for a pork chop and Lita plumped for stew and rice. At the same time we ordered some banana pancakes for dessert so Ally could allow for this. This was at 7.30 pm. At 8.30 pm we ordered a cheese sandwich to come quickly, as we were now mindful that it looked like a long wait for the proper food. The whole order came piecemeal from 10.30 pm and had so many problems it was just about all sent back. We said we would pop over tomorrow to discuss how much we would pay.

The next day dawned and it transpired that Ally and about half the staff had resigned. The rest of the staff also want to leave but couldn't as they had not been paid yet. Rosie, the wife, was in an incredible huff and the last we saw of her she was peeling carrots. We ate at our resort the last couple of nights and avoided Talisay, so who knows what eventually transpired.

Unlike the trip there our journey back was uneventful and we spent a night in the luxury of the Manila Hotel before flying back to Hong Kong. There was one final transport issue on the holiday, which was that on arrival at Hong Kong we were greeted by some sort of taxi foul up, presumably due to the weather, which was terrible. There were the longest queues I had ever seen, and hardly any taxis arriving. After five minutes we decided to go and try outside the airport hotel, reasoning that if that was just as bad we could at least go in the bar for a couple of hours, and hopefully let things sort themselves out. When we arrived at the hotel entrance we were very surprised to see that no one else was waiting. Because of the weather it still took five minutes for a taxi to arrive, but that was miraculous compared to the wait we would have had at the airport.

Chapter 19

The final weeks

I had five days in Hong Kong before my business trip to Florida. I used them to start the ball rolling on moving back to the UK, having arranged before I had gone on holiday for three shipping companies to come and give me estimates. They all felt that what I had would fill a full-size container, so the cost of getting me back would be very different from bringing me out – when I just had a tea chest! Datewise, I had been asked to be back in early March. I had mooted the idea of having eight weeks off before starting in the UK, but there were apparently some key items London wanted me to pick up ASAP, and they preferred me to take no more than three weeks. I decided that if I could not have a mega-holiday I wouldn't take any, as I had done very well for holidays in the last year and was actually quite happy to go straight back. I reflected that not getting the big holiday break might make the company more favourably disposed to the size of the upcoming removal bill, but then decided it wouldn't.

The trip to Florida had two attractions. The business part of it was going to be interesting – I was undertaking a high-level evaluation of a product from an Orlando-based company for which we were considering becoming an agent. Secondly Orlando, which I had not been to before, was the location of a number of major theme parks (including Walt Disney World) as well as Cape Canaveral, NASA's main space launch facility at the Kennedy Space Centre. I had allocated three days at the company (to review the product itself, its existing customers and the development and support capabilities) and then planned to have two days' holiday to visit the parks and space center. The one thing I was not looking forward to was the amount of travel.

I left Hong Kong at 11.30 am on the Saturday morning for San Francisco and had a very pleasant surprise at the airport when I was upgraded to First Class; nice at any time, it was particularly so on this occasion as I had a fifteen-hour flight. Due to crossing the dateline I had the novel experience of arriving at almost the same time I had left, 10 am on Saturday morning. Due to flight connections I had to stay overnight in San Francisco, and the next morning took an early flight at 8 am to Miami, where I changed planes for the one-hour flight to Orlando. With time changes and the eight-hour journey from San Francisco, I didn't arrive in Orlando until 7.30 in the evening. I was met at the airport by the director of the company I was visiting. We had a couple of drinks in the hotel bar, and feeling quite tired I opted for room service and an early night, rather than going out for dinner with him.

I had a very enjoyable and productive time going through all the areas required to complete my evaluation, and managed to finish as planned on the Wednesday afternoon. Thursday morning I hired a car and went to Walt Disney World. This had two sections then, the Magic Kingdom and EPCOT Centre. I had seen much of what was at Magic Kingdom at the Tokyo Disneyland so opted to spend the day at EPCOT; no surprise they always used the mnemonic, as the full name was 'Experimental Prototype Community Of Tomorrow'. This had two main sections, a group of pavilions setup by major corporations and showcasing the latest technology, and World Showcase, where different countries had built environments to reflect a view of themselves. France had a Paris-like square with shops, China a large pagoda with a 360 degree surround cinema, Great Britain a country village with old shops and a pub and about another nine countries were represented.

When it was time for lunch I decided I would try out the British food at the pub. Named 'The Rose and Crown' it had been done fairly well in terms of interior design apart from the horrible and unauthentic outfits worn by the serving staff. These looked like something out of a pantomime and completely spoiled the impression. The menu had a number of typical pub staples and I chose Shepherd's Pie together with a pint of Bass beer, both pretty good and served by genuine British staff; I had a chat with one of them and he told me they came out on one-year contracts and had a good time socialising with all the other temporary staff.

On the Friday I went to the Kennedy Space Center about 60 miles away, as there were a couple of good tours of the Shuttle launch facility and Cape Canaveral. On the drive there I had some fun when I realised the car had cruise control, the first time I had seen it. There were no instructions, but from reading magazine articles I had a basic idea of the setup actions and after a few minutes of playing around had it working.

On arrival I found that the tour of the air force base where the early space missions were based was not available as they were testing cruise missiles. However I joined an excellent two-hour tour of the Shuttle facilities including seeing the next Shuttle being assembled. The highlight though was a film in a special IMAX theatre (the first time I had experienced this) with a screen some five storeys high. Most of the footage had been shot by the astronauts in space, the quality was excellent, and it provided a very good impression of what it was like being there. We were told that access to the space facility was first available in 1963 when, following an ever-increasing number of people visiting the Cape Canaveral area, the public were allowed to drive their own vehicles on a predetermined route around the air force base between 1 pm and 4 pm on Sundays. In 1965 this was expanded to include areas of the Kennedy Space Centre and subsequently the visitor center was built.

The next day I was flying back and, as I had experienced previously on my trip to Hawaii, crossing the dateline on the way back to Hong

Kong was not just a long trip in hours flown but also in time impact. My flights back took 22 hours, but I lost over 43 hours on my diary, leaving Orlando at 1.40 pm on the Saturday but not arriving in Hong Kong until 9 am on the Monday.

I had five days before leaving on a trip to Tokyo, and with Lita back from the Philippines it was nice to have even these few days of relative normality after almost four weeks of being overseas. The shipping quotes had arrived and sure enough they were fairly eye watering - all around the £3,000 mark; I had to admit I was surprised at just how much I had accumulated in only four years. We also kicked off the process of the paperwork to get Lita into the UK. We would apply for a fiancée visa, which allowed her to stay in the UK for 90 days, and she had to be married in that time to remain. It seemed best for her to stay in Hong Kong while waiting for the visa to arrive rather than going back to the Philippines; we had been told that it was likely to be a more fraught process going via the British Embassy in Manila rather than the authorities here, given that Hong Kong was administered by the UK. Our good friends David and Gloria came to our aid here, generously volunteering that Lita was most welcome to stay with them once I had left, which removed a key concern we had. Unfortunately George and Betty, her old employers, who still treated her almost like a daughter and would have been more than happy for her to move back with them, were relocating to the US at the same time as I was off.

The end of January was Chinese New Year with the actual day being Thursday 29th, giving rise to a four-day holiday. That week one of my cousins had been in touch to say that her parents in law were on an extended holiday and were in Hong Kong from the Saturday to the Wednesday, and she wondered if we would have a chance to meet up with them while they were there. They were booked into the YMCA apparently but I told her that it would be no problem for them to stay with us, so we agreed to pick them up there at 10 am on the Sunday, as we were busy the previous evening when they were arriving.

Joyce and Donald proved to be a lovely couple and easy to get on with. They were very intrepid travellers, picking the most interesting way of seeing the world rather than the easiest or most comfortable. This couldn't have been more clearly demonstrated than by their description of a big trip around India they had made the previous year. This had been done by railway, often eating from the stalls on the platforms, with Joyce's luggage consisting of one small soft bag. In this she had one change of clothing and a simple black dress in case they needed to be smart! We took them for dim sum and they bravely tried to use chopsticks for the first time, and then for a drive round the New Territories. We had dinner together on the Tuesday at the Jumbo floating restaurant before they left the next day for Australia.

The day after they left we were woken at 2.30 a.m. by the phone. Quickly answering it in a bit of a daze, thinking what major issue has resulted in a call at this time, it turned out to be one of my sisters. 'Hi Bernard' Marion said breezily, 'have you had your breakfast yet?'

From her tone it didn't sound like there was anything serious amiss, which relaxed me somewhat.

'Well no I haven't, given that it's 2.30 in the morning,' I replied.

'Oh no, I'm really sorry' she answered, sounding genuinely embarrassed. 'I never call you so I've mucked up working out the time'.

'It's ok, I'm awake now and all ears for why you are phoning,' I said with good grace.

'Well my friend Sheena, who you know, has managed to get a courier flight to Hong Kong. She arrives Friday morning at 9.15 a.m. and I wondered if she could stay with you and Lita,' she explained. 'She doesn't earn much so while she could find somewhere cheap to stay I said I would call you and see how you were placed, she's leaving on Wednesday.'

'That's ok' I replied, 'but she'll have to look after herself as we're busy at the weekend and Monday I'm off to Tokyo. But I will be able to pick her up at the airport'.

'That's fantastic, she'll be so pleased,' she said, and carried on, 'I'm so envious, I wish it was me'.

We said our goodbyes and I tried to get back to sleep.

Well I had some fun and games meeting Sheena at the airport.

When I checked, the flight was delayed to 9.45 am, but even though I left later to allow for this the traffic was so light I was there by 9.15. By 9.45 the plane had landed and because the airport wasn't busy and Sheena only had hand luggage (being a courier flight), I expected her to come through just after 10 am. The First Class passengers started coming out at 10.05 and by 10.20 all the passengers appeared to have exited. By 10.45 I gave up, even though I had allowed for the fact that as she was on a courier flight she might be delayed by paperwork, though surely not by an hour. As I didn't know her surname I couldn't even check the manifest to see if she was actually on the flight.

I went home to pick up my case and while unlocking the door I heard her leaving a message on the answerphone. I frantically unlocked and opened the door and dived at the phone, but I was a couple of seconds too late. Her message said she was going to try me at the office, so I called there immediately, to try and get the receptionist before Sheena rang. She had been very quick as I missed her there too. I pondered what to do and decided the best thing was to go back to the airport, but in case she called again I changed my answerphone message to say 'if this is Sheena calling please stay at the airport, I'm on my way'. Thankfully there she was waiting when I arrived. It had been an administrative problem – DHL had messed up the paperwork and she had had to sort it out, and had not been able to get a message to me.

On Sunday 8th I flew to Tokyo for the last time and had a busy couple of days which finished pleasantly with a goodbye party that our agents gave me. Back in Hong Kong I had to finalise the packing and shipping, having selected the company I would use. I also had a couple of meetings to sort out my income tax, firstly with the accountants and then with the government tax office. I also decided on my leaving date, which would be Thursday 5th March, flying back via Bangkok where I would spend four days, as although I had been there on business a few times I had never had the time to see the sights properly.

On the not so auspicious date of Friday 13th February, Lita and I had a farewell dinner with Bob and Sandie. They had become very good friends and were relocating to Singapore, flying there the next day, so this would be the last evening we were all in Hong Kong. We had decided to go to the Repulse Bay Hotel and eat at The Veranda, which we had booked a few days before, as it was very popular. This was not actually a hotel but a replica that had been opened in 1986. In yet another of the sad stories related to attractive colonial buildings in Hong Kong, the original Repulse Bay Hotel built in 1920 had been demolished in 1982 to build apartments. This had been an upmarket hotel, very attractive, and in a great location and consequently it had a good number of famous and important guests over the years. Having demolished it the owners of the site then decided that it would be a good idea if the new development did have some link back to the historic hotel, so a copy of the main building was constructed, but the only facilities were two restaurants, one indoors and The Veranda, which had been one of the top Hong Kong dining locations in the days of the original hotel.

On Wednesday the 25th February, the evening before the packers arrived, we had my farewell dinner with the staff. Never having been involved with professional movers I was amazed the next day to see the process of packing. No wonder I needed a 40 ft container, everything was wrapped really carefully in layers of different material, often starting with tissue paper, then corrugated or brown paper ending up with each item becoming three or four times its original size, particularly with glasses or china. Some of the more valuable or fragile items were individually crated or had custom boxes built for them. The packing also needed to allow for the fact that there were effectively two shipments. As I had a fully furnished house in the UK (which I planned to sell on my arrival), most things were going into storage. But I wanted to have access to a number of items as soon as they arrived in England, for example my computer and my clothes. The packing took four working days, finishing on Monday 2nd March, and on the Tuesday everything was shuttled from the apartment to where it would be loaded into the container. Thankfully it was a dry day as during the course of it all my items were sitting outside reception in the open waiting to be loaded onto the van.

On the Friday night in the middle of the packing we were going out with relatives, an aunt's sister and her husband from England, who were in Hong Kong for a couple of nights. We met up in the main restaurant in the Excelsior Hotel, where they were staying, and incidentally where I would be for my last few nights. This was one of my favourite dining rooms and as the hotel was also our corporate hotel I was quite well known there. They were suitably impressed when the maître d' greeted me by name, as they had booked the table, and we had an excellent meal as with my cousins' parents-in-law three weeks earlier, finding them very easy to talk to. While saying goodbye at the hotel entrance they were impressed a second time when I went to my car, parked in one of the only three spaces in front of the hotel – well, we did put a lot of business with them, so this did result in the odd perk such as this.

I had two more interesting evening events before flying out. On Tuesday, two nights before I left, Lita and I went to Gaddi's. This was the top restaurant at the Peninsula Hotel on Kowloon side, one of the Grande Dames of Hong Kong hotels and famous for its fleet of dark green Rolls Royces. This was to be my last meal with Lita and I had chosen Gaddi's not just as a special place, but because, in keeping with its very expensive fleet of cars, it was arguably the priciest restaurant in Hong Kong. This was relevant because in September 1983 during the financial crisis, as mentioned earlier, I had ended up selling some gold Krugerrands I owned at a loss, but I had kept one and promised myself that I would either sell it at a profit or blow it on an extravagant meal before I left Hong Kong for the last time. As the peg between the Hong Kong and the US dollar had held it was still worth less than I had paid, so its time had come. Being worth somewhere around £250 in 1987 this was an enormous amount to spend on dinner for two, and in reality I could only run the bill up to these levels through extremely expensive alcohol. I decided this was going too far; I would drink very good wine and have a special cognac afterwards but would be moderately sensible. The meal was very memorable, including the most expensive items on the menu, but it left me with a decent amount unspent.

The reason Lita and I had our farewell dinner two nights before I left was that on my last night we had been invited to a wedding. William, one of the consultants in the office, had very kindly invited us and it was going to be a full-blown traditional Chinese affair, the first I would attend. We had a wonderful time and it was a tremendous way to say goodbye to Hong Kong and all the experiences I had while being based there.

Sadly the next day I said my goodbyes to Lita. It was very frustrating having no idea how long her visa would take and therefore when we would be together again. The officials in Hong Kong had turned out to be very understanding and helpful, but unfortunately it was the UK end that was the problem, basically a black hole with no interest in providing a decent service. I didn't know it then but it would get worse. I would waste hours and hours at the Immigration Office in Croydon, trying to find out why nothing was happening, until finally they accepted that Lita's application had been lost. Given this, I had to go ahead to sell my house and find a new one without her direct involvement. My house was in Bedfordshire, some way north of London, but while I had been in Hong Kong the company had moved from the centre of London to Wimbledon in the south. This was a terrible commute taking over two hours each way by car, and then I had to do the same thing most weekends to look at property, as we clearly had to live somewhere near the new offices.

The M25 motorway around London had been completed while I was away and it transpired that this had caused prices within it to go up sharply, and it was soon clear that to get the best value for money I would need to look further out from Wimbledon then I had planned. While all this was going on we did get some time together in June as I had a business trip to Hong Kong, Sydney and Singapore and stretched my time in Hong Kong to almost six days so we would have a decent amount of time together.

Eventually the day arrived when, at the end of July, I was at Gatwick Airport to meet her. We had a few days in my old house before moving into the new one, and in October we were married, but all that is another story.

My trip back via Bangkok did provide one final noteworthy incident before I left Asia behind. I stayed at a good hotel, the Dusit Thani, and after checking in and unpacking I was on my way down to the lobby when I passed the time of day with an attractive Thai girl who was also in the lift. We carried on chatting after we had got out and it transpired that Su (full name Temsuda) was working for a travel agency owned by her uncle while she was waiting to join Thai Airways, the national airline. She said she would be happy to give me some ideas on how to structure my sightseeing, as she had an hour before she was meeting her next customer, so we went for a coffee.

We got on very well, and after she had found out that I was engaged and on my way back to the UK to get married she said that she had no customers for the next two days and would be happy to take me around Bangkok. She explained that one of the reasons for working for her uncle was to improve her English, so it would be good for her to spend time with me, and there would be no charge. This was clearly a wonderful opportunity so I jumped at it, but of course I wondered how it would be received, not just by Lita, when I told people I had spent two days with a young attractive Thai girl in Bangkok!

Not only did Su turn out to be an excellent guide but she had her own car, quite something in Thailand for a young single girl, which made getting around very easy. Both evenings she took me for dinner to very nice Thai restaurants. I would have preferred to go to more basic places as hers were aimed at tourists; I didn't however have the heart to say this as she clearly wanted to show off Bangkok's best side, and also it transpired that she knew the owners of both restaurants, who were friends of her father and uncle. Given this I didn't even have to pay for her meal, as it was on the house.

Jumping ahead in time, Lita was of course 'interested' in Su when I told her of my time in Thailand. Only just over a couple of years later however, travelling with our first child to stay with David and Gloria, who were now based in Bangkok, they met. Su had joined Thai

Airways by then and having left the plane last as we had to wait for our pushchair, we were stuck at the back of an enormous immigration line when Su arrived. She hugged us both and took us off to the VIP channel, bypassing all the queues!

www.ingramcontent.com/pod-product-compliance
Lightning Source LLC
Chambersburg PA
CBHW061229070526
44584CB00030B/4052